CLAU

MW01105271

GiraffeNeckSoup

A Spherical Perspective
Into The
Betterment & Advancement
Of
Humanity

To My beloved sister in spirit, Barbara

In Gratitude beyond words!

"Self-Help for Humanity"

Also by Claude La Vertu:

-Claiming & Maintaining Peace Of Mind

-The Relationship Companion

-The Affirmative Companion

-The Success Companion

-Clairvoyant Being

-LoveDare (Novel)

-A Better Man (Novel)

<u>GiraffeNeckSoup</u>

A Spherical Perspective
Into The
Betterment & Advancement
Of Humanity

ISBN 978-1-4357-9547-1

Claude La Vertu Media Collective

www.claudelavertu.com

For My Sister Patty

My Confidante – My Best Friend

veritas vos liberabit

ACKNOWLEDGEMENTS

In gratitude for the very important people to which whom without this book would not have come to be.

The very first person I must acknowledge is my sister, Patty. The most intelligent person I know, Patty is courageous and strong, beautiful and refined, tough as nails yet always and ever a lady. Since childhood she has been my absolute best friend and the person to which all people in my life are measured. She's a devoted mother who has committed her life and her heart to her children, and as a loyal, dedicated wife to her husband, she's beyond anything most men could ever hope to deserve. During the time I wrote this book, just as always, Patty more than anyone was my rock. She supported me throughout my journey, never wavering in her integrity to our friendship or to her family. She listened to me tirelessly and deserves a medal for enduring my *weirdness*. Patty always shares in the good times and keeps me laughing during the tough times. Always encouraging me to keep writing and to remain a gentleman no matter what may arise. If anyone deserves credit for this book's fruition, it is undeniably Patty. When all is written, said and done; when I move on from this place, if God find's me suitable for the heavens, it will be because of my sister Patty.

Karen Ann Wood-Moore; an unreasonably beautiful woman with an immeasurably good soul, who has always let me be me, and who played the role of surrogate sister when I needed it most. Thanks for feeding me, with food, ideals & love. My mind, my heart, and my belly thank you!

There are many people who supported me while I wrote, who listened to me and shared ideals, who fed me when I was too busy writing to think about food, who prayed and meditated with me, who laughed and cried with me and encouraged and challenged my many ideals. Among these good people are Ryan Lange, Amber Juba, Mary-Ann Kren, Robert & Elizabeth Burgess, Sue Cheek, Dorothy Turk, Judith Plummer, Sam & Jacqueline Beamish, Karen Tesolin, Denise Hickey, Catherine Bailie-McGrath, Rodney DeSouza, and, Barbara Schreiner-Trudel.

A very special thank you to all the good people of Trent Hills, Northumberland County in Ontario, Canada.

I would like to especially acknowledge my nieces, Celine and Elise, for their unconditional love and constant support. And my very dear friend, Olivia Perkins, whose faith carried me when my own faith threatened to buckle during those dark days of profound obscurity.

Beyond these fine people, I wish to express my uttermost gratitude and immense love to my siblings; Joey, Yves, Suzy, Patty, and Keith, all of whom were the hero's of my childhood and remain an inspiration to this very day. Thank you also to my mother, Marcella, for giving me life, and for doing what I sincerely believe was her absolute best.

Finally, to Allan Perron, whose friendship has been the most beneficial and healing source of light and love I have ever known. Thank you for your support, your faith, your encouragement, your divine friendship, and your love.

Thank you, and bless you all...

Namaste

INTRODUCTION
=GiraffeNeckWhat?=

**A giraffe has a black tongue twenty-seven inches long and no
vocal cords. A giraffe has nothing to say.
He just goes on giraffing.**
~Robert Fulghum

When I began sharing with people my decision to name this book GiraffeNeckSoup, the response from most was usually a laugh followed by an inquiry into why I'd give such a silly name to a book of such serious subject matters. My response was; *because it makes people laugh!*

I first came up with the book's title when I was learning Spanish and explaining to friends that I don't eat meat. Jokingly, I thought about the most absurd meat I could consider eating and then explained that the only meat I eat is fresh giraffe meat, especially the meat from the neck which, as I explained, is always best served in a soup; a meal I referred to as *Sopa con carne de cuello de jirafa*. I also suggested; *if God didn't want us to eat giraffe neck meat, he wouldn't have made it so darned tasty! (Disclaimer: Please do not eat giraffes!)*

Shortly thereafter, while pondering the assortment of thoughts someone with my inimitable perspective ponders, I considered how unfortunate it would be to *not* name my book GiraffeNeckSoup, and so I did! Humor is the only reason for the title; because it's silly and it makes people laugh. Otherwise, I know little about giraffes other than they're tall and cute and if you put a cookie on the roof of your car at the safari, they'll eat it (and distract you while the monkeys rip the trim from your bumper).

I believe that God (in whatever capacity God exists) has a sense of humor. This theory is supported by the fact that laughter is so healing and regenerative to our bodies and minds. This theory is further supported by things like the size of the avocado pit, the very existence of the duck-billed platypus, and the restrained veracity of the whoopee cushion – even if the humor I acknowledge in these things is merely a result of my own idiosyncratic perspective. Whether or not these factors truly support the theory of God's sense of humor, nothing supports the theory more than the results of what happens when we search for *Truth* without a sense of humor. Truth, whenever we come across it, is often painful to acknowledge, and it has become clear that we need to lighten up a little (or a lot) if for no other reason than to be able to deal with the seriousness of what we may discover, and to survive the journey.

Before resuming, I should mention that I refer to God often in this book, and in order to keep things simple, I refer to God as He/Him/His and as God. I do this because it simplifies things and should in no way imply that I think God is a dude, and should in no way imply otherwise. It's just a term. Also, I did not write this book with the hopes of people agreeing with me or to get anybody's approval. I approve of me and God approves of me; that's good enough for me! I wrote this book with the best of intentions to encourage people to think and to unite us all. My indifference also applies to whether or not people believe in God, and how they refer to God. <u>This book is for everybody!</u> I respect everybody's right to believe what they believe; especially those on a journey of the search for *Truth*, and who are on said journey out of love rather than out of guilt, fear and the need to follow in the shadowy footsteps of others who do the same.

Insofar as nobody has ever succeeded at proving that God exists, so has nobody ever proven that God doesn't exist. In my unbiased research into both sides however, I recognize that there is more evidence which suggests that God does exist than which suggests otherwise. Either way, I'm not out to prove anything; I am simply sharing some of what I have come to understand about *Truth* and the meaning(s) of life.

Because most of the ideals in this book were relayed to me in *energetic terms* during meditation, deep thought and prayer, I was faced with the challenge of translating literal energy into words, and thus, the real challenge was to find ways to describe *Energetic Truths* without compromising their core value. Fortunately, the messages were of simplicity and logic, so I've kept it all simple and logical.

When I speak of ideals being *energetically* relayed – as much as I am my own individual person (little more than a geek with some fashion sense) – I am exactly like everyone else; I just happen to spend more time with God and in thought than with anything else. As such, I have merely tapped into that realm of which every human is capable and invited and encouraged to tap into. This place is as much within us it is as around us, and it is as deep as it is wide, and it is filled with knowledge beyond our imagination. The knowledge is beyond most people's current understanding because we rely so much upon words, yet the information within is energetic, and thus we must be attuned to it in order to receive it. On my journey to do my part to better the world, I have relayed these ideals.

The rest is up to each of us to make our search our priority.

I have been challenged by many and have challenged myself about these ideals, and since I realize that any mediocre ignoramus can consider the immediate obvious; *a spade is a spade*, I knew I had to look deeper than do most others. When it comes to subscribing to the deductions of the common populace, I can assure you; I didn't spend years thinking, praying, meditating, writing, editing and resisting the frequent urge to throw my desk through the living room window without having it occur to me that I could be wrong and that maybe everything is just chaos and coincidence. This, after all, is what an intelligent person does. That said, after considering the immediate obvious, I placed all those ideals aside and went beyond. This book is the result of going beyond the *immediate obvious,* and going beyond our current *"reality"*.

This book is not about believing; it is about *being* and *doing*. Spiritual convictions are not required. It's more about integrity, commitment and discipline than anything else. For the record, I believe that all religions hold basic *Truths*, yet I am beyond the restrictive principles of any one religious, political or scientific ideal, thought or organization, and beyond the alleged brilliance of their discoveries which humanity glorifies largely out of the lack of knowledge of the falsehoods that are the foundations of many of those discoveries, and of the limitations which they imply. In my life and in my search for Truth, I subscribe to the covenant of the motive which fuels my commitment to my search. The motive is to discover, observe and know *Truth*, and to do my part to shed light on the path which is the bread of life which all humanity craves.

There are no shortcuts...

When you become the person God intended you to be,
then you will have the life God intended you to have.

There is no other way...

CHAPTER I

=ConsciousAffirmativeLiving=

Taking humanity to the next level...

I want people to stop hurting. I want them to stop hurting themselves and each other. I want them to think more profoundly than ever before. Everybody. Each of us. All of us. This is the reason for this book. There is no other agenda. I am not looking to sell a religion, cult or sect. I am looking to help stop the hurt and encourage the kind of affirmative thought process that will cease the hurting, revolutionize our world and propel humanity to the next level.

My primary intention in relation to this book is to encourage people to *think*. Yes, I'd like for people to understand the importance of *living affirmatively* on an honest, moment-to-moment basis, as well as what precisely the process entails and the inherent good it yields. Nonetheless, this book is primarily about getting people to think. If in the process this book can bring clarity and a much needed light to humanity, great! However, I believe the light we seek won't be brought to us by a mere book, for the light we seek is an understanding; a gift, available to every one of us for the taking. We just need to be honest and be willing to do the work. Once we understand that as much as we're all one and the same; that we're also individuals, we then realize the power that one individual has to change things for the better and the crucial import-ance of *reaching within*, finding our best *self*, and bringing it out into the world (which encourages the masses to do the same). This, in the midst of all we pursue, is a great part of what completes each and all of us.

The *reaching in* process entails that we dwell exclusively within the realm of *inherent affirmative possibility*. To do this requires that we surrender attachments to our obsolete and inaccurate ideals about our existence. Inasmuch as we must dwell on what we *do* know about life, we must acknowledge that much of what we base life on is found-ed merely on what we *assume* we know to be truthful and/or accurate (archaic religious practices, outmoded forms of government and our individual and collective myopic perspectives, to name some). In this discovery lies one of the greatest threats to the potential greatness of all of humanity. Once we adjust our perspective and our thinking to the point where we can acknowledge more than our current reality, things *will* change, and we *will* see, feel and touch the light. I say *once we advance* because I am entirely convinced that *we will* advance, and I for one intend on being part of that generation of humanity that bridged the gap between intelligence and knowledge, between spirituality and religion, between money and economics, between society and humanity, between the good and the greater good, by taking that giant leap towards the *greatest good*. I intend on being part of that generation which took the selfless leap of faith. That generation which finally decided to wake up and *think!*

Although many have heard of *spiritual consciousness* or *conscious living* (positive thinking, spiritual awareness, etc.) and assume they're living consciously and affirmatively, in actuality, few people including most so-called *spiritual* people truly live in a manner which is either conscious or affirmative, and consequently, their efforts to achieve true spiritual enlightenment and basic success is a fruitless endeavor. The purpose of this chapter therefore is to explain the basic concept of *Conscious Affirmative Living.*

Living consciously and affirmatively is exactly as it sounds: Living in awareness of what we think, say and do; doing so in the most affirmative of ways. In a nutshell, *Conscious Affirmative Living* means thinking, speaking, being and acting affirmatively in the conduct of awareness. It means practicing any or all religions, or none of them, with integrity, commitment and discipline, in a manner which is respectful to all life. It means listening to our instincts and intuitions, and our hearts and minds; individually and collectively. It means absolutely no judgment and extending compassion to all. It means every word uttered being of an affirmative nature and every thought being dwelt within the realm of inherent affirmative possibility. It means working honestly, dealing with honest people, making good on one's word and committing to the fulfillment of the Commandments implied by living for God and loving thy neighbor. It means loving the unlovable, soothing the unhealed, teaching the unlearned and harmoniously surpassing the barriers of limitation which keep us from our greatest selves and from each other and from *Truth* and from God. *Conscious Affirmative Living* is a process. It is what God does: God gives life,

God creates, and God dwells within the realm of affirmative possibility. God at all times is conscious, aware, loving, creative and affirmative. To do or to be otherwise, God would cease to be God. As with anything, *Conscious Affirmative Living* takes practice. Not because it's difficult to do; it's actually quite simple, but the difficulties lie in our stubborn refusal to surrender old habits, relinquish old beliefs and release our ego's constant need for approval.

To anyone remotely familiar with religious science or positive thinking, the concept of living consciously or affirmatively is not foreign, but even in their attempts to live according to their basic ideals, most *spiritual* people fail to achieve significant enlightenment or life-success because they don't recognize to what extent their thoughts, words and actions must be altered. They also don't really know what they truly want, and/or don't feel they deserve it or that it's possible or that it will linger. Furthermore, there is an inexact rumor which suggests that one can just *will* material wealth or love out of thin air, but a basic truth remains; *nothing comes from nothing!* Everything is possible and attainable, but valuable *riches* don't come from nothing. Their energies already exist, and they dwell within the realm of inherent affirmative possibility; a realm one cannot arrive at or extract anything from by *pretending* to be spiritually enlightened. To make it appear for real, one must abide by the doctrine for real. One must really go there! To really go there, one must start with a commitment to honesty.

Regardless of humanity's current stagnant appearance, the fact remains that it is the inherent nature of humans to seek to advance themselves, each one personally, all globally. As beings who seek to advance ourselves to our ultimate potential – if we wish to see any real progress in our lifetime – it's vital for us to recognize that not only is education the key to the advancement and survival of all humanity, but that *honesty* is the key to the advancement and survival of all knowledge. One certainty I have come to recognize about nature itself is that it's the very *nature* of *nature* to be unbiasedly honest. Like our innate desire to advance ourselves, honesty is also a naturally innate component of *human* nature, but a component of our nature we humans rarely employ naturally; usually due to our addiction to approval and our egocentric desires. Humanity's lack of employing honesty (personally, collectively, globally, politically, spiritually) is perhaps the one thing that holds us back more than any other concept in existence, and consequently, we cannot discover truth or ultimately advance beyond our current condition. In our failure to be honest, all of humanity – at best – languishes in repetitive cycles. At worst, we stagnate, we regress and we die.

Humanity's failure – personally and globally – to be completely honest about everything is the principal reason why there is little in life that we can genuinely rely upon to be consistent and true, but when it comes to the survival and advancement of humanity, the *honest* search for, and research into, *Truth* is key. With all the hearsay about what *Truth* actually is or isn't, it's not always clear where to turn or who to listen to or what to believe. Everyone has their motives for what they're selling, and those motives are not always honest. Three things, however, that are guaranteed constant and honest are nature, science and change. These factors never lie. They honestly tell the truth about where we've been, where we are going and where we are now. The greatest component being the *where we are now* factor. It is crucial to acknowledge this because it is the only place and time where we ever have any power to change our course: *Here and Now!*

Our failure to be completely honest about everything is the principal reason why there is little integrity, discipline and commitment circulating in our world today, and as these factors are the tickets to true enlightenment and success, it's quite evident why so many people; religious and otherwise, are struggling. Even those who are entirely familiar with the concept of *Conscious Affirmative Living* fail to achieve enlightenment and success for reasons other than they aren't trying; reasons habitually having to do with compromised intentions. For example, we assume that our *awareness* of conscious living means we're *living* consciously, but "knowing" is nothing without "doing". Living consciously is not done weekly or hourly. It's done constantly, moment to moment. One cannot be conscious for one hour per week and expect to achieve their goals because of that one hour. Conversely, one cannot sit in affirmative contemplation all day long doing *nothing* and then expect *something* to happen. We know that anything worth having is worth working for. In this age of *easy to acquire disposable everything*, very little has real worth and is consequently not worth working for, and what is worth working for seems unattainable because we're out of practice about where to begin, and we don't want to commit, and we're undisciplined. It must be understood that anything worth having requires integrity, honesty, discipline and commitment, and it *must* be worked for. This is where *intention* and the real value of any meaningful thing or worthwhile endeavor come into play.

Although integrity, honesty, commitment and discipline are key driving forces behind every great accomplishment humanity has ever known, intention itself is a powerful tool, but like our subconscious mind, our intention is mostly on auto-pilot because we've either not taken charge of this active "live-wire" or we've plugged it into ideals that are not in alignment with what we truly desire. Or, we've plugged it into fear. It's impossible to achieve true enlightenment and/or true success while we're at the same time trying to achieve something that is not in harmony with our true selves or we're constantly living in fear. The fact remains, however, that most of us pursue goals that have nothing to do with our actual dreams and more to do with seeking approval, and this ever-elusive approval factor is not at all in alignment with the realm of affirmative possibility, because it is ego-driven, and it is not pure.

People dream of being celebrities for the mere idea of being famous when in reality what they truly desire is approval. They aspire to become doctors or lawyers in hopes of becoming the rich person they couldn't be when they were kids, still seeking acceptance from peers, hoping to defeat their deep-rooted insecurities about the way they felt in the past. Approval addiction is the main reason many people don't establish or maintain boundaries where relationships are concerned. In this unending search for approval, it's impossible to bring the best of ourselves to our careers or to our relationships or to the world. It's also difficult to be recognized for something we're just *good* at doing, when others are succeeding at it because they're *great* at it — because they're actually *living* it and not just fantasizing about it. Many people also pursue compromised goals because they know it will ensure their failure, thereby succeeding at being the failure they were always told they were. This applies as much to careers as it does to homemaking, childrearing, relationships, finances, health and everything else we struggle with under the watchful eye of family, friends, neighbors, peers, and even strangers.

Whether our endeavors are of a spiritual, financial, professional, material, physical or emotional nature, confusion plays a huge role in our lack of realizing success. Our confusion is vast and is as well rounded as it is well founded. It holds us back and keeps us in a stagnant rut, as does any product of fear. The key to moving towards our greatest *self*, and towards our goals and dreams, is to be honest about what we truly desire, and then move forth, affirmatively maintaining our faith, holding ourselves accountable for our actions, doing what's right and doing what we know we'd do if God were standing right beside us. This process actually brings confusion to order.

Our confusion is generally fed by fear, and nowhere is this more evident than where spiritual convictions are concerned. On one hand, we're told how the Lord is always there for us; on the other hand, we're told how God is angry with us. On one hand, political leaders speak about God in order to get our vote; on the other hand, they have no control over their own household, or their children, or their relationships or their *self* or their integrity where it applies to their alleged commitment to serving God. On one hand, we have new-found scientific evidence that we can control our lives and strengthen our faith through mental conditioning; on the other hand, this evidence comes from the same sources which are proving that God isn't exactly as the Bible portrays, thereby compromising the very spiritual convictions we're looking to strengthen. Beyond spirituality; on one hand, Dad wants you to be a doctor; on the other hand, you want to be a dancer. On one hand, you need your job; on the other hand, you can't take the boss' abuse for one more day. On one hand, your mind is telling you that you're the worthless brat your mother, father, teacher said you are; on the other hand, your heart is telling you that you are the precious glimmer of hope God intended you to be; a glimmer of hope humanity's been waiting for. In short, it is in remembering that we really are, each of us, that glimmer of hope bestowed upon humanity, that we can do away with all the confusion and simply believe that we can have – and that we deserve to have – all that we desire; regardless of what anybody has to say about it, and that God is one hundred percent behind our every dream and goal and endeavor.

When we hear about how successful people *made it* because they truly wanted it, we don't always understand precisely what that means, especially in light of our own numerous failures to achieve our own goals, and in light of how bad we want what we seem to want. Take for example finances. Most of us would declare that we'd rather be rich than be poor, but for most of us, our actions do not walk the same path as our declarations. On one hand we say we want to be rich, but on the other hand, we think money's evil, or that it's unattainable, or that we're unworthy, and in the process we justify our poverty and nickel and dime ourselves so deep into debt that it only makes the prospect of wealth that much more unattainable. For those who did make it to the top, whether a crew leader of a fast food restaurant, an award-winning actor, a corporate CEO, or a prize-winning novelist; they had to *walk the walk*. Even in the midst of prayer, chanting and endless affirmations, there came a time when they had to shut up and put all their energy into the *walk*!

For some, walking the walk means leaving an executive position to wash dishes for a living. For others it means leaving loved-ones. For some it means going for broke, for others it means looking crazy. For all it means blood, sweat and tears, and relinquishing who we are for who we could become. Every step along the way towards our dreams means crashing through limiting ideals about ourselves; ideals placed before us by others who were lost in their own limitations or are so jealous they can barely see straight. For each and all of us, it means doing what we know we are meant to do, and it means putting the prize first and keeping our eye on that prize. This is where integrity, commitment, discipline and especially the power of true intention come into play and bring value to our desires, goals, dreams, endeavors and achievements.

The key to affirmatively harnessing the power of intention and the power of your own will is to put your intention and your will to use while continually speaking God's language (affirmative, creative, conscious). Among the following chapters is a chapter dedicated to the law of attraction, so I won't delve deeply into the subject at present. I mention the law of attraction now however, because it's important at this juncture that all who read this understand that God or The Universe or whatever term you use, is one hundred percent on your side. God's word is affirmative. It is always *"yes"*. Like electricity that is unbiased to whatever you plug into it to be electrically fed, God will always reply *yes* to your endeavors because it is a promise, and it is the law. That said, consequence is also a promise, and it is also an indisputably unavoidable law, so we must choose wisely.

Taking into consideration that nothing comes from nothing, it's important to realize that there is always pay-back; *cause and effect*, and we cannot hide from it. God is all around us and within us, and we cannot hide from God. We cannot hide from the bad or from the good we've done. The energy that results from what we've done, good or bad, will find us. This is not a scare tactic; this is a reminder that *what goes around comes around*. With this data comes great power, for when we curse, damn or judge others, that energy returns to us. Conversely, when we bless, pray for and praise others, that energy is also returned. In all cases, all energy returns to us multiplied, many times over. This energy exchange process (with its compound interest-like results) beautifully illustrates why and how the universe is in constant expansion, and why and how it affects each of us personally, and all of us globally and universally.

The concept of *Conscious Affirmative Living* and dwelling within *inherent affirmative possibility* isn't restricted to people of spiritual faith. Being kind, disciplined, committed, compassionate and grateful is, before anything else, a state of mind. Whatever your spiritual convictions how-ever, including if you have none, know that getting the most out of your convictions for a greater life will always be dictated by how you employ your convictions. There is *Truth* in each religion. There is *Truth* in having no religion. God – in whatever capacity God exists – speaks through every religion and through every *thing*. Hearing what God has to say requires only that we speak God's language, which as the Divine Creator is clearly and absolutely *conscious, creative and affirmative*.

Ultimately, this kind of thinking, being and doing is the state of mind which must be nurtured in all of us, throughout humanity, throughout the coming ages. This is the kind of thinking that will help us move forth. These are the kinds of ideals which will take humanity to the next level, and stop the hurting...finally and forever.

Before proceeding to this next chapter, I wish to reiterate that I utilize the term "God" and I refer to God as He/Him/His. This term is respectfully employed to simplify clarification of ideals and is intended to refer to God in whatever capacity God exists (God, Goddess, Universe, Spirit, Energy, Life, First Cause, The One, Heavenly Father, Higher Self, Consciousness, Etc.). I utilize this term with utmost respect and reverence to all faiths, and it is my hope that it is received as such.

CHAPTER II

=TheMission =

Why we're here and what to do about it...

When one *spherically* contemplates the true oneness of all that is, one cannot help but recognize that there clearly is an omnipotent multitude of reasons for human existence. As such, there is not "one" *meaning of life*, but rather, there are countless *meanings* of life, or, *reasons for life*, especially for humans.

Being human offers, among other things, an opportunity to experience time in a linear form, and to experience free will, and a chance to be a separate individual beyond God. We come here, we get to do what we want to do; make dreams happen, or waste our days watching TV, or kill people, or save lives, or do whatever else we want to do. It's kind of like attending the ultimate amusement park where absolutely nothing is impossible, for better and for worse, without limits. That said, insofar as there may be many reasons for why we're here, there is a grander picture. So, without much ado, my theory as to why we're *mainly* here is this: *We're on a mission to ensure God's perfection by being, doing and experiencing all the things God can't be, do and experience as a result of omnipotent perfection.*

Here's my reasoning: Perfection is God's only link to any possible *imperfection*. For example, if God *knows* everything, how can God *learn* anything? If God can't learn anything, wouldn't that limit God, thereby rendering God imperfect? Perfection also implies possessing everything including divine patience and acceptance. But how does a perfectly patient and accepting being experience anger for example? Anger, after all, is a state of mind caused by unmet expectations; something which an all knowing, all patient, all unconditionally loving and divine being could not experience.

In developing this theory, I did consider that God has existed long before most of us can fathom, and it's possible that God did learn *everything* over the past billions of trillions of years (give or take a week due to red lights and daylight savings time), and this alone could feasibly make God perfect. However, even if the latter is the case, the fact remains, if a being does not continue to learn and grow, it dies. If a perfect being cannot learn, even if it is a result of his own perfection, then his *incapacity* to learn renders him imperfect. Therefore, in order to ensure God's continual growth, and to maintain the title of perfection, God must continue to learn. That's where we come into play. To better explain, imagine that you're an all-knowing being, and you realize that your very survival depends on imperfection, ignorance and continual learning, but you are perfect, you already know *everything*, and there is nothing left to learn (and maybe you're a bit bored)...What would you do?

Is it possible that God came to this realization at one point? If so, is it possible he sacrificed himself, in part or in whole, throughhout the universe, whether through the *Big-Bang* or some other way, on multiple levels of dimensions, frequencies and consciousness, manifesting in, and as, everything from rocks to plants to humans to animals to space/air/fire/water to extraterrestrial life to giraffe spots to airline seat-sales? Is it possible that God cast himself into absolute ignorance in order to continue learning? Is it possible that we're all merely God-Pods (little pods filled with *God-Energy*) experiencing/learning on God's behalf? Is it possible that we are God's final link to perfection, and thus, not to put too fine a point on it; is it possible that we don't need God as much as God needs us? If so, it might explain why God never gives up on us, no matter what! If imperfection is in fact the core motive behind our existence, it does bring into question what the point is to living affirmatively. As I understand it, living affirmatively is the key factor to making the journey worthwhile. To simplify; anyone can be bad, but it takes work to be good. This is why being good is rewarded. So, if I'm right, and if we must be imperfect, we might as well reap the benefits that come with being *affirmatively* imperfect.

We're also here to learn about, and to develop, aspects of love beyond that which already exists. In effect, we're playing a role in the evolution of *unconditional love*. Yes, unconditional love is already perfect, but as perfection implies the necessity to change and grow, unconditional love must subscribe to the evolutionary process (perpetual transmutation), and that's another reason for being here, and it highlights the importance of human existence throughout the entire universe. We couldn't possibly participate in this divine process if we were all born remembering the *Love* from which we came and to which we return, which is part of the reason why we're here with no memory, no manual and little guidance. This process may imply bumps, bruises and tears, but in accordance with the law of cause and effect, everything we endure in the name of our journey is compensated many times over. Part of that compensation entails unconditional forgiveness. It should be noted that *error* and *intentional evil* (sin) are two separate concepts. Sin is when we do what we know we shouldn't be doing in the name of our ego, whereas error is a price we pay for intentionally growing and developing for the betterment of that which lies beyond ourselves. Cause and effect rewards us for having to make errors and dealing with unpleasant results. When we err with a motive to do good, we're actually *giving*, and as such, because it's an inherently affirmative process, there is an affirmative payback.

Whatever the rhyme or reason for our being here, there's a common misconception about how easier life would be if we knew the actual *meaning* of life, but such profound knowledge comes with vast responsibility and requires action in order for it to signify or accomplish anything, otherwise, knowledge without assuming responsebility and taking action is merely idle data. Furthermore, we already know how to take better care of ourselves; how to better treat others, how to be generous, honest, integrous, disciplined and committed, and we know the affirmative payoffs these actions yield, but we don't do those things, or at least we don't do them often or consistently, so it stands to reason that if we're not applying ourselves to the little things, then knowledge of the bigger picture; like the meaning of life for example, regardless of what it is, would be useless to us, because that's what data is without action; *useless*! If you are building a house and you have the schematics, it's not the schematics that are going to build that house; you must take action, you've got to get to work. Otherwise, the schematics mean nothing.

We might not all be in agreement about or recognize why we're here, but we all have enough intelligence to recognize that being civilized and working together and doing our part will take us much further beyond our current understanding of ourselves, and catapult us to the realization of our absolute mission. In actuality, regardless of what anybody has ever implied about achieving anything in life, whether it's achieving financial success or raising happy children or connecting with God or awakening humanity or actually discovering the true meaning of life, or arriving at anything else we wish to accomplish this day or this year or this lifetime; there's always work to be done. As previously mentioned, only nothing comes from nothing. In order to achieve something, one must actually *"do"* something, otherwise we stagnate, we regress and we die.

As for *"nothing from nothing"*, I have come to recognize that it is impossible for *nothing* or *nothingness* to actually exist, and that there is no such thing as *nothing*, and therefore by virtue of the concept of the law of attraction (like attracts like), we're never attracting *nothing*, which means we're always attracting something. If this understanding is correct, then we'd better get conscious really soon; all of us personally and collectively, because based on what we're doing, saying, thinking and feeling, what's coming doesn't look very pretty!

If in fact there's no such thing as *nothing*, then there is only *omnipotence* existing *omnipotently* in all places, on all planes, throughout all of existence, including beyond that realm of where we think it all began/begins (that rhetorical void of nothingness which resides just beyond that place where we imagine the universe ends – because of course, if we can't imagine anything there, then there must be nothing there, right?). According to my theory that *nothing* can't actually exist, in the beginning there had to be *something*, even if that something was/is a vast realm of energy waiting to be utilized or occupied. I have come to understand that this *place* which seems to be *nothing* is actually omnipotent *possibility* and *probability* in its purist form, and it is the affirmative realm of possibility, and it is God. It has always existed. We only rack our brains over attempting to conceive of where it came from or where it began because we apply the concept of linear time to everything we contemplate. However, insofar as humans restrict everything to the concept of linear time, linear time is the creation of God, and as such, God is not restricted to the concept of linear time. God has simply *always been.*

When it comes to my personal search into anything, it's important for me to be unbiased, logical and honest. In keeping with my mandate, I must admit that my theory as to why we're here could be just that; a mere theory. In the same rite however, it's very possible that I am correct in my estimation. That we're all *being, doing* and *experiencing* on behalf of God. Of course I've considered other possibilities. I have to; it's what I live and breathe for. It's what I do. Yes, it is possible God doesn't exist, and everything is all chaos and chance and survival of the fittest. Maybe we humans aren't as precious as we'd like to think. After all, every living thing wants to survive; humans, dogs, giraffes, mosquitoes, worms, bacteria, cancer cells. We all want to survive, live, consume, produce and reproduce, and we all have the right to do so, and the outcome is seemingly based on who's got the upper hand, which animal runs faster, who can afford the chemo, who wraps their rascal on prom night, and who knows who, among other things.

In my less than profound imaginings, I've considered that we humans are possibly just a result of a random mutant form of bacteria that got pooped out of a monkey's butt and then got struck by lightning on a full moon of a summer solstice, igniting the beginning of a new species that would evolve into humans (sorry for the ill-mannered narrative, but a scientific mind isn't always a pretty mind). However, when one truly observes the *rhyme & reason* of human nature, not to mention all of nature in general, one cannot deny the presence of universal law's sense of *intelligent rationale* (and outright humor) which brings chaos to order. Sure, chaos still exists, but in the same manner of which light and dark need each other, so do *chaos* and *order*, as both have an important role to play for the sake of all of creation. Nestled comfortably behind that sense of *intelligent rationale* is a "reason" for it all.

Regardless of whatever theories we've considered and imagined, we cannot deny that there really is a reason for everything. Birds need to mate, so they were made colorful to attract mates. Bees need nectar, so flowers are fragrant and colorful to attract bees. Beavers are given the illicit penchant for chewing; otherwise their lower teeth grow until eventually piercing their upper palate and penetrating their own skull, while at the same time those same lower teeth never stop growing in order to accommodate their illicit penchant for chewing. These are just a few illustrations of the brilliant considerations behind nature's *intelligent* designs.

My point is that there's simply too much evidence of thought, logic, reason, creativity and intelligence behind nature's designs for it to be all by chance. In all honesty, I would like to believe that it's all chaos and that it doesn't matter what we do. This would make everything so much easier. I'd only have to worry about me, I could do whatever I want to do and not care about the consequences of my actions because it wouldn't matter. I have however, come to recognize otherwise. That it does all matter; every single thing that we do and say throughout every single moment, and that we humans, along with every single thing in existence, were and continue to be crafted with integrity and love and a caliber of quantum consideration beyond anything we currently allow ourselves to recognize.

In all my searching, I have come to understand this constant: As we search for *Truth* and meaning, we must always remember to leave the concept of limitation out of the equation. Just because most minds cannot conceive of where and how it all began, or that something intelligent created it all, does not mean there wasn't a beginning (or occurrence), or that *intelligent thought* wasn't behind it all. And it's tremendously arrogant to assume it all began, or occurred, with *nothing* just because we cannot imagine *something*. I find it absurd that scientists are as adamant to deny the concept of *creationism* in the same closed-minded extreme which religious addicts are adamant to deny the concept of *evolution*. Whether through religion or science, one cannot make *True* discoveries about *Truth* when one's mind is closed, because the missing links to all the greatest discoveries which are waiting to be *discovered* can only be revealed through an open, unbiased *spherical thinking* mind. Like politicians, scientists and religious extremists would rather endeavor to prove the other side wrong than come together and discover their very common ground. That which I have come to recognize is that both sides have been correct all along. Creationism *and* evolution are both valid theories; two phenomena brought together through universal *intelligent rationale* to serve Divine Purpose. In other words, something was created for a reason, and it had to (and has to) evolve. Pretty simple, actually.

All that said, it's important to understand that just because you might know why you're here doesn't mean the journey will be easier. In fact, it generally makes it a tad more challenging, but as challenging as any knowledge may be, when you discover that you're feasibly living and learning on behalf of God, it places your everyday thoughts and actions into greater perspective, not to mention, it somehow makes the difficult times bearable and less frequent and the good times better and recurrent.

Again, knowledge is important; knowledge is precious even, but knowledge alone is merely a component of our existence. For anything affirmative to happen as a result of knowledge, one need only take affirmative action, one step at a time. One needn't be scientific or masterfully spiritual, or sacrifice all material possessions (our mission may be the same, but our paths are habitually unique). Ultimately the key to change for the better throughout all of humanity is for each person to take responsibility for the actions we choose to take from this moment forth, and to take responsibility for what we make priority in our lives. If we live every day taking responsibility for our lives; our current situations and every decision we make and the actions we take, and we set the example and start the trend, then taking responsibility would feel as natural as thinking about water when we're thirsty.

Humans haven't forgotten how to take action or how to make things happen or even how to communicate with God or with each other. We've never lost our ability to communicate and take things to the next level, it's always been there; we're born with it. We're simply out of practice. Thinking for ourselves, being completely honest about everything, taking responsibility for our lives and our actions, and prioritizing what's important in our lives; everything from deciding between playing video games or studying, to deciding between a doughnut or an apple, to the excuses we make for not doing what we know we should do, only seems difficult because we're out of practice. Like anything else however, once you get into the zone, it becomes second nature and you wonder how you ever got along without it. From observing humanity and the state of our planet, it has become apparent that we aren't getting along without taking action; we're barely surviving, and most of us are surviving the negative ramifications of *our own* negative actions; the way we handle our finances, our relationships, our health, our politics and so forth. This astonishing survival is not *because* of us but mostly *in spite* of us. On an affirmative note, this realization is a shining testament to our astounding resilience. On a realistic note however, it seems we're toast! Nonetheless, I personally do not subscribe to the collective delusion of *reality*, and beyond this, my faith in humanity is vast beyond measure, so I remain devotedly optimistic.

The key to taking total responsibility is for each of us to simply start small. By this I mean, start by shifting priority from doubt to faith, from spending to saving, from rage to kindness, and for those ready for a big change, shift everything from fear to love. My advice to everybody is to start with the affirmative shifting you can handle and leave the bigger shifting for when you've mastered the small stuff. I realize this sounds simple on paper, but as it's always the little things that are most important, it's clear that we've got our work cut out for us. We're trying to be slimmer, prettier, younger, richer, etc, and in our process of attempting to master our lives, we master insecurity, self-loathing, self-hatred, self-mutilation, to name only some. Then there's what we do as a result of this process; trying desperately to become someone who will mask the undesirable something we've been hiding behind, thereby never getting to know ourselves or the gifts we each have to bring to the world, and so the cycle continues and our mission as humans is never recognized, and it compromises our lives and our relationships with everybody and everything.

Further along in this book is a chapter dedicated entirely to the concept of relationships, and although the chapter touches on many aspects of relationships in general, per-haps the most important message within the chapter is the importance of mastering our relationship with our own *self*. I mention relationships now however, because without mastering our relationship with our own *self*, it is impossible to bring the best of ourselves; the *God-Within*, to the forefront of our lives for the benefit of experienc-ing our best lives and for the betterment and advance-ment of humanity. Before setting forth to master our relationships with our families, our neighbors, our friends, our spouses and our children, we must first master our relationship with our *self*; what we put into our minds and bodies, and mastering our habits, vices, addictions, words, thoughts, feelings, education, and especially the lies we tell ourselves and everybody else about who we are. When we master the relationship with our *self*, it profoundly affects all our relationships. This process when carried out by just some of humanity, affirmatively affects all of humanity, and it affirmatively affects the entire universe.

If we'd relinquish the arrogant, ego-based, know-it-all thinking which is responsible for the way we stagnate; by this I mean relinquish our attachments to animosity, arguments, drama, hatred, blame, jealousy, resentment, and especially our addiction to approval; all of which ultimately keeps us from *Truth* and from becoming our definitive selves, then we'd discover a shift in our commitment in what we deem important and our consequential commitment to our search for *Truth* and mastering our relationship with our own self. This would be just the very beginning of healing and advancing all of humanity towards its greatest potential. This one single process of healing, bettering and nurturing our relationship with our own self would propel all of humanity towards global consciousness unlike anything most of us can currently fathom. The affirmative, innovative, breakthrough discoveries this process would yield during just its infancy stage would have more impact on the planet than if every single person worldwide – military and civilian alike – would instantly drop their arms and pick up a soccer ball. Moments beyond the infancy stage of a global conscious shift of this magnitude, our current stagnant reality would be virtually unfathomable to us. The best part of this ideal is that we don't need the entire world to make it happen; it would only take a small fraction of the world's entire population to get the ball rolling. A very small portion. We just need that small portion of people to commit to the journey: The journey within...

Beyond relationships, sometimes the biggest shifts take place when we attempt to change our lives when we feel we're in too deep. For example, when we've done something illegal, or we've hurt somebody deeply, or we're at death's door. The truth of the matter, however, is that it's never too late to change! This is about making the change where we are, right here, right now. Often we want to make changes in our lives, whether it's finances, diet, better parenting, walking a legal path and so forth, but we feel like we're in too deep, or that it will take ten years to rectify the problem. If we're walking a dark path and decide to walk in the light, many steps towards the light may still be surrounded by darkness, but it's during these times that we must dwell in the realm of affirmative possibility and keep believing and always keep going. In the process, we must remember to keep affirmative words, thoughts, feelings and actions at the forefront of all we do. We must be conscious about whom we let into our lives and about whose lives we enter into, and most importantly, we must face our issues *head-on*. Furthermore, if you think a process of change will take ten years, keep in mind, if you plan to be around in ten years anyway, you may as well get started! Finally, we must keep learning beyond what we know and beyond what we *assume* we know.

As mentioned in the introduction, one of the greatest threats to all of humanity is that we are living our lives based largely on what we *assume* we know as opposed to what we *do* know. To put what we do know into perspective; with all our knowledge, we're more misinformed than we are informed. To place into perspective what we *do not* know, consider the following: Imagine the concept of infinity as it applies to space. By this I mean *literal space* in all its infinite mass, volume, depth, width, length, height and so forth. Most humans cannot conceive of where space begins and where it ends. Because our current concept of space is non-containable and seemingly goes on forever, we cannot imagine that there is anything *beyond* the realm of space, and thus, we accept this perspective as fact. However, once we advance our thinking to the point where we identify infinity as a mere *component* of all there is, rather than identifying it as *all there is*, we would then recognize that infinity is merely one single component among billions of trillions of additional components working harmoniously together as the true universal oneness that is God.

Because our concept of space is limited to what we *allow* ourselves to see, we're limited to what we could discover about what lies *beyond* space. In expanding our concept of what lies beyond the realm of infinity as it applies to space, we'd discover that, to the consciousness of *all that is*, what we consider to be infinity is about as significant to God as what we consider an atom on a flea in the fur of a mouse in some land of which we've never heard. If we'd get to that level of consciousness, we'd begin to understand the astonishing vastness of the infinite love God has for that one precious atom; a love as big as what we'd consider to be infinity as it applies to the entirety of space. If you get this example, then you are barely beginning to scratch the surface of the immense role you are playing in the universe. And, if you can imagine God's infinite love for that one precious atom, try for a moment to imagine God's infinite, unlimited, unconditional love for you.

Why we're here may not be apparent to anybody. The answer to that question may never come, or perhaps I've nailed it within the first lines of this chapter. Either way, if the answer does exist, one thing is certain; the only way we'll ever find it is to dwell in the realm of absolute *affirmative possibility*, for this is clearly where God dwells now, has always dwelt, and shall dwell forevermore.

Many people with whom I've discussed these ideals and principles; dedicated scientists, theologians, clergy and humanitarians alike, have agreed with many of my theories but tend to believe that our species is not ready to take on the commitment required to propel humanity to the next level. I believe, however, that we *are* ready, and we're hungry for it, and we're long overdue. I believe that as a people and as a species, and as entities and missionaries of Love and of God, we are ready for this responsibility. I believe we are here to do a job and that we are capable, and we're ready to take humanity to the next level...

CHAPTER III

=TheMind=

To limit the mind is to limit everything...

Although there remains substantial confusion about the precise manner in which the mind functions, it is my strong opinion that we humans truly warrant a well deserved pat on the back for not only attempting, but for actually *succeeding* at figuring out so much about something of which we use so very little. Considering our ongoing archaic thinking and limiting beliefs about God, the world, and ourselves, and the tragic way we live our lives, we have somehow figured out enough about our minds to have survived, or dare I say, advanced to this point, and for that I say, KUDOS TO US!

There is no shortage of people out there who spew negative *non-factual* facts about humans and how slow we are to develop in comparison to most animals, but those people's perspectives and their outdated findings are the results of what happens when people don't look deeply enough beneath the surface of what *seems to be*. Most of us can appreciate how astonishing it is that a new-born giraffe can stand up only an hour after it is born, and that it can eat only seconds after it stands. Well, if the only things humans had to learn were to stand up and eat, we would get the hang of things sooner, but there is more to humans than mere standing and eating and basic survival. Our survival instincts do make up a vast sum of our nature, but there is so much more to the complex nature of humans, and based on what we are capable of learning and doing, not to mention all we resiliently endure as a result of what we must face in life, it's truly a wonder we don't take even longer to develop.

Humans write, speak, read, cook, knit, golf, drive, and do countless other things that don't even scratch the surface of what animals *cannot* do. Yes, we've taught cats how to use toilets, horses how to count, and apes how to communicate through sign language, however, what animals actually learn when we teach them to do what humans do is to imitate human behavior. Even if a horse learns to sew or a dolphin learns to fry an egg, an animal will never naturally do all that one human does. Not only because it's inherently not interested, but because it's not designed to do so, and it's not in their nature. The point is, *we* take the time to develop because there is so much in humans to develop. We are not slow; we've merely got a lot to develop.

With so many books out there about self improvement, the law of attraction, quantum physics, the power of thought, the mind in general, and let's not forget the Bible, it's somewhat challenging to offer up fresh and informative knowledge to feed the minds and hearts of those who are on a consistent quest for answers. Most recent books on the subject of *the mind* merely offer up the very same information but delivered in different terms, presenting facts and theories in a different order, just like the countless rows of self-help books you'll find at any book store. Repetitious as they may be, many of those books serve a purpose because although they might be saying the same thing, their delivery speaks to different people. One common problem with many and most of those books is not with their content, but rather, the people who read and accept that content as fact or truth without challenging the ideals, and the people who base their lives on the misinformation therein without truly thinking about it. Then there are those who apply a newly learnt concept to their lives (meditation, law of attraction, prayer, diet, etc.) but don't adjust other areas of their lives (belief, trust, devotion, discipline, exercise, etc.) and come to the conclusion that what they've read is a big crock of sugar-coated cow-dung. My goal with this chapter isn't just to offer up new ideas, but to also bust a few myths about the mind. Myths upon which even seasoned scientists have based, and currently still do base, their life's work.

Contrary to popular belief that the mind functions affirmatively only if we think affirmatively and negatively only if we think negatively, and contrary to popular belief that the mind doesn't acknowledge negative commands such as *no, don't, can't* and *won't*, to name just some, I have come to recognize that the mind, like God, only functions affirmatively, regardless of what one thinks or says, and inherently so, and here's why:

Your mind is a creator. It is your direct link to God The Divine Creator. Creating is all that the mind can do, and it can only create anything and everything *affirmatively*. Even immense catastrophic destruction of the most evil variety is a type of *affirmative* creation. Any *intention* to devastate or to destroy is an intention to accomplish something, and although the desired outcome may be of a negative nature, any intention to accomplish anything is an *affirmatively creative process*. Any endeavor, whether good or bad, takes affirmative action to become reality. Without affirmative action, nothing happens.

To clarify this theory, imagine a girl is teaching a boy to ride a bike. For the lesson to take place, the girl needs to first think about what is required and then take the appropriate action. Conversely, imagine the girl dislikes the boy and wishes to harm him. Again, creative thought and affirmative action are the basis upon which the girl may succeed in either undertaking. In the case of the girl's negative undertaking, some would argue that her actions were negative, and that even her thoughts were negative, and her mind worked negatively to produce the negative outcome she desired to achieve, however, inasmuch as her desired outcome was of a negative nature, the fact remains that the desired negative outcome would only happen if she took *affirmative* action. This affirmative action includes *affirmative creative thinking* and *intention* in order for her to succeed in her unloving undertaking.

When understanding this concept, it's important to not confuse the mind itself with thought or intention. If you can imagine a computer system, you can imagine that thought or intention is the software (*the program*), whereas the mind is the hardware (*the computer*). Thought, feeling and intention (*all software components*) are what we feed the mind (*the hardware/computer*). The computer affirmatively processes whatever software it is fed.

Another way of looking at the mind and thought or intention is to imagine the mind as a DVD player, and thought as a DVD disc. Whether the program on the disc is about a positive subject – say perhaps miracles – or a negative subject – say perhaps massacres – the DVD player functions in the exact same manner in order to present the program, remarkably, without any bias whatsoever. The DVD player will never laugh or cry while it plays the content, and it does not judge the content, nor does it judge the viewers' response to the content. It just does its job. The DVD player is not good or bad for not responding to what it exposes, it merely operates as it's designed to operate; it actively and affirmatively processes whatever positive or negative data it is fed, as does the mind.

When we apply this example to the mind, it gives us a better understanding of how our mind attracts to us – in a completely unbiased manner – experiences and events which are harmonious with what we're thinking, feeling, saying, believing and doing. The mind, like a computer, is designed to do a job regardless of the program. Like a computer, in order to expand its ability to accommodate a greater program, we need only expand our thinking in order to accommodate greater consciousness. This cannot happen if we're all in agreement with what the mind *cannot* accomplish. This happens when we acknowledge the mind as omnipotent. I'd also like to interject at this point that the mind, although unbiased in it's willingness to process what it is fed, *is* completely affected, or *infected*, by the program it processes. A DVD player won't be affected by the horror flick you choose to watch, but whatever thoughts touch the mind impacts the mind.

One massively erroneous and therefore dangerous myth about the mind is the theory which suggests that the mind cannot register negative terminology, for example, words like *no, don't, can't* and *won't*. I say this theory is dangerous because it suggests a limitation of the mind. It also implies that because we didn't find a better or more accurate rebuttal to this theory, it's okay to accept the theory as factual. This thinking is as dangerous to our existence as is our perpetual tendency of presuming fault with anything we do not comprehend. It is my theory that not only can the mind register these negatives, but it registers them perfectly well; as well as anything else the mind can register. I also think it's preposterous to consider that the mind, on a subconscious level, in all its astonishing brilliant omnipotence, is unable to register anything. The very fact that negativity is so rampant in our world only underscores the idea that the mind does in fact register negative terminology.

A simple way to explain this theory is, whereas the *conscious* mind comprehends the word *don't* as a negative, the *subconscious* mind registers the word *don't* as a symbol rather than a word. A symbol that represents a command; an affirmative way of carrying out a specific action. We tend to assume that the subconscious mind comprehends words in the same manner of which we comprehend them consciously, but the subconscious mind processes information in far more advanced ways than does the conscious mind. Of course, by far more advanced, I mean simple.

When we first learn to read, we're introduced to a series of unfamiliar symbols that we quickly learn are called letters. Later we group letters together to form other symbols called words. Eventually, we learn to group words into a series of symbols called sentences, and then with these we form paragraphs, pages, volumes and so forth; all merely symbols to the subconscious mind. Even verbally, words are not really words but merely sounds made by manipulating our tongue, lips, cheeks, jaw, breath and vocal cords. To our subconscious mind however, a verbal word is a symbol. On a conscious level, we've learned to recognize words as words, and letters as letters, but the subconscious mind continues to recognize sentences, words and letters as symbols, and those symbols each represent a *signal* to the subconscious mind.

Perhaps as exciting as a basket of puppies on caffeine in a kindergarten class is the perspective that everything the mind understands about these communicative symbols is based one hundred percent upon the training or the *conditioning* of the mind, and the words *no, don't, can't, won't* are no exception. If the mind could not conceive of nor understand these negative terms, we would not be able to speak them or understand them when they're said to us. Furthermore, we understand negative words because we are taught their meanings. For example, whether the word *giraffe* is presented to the subconscious mind verbally or visually or physically; whether through spoken word or print or brail or sign language, there is absolutely no real correlation between these symbols. The symbol correlation or "word association" is merely about affirmatively imposed perspectives; in other words, *education*. We tell the mind how it is, and the mind complies. There is absolutely no correlation between the vibrational frequencies of the spoken word *giraffe* and the optical symbol of the word *giraffe*, or the feel of brail which represents the word *giraffe*, or the mechanical movements of the hands in sign language which represent the word *giraffe*. These symbols represent little, if anything, without first training or conditioning the mind. Nobody knows what the word for giraffe is until they are taught that it is such. This same principle applies to any communicative form of the words *no, don't, can't, won't* and so forth.

Since our minds are predisposed to learn and absorb everything as fact, it takes very little for us to condition our minds, and therefore all of humanity, in and out of any perspective. Understanding how easy it is to manipulate communication and how easy it is to be manipulated by communication should be our greatest incentive for improving upon and extending diligence to everything we say and think, and what we feed our minds.

To the subconscious mind, language is merely a series of signals which means about as much to the subconscious mind as what hearing a fire truck's siren means to you consciously. It's not something you can see or touch or read, but you know the sound's frequency means *urgent!* It is this way because you were taught this. The same thing applies to what you understand on a hot summer day when the bells of an ice cream truck are within earshot. Even a two year old can differentiate the meaning of a fire siren from the sound of bells. Apply this to the sound of laughter or the sound of crying; all merely sounds, yet their vibrational frequencies send out signals that even the simplest person can understand.

Where *double negatives* are concerned, in the same manner of which you can't *not* think of laughing as I suggest *don't laugh*, the subconscious mind can't *not* recognize the word *conditional* as a command when the term *unconditional* is used. To the subconscious mind, the word *un* does not cancel out the word *conditional*; the word *unconditional* is recognized by the subconscious mind as two negative symbols; *un* & *conditional*, and both negatives become part of your creative intention. This, for example, is why the term *unconditional* should be replaced in prayer, meditation and especially affirmations with the term *omnipresent*.

So, contrary to current theory which suggests that the mind doesn't hear or register negatives, the mind in all its infinite brilliance does hear the words *no, don't, can't, won't* and so forth, and it processes these symbols and their signals affirmatively. A simple way to understand the process is to imagine that Mary tells David to remember his umbrella. With this affirmative directive, David's subconscious is programmed to remember the umbrella, even if throughout his entire day he's consciously unaware that he's carrying it. However, if he responds with, "I won't forget my umbrella," he's sure to forget his umbrella. The reason for this is because not only did David override Mary's command to *remember* by following up with the command *forget*, but he also reinforced that command with a symbolic directive, telling him not only to forget his umbrella, but also *how* to go about forgetting it; the *how* being the symbol *won't*. To the subconscious mind, the word *won't* doesn't mean *won't*; it's merely a symbol which signals a reinforcing directive (*"extra"* forget). If David said he'll *sadly* forget the umbrella, his mind will be programmed to forget the umbrella during a sad moment during his day. Even if David's day goes by without a sad moment, his mind will create the necessary moment, even if it means causing old sad memories to resurface in order to provide the sadness required to carry out the undertaking. In this case, David said he *won't* forget the umbrella, and as such, the word *won't* is recognized as a directive, almost as good as saying *"reinforce forgetting the umbrella"*. As the mind will always affirmatively process a directive, it instructed David to absolutely forget the umbrella. In short, the subconscious is a very clever thing and it will always figure a way to affirmatively process whatever it is fed, including anything we consider to be negative. It does this at all costs, not because it is *for* or *against* us, but because to do so is simply its job.

This subject may seem somewhat insignificant in the grand scheme of all things, but the threats that lie in humanity's act of dwelling upon limiting beliefs about our mind's inabilities – beliefs resulting from inaccurate facts about the nature of which the mind functions – are the cornerstone upon which all of humanity's detrimental beliefs sit. Detrimental beliefs that have been since the beginning of time nothing short of humanity's impending self-imposed threat of its own demise. The danger that lies in the theory that the mind cannot register something is to humanity, limiting beyond reproach. The theory that the mind can and does register everything is supported by the mere fact that the mind *creates* everything. Furthermore, the danger that lies in the theory that the mind is incapable of recognizing *anything* is to acknowledge the mind as other than affirmatively creative. To do so is to acknowledge the *Greater Thing*, The One Divine Creator to which all of our minds are connected, as limited.

Something about the subconscious mind that very few people are aware is that the subconscious mind doesn't know the difference between right or wrong, nor does it know if what it is seeing is real. In fact, just by my telling you that there is a blue giraffe sitting next to you right now, you might not consciously believe it, but your subconscious mind does. The beauty of this discovery is that it broadens our perspective on the way we see everything, especially reality. When we broaden our perspective of reality, we discover that reality doesn't actually exist, and we understand that *perspective* is all there is. Furthermore, when we discover that perspective is all there is, we realize that what any and every society, and all of humanity actually, sees as reality is merely a *mass perspective*; everyone choosing to look in the same direction. Nowhere is this more evident than in the world of consumerism; fashion, automobiles, cosmetics, food, entertainment, etc. Place it on a magazine cover and say it's all the rage, and you've got an instant hit! What's exciting about this discovery is that it proves that all of humanity has the ability to look in a same direction and walk a same path, and thus it is feasible for everyone to see the light. In the next chapter about the law of attraction, I cover various additional aspects of how the mind works, but before you proceed to that chapter, I wanted to present a basic understanding of the subconscious mind.

Among other things, it's the job of the subconscious mind to yearn to experience, to do as it is told, to figure things out and process what it is fed as fact, and find a way to turn ideas into actuality. Whether the subconscious witnesses you experiencing something, or it witnesses another person experiencing it, it is unbiased. It yearns for the lesson, and it will send you in the direction of that lesson based on the signals you send it, and it does this in harmony with all universal laws and with Divine Purpose. As much as the mind has its work cut out for itself, it is up to us to consciously study ourselves and to bring ourselves to a better understanding of how we function in order to affirmatively wield our minds for harmonious life experiences and for the advancement of humanity.

It would be wonderful if every single person could pick up a book; either about self-improvement, or the environment, or the law of attraction, or positive thinking, or health, or about some form of conscious growth, and for all of us to grow together from that one book. For each book however, no matter how great it is, its varied ideals are no match for the diversity of our minds. We all think and feel and assimilate information differently; this is why everybody doesn't share the same ideals about movies or music or sports or food or experiences. One main reason why one ideal about conscious awareness cannot possibly apply to every person's mind is because the subconscious mind of each individual, just like with each conscious mind, is *distinctive*. Each person's subconscious is designed to function identically, but each mind is nonetheless individually unique. A simple example of this concept is to consider the following:

In one year, several millions of one brand and model of minivan have been designed in the exact same manner and to the exact same specifications and manufactured with exactly the same methods and with the same ratios of plastic to metal to glass to fabrics and so forth; all incredibly within the same proportions within thousandths of a millimeter. Of the several millions of minivans however, produced that year, the fact remains, no two are in any way alike. Each and every single component which comprises every single minivan; every metal body, every plastic gauge-lens, every glass windshield, every seatbelt; all of it consists of completely separate atoms and molecules and therefore, regardless of its visible sameness, every single minivan is one hundred percent unique from another. Beyond this, when measurements of each component are observed beyond the thousandths of a millimeter, it becomes obvious that the microscopic volume of each component, and therefore each minivan, is also unique. If this is the case for something that doesn't think, feel, grow, learn, or hold a perspective, imagine what this means to the subconscious mind of each and every single thinking, feeling, growing, learning human being who each possess a unique immeasurable consciousness.

Perspectives are largely created by the subconscious mind, but the perspective of the subconscious mind continues to be fueled by the conscious mind. When we understand that each subconscious mind – although connected to a greater collective consciousness – is unique, it becomes evident why one self-help book won't appeal to or help everybody. Our concepts of what defines an ideal life-experience go well beyond the ideals which motivate us, not only because we're not all motivated by the same things, but because our motives are as much dictated by the physical and metaphysical make-up of our brains and minds as they are by the experiences which mold our thoughts.

Many researchers suggest that humans have just so many thoughts in a day. Some say 50,000 thoughts, others suggest 75,000 thoughts, and that it is impossible to acknowledge all of them. I personally suspect that those numbers are highly underestimated, because when I consider what I think about in a day, there are thousands of thoughts that come up during that one thought process of considering my daily thoughts. In my estimation, there have to be millions of thoughts flowing through our minds each day, especially when taking into consideration the various levels of consciousness upon which we think. I personally am a deep thinker; it is what I do, so it stands to reason that if I think more often on a conscious level than would a non-deep thinker, I probably think more on a subconscious level as well, thereby increasing the number of thoughts I have in a day compared to a non-deep thinker. Just taking into consideration that there are 86,400 seconds in a day, and that we think nonstop, even as we sleep, and considering that a thought can last a nano-second thereby implying that the mind can conceive of multiple thoughts per second, I don't see how anybody with regular basic faculties could only have on average 75,000 thoughts per day. I do agree with scientists that for many of us, most of our thoughts are of a negative nature, so whether we're thinking 50,000 thoughts per day, or its one million thoughts, if most of them are negative, and if we're not recognizing it, we're fighting a losing battle.

While we have the power to control our subconscious to believe anything we tell it, it's evident we're not using this power, and in our reluctance to gain control of our basic consciousness, our subconscious is on autopilot, having a field day at our personal expense and at the expense of all humanity. We've come to a point where we've permitted our subconscious to have total power over us, and it controls us, and it does this because it wants to play, learn and experience. Unlike us, the subconscious mind never sleeps, so it's time for us to wake up and get into the game, if for no other reason than to enjoy the game...

So, let's play!

CHAPTER IV

=LawOfAttraction=

As ye see it and believe it, so shall it be...Maybe...

During the writing process of this book, there were several times at which I questioned the truthfulness of what I was writing, and the integrity of the various facts I was relaying to make my point. At no time, however, during the writing process did I struggle more than while writing on topic of the law of attraction. Let's face it, after all, I wasn't writing a cook-book or a do-it-yourself book; something where if a reader followed the directions is pretty much guaranteed to yield immediate bona fide results, and thus, it was difficult to convince myself that I was on the right path. (For anyone unfamiliar with the concept of the law of attraction, basically, the law implies that *like attracts like*, and therefore, where it applies to the mind, whatever we think about and act upon – good and bad – we attract into our lives.)

As I struggled to move beyond my own doubts, even after much success with consciously manifesting some absurd things into my life if for no other reason than to see if I could do it, or at least to prove the theory was a myth, my doubts still remained. Even after successfully manifesting things like daffodils in a snowstorm, a large house in the countryside, and an actual Rolls Royce (just to be sure), there was a point where I completely doubted the theory. It was during that period I discovered that the best medicine for doubt is rebellion. So, for a short period, I researched whatever information I could find which could logically dispute what I knew about the law of attraction, and I was committed to considering any-thing that anybody said or published which supported the theory that the law of attraction is a myth. For one, I wanted to know if I was barking up the wrong tree, and for two, I most certainly did not want to encourage people to consider something to be true that was not. *"Who knows?"* I thought, *"Maybe the house, the daffodils, and the Rolls Royce were just a fluke!"*

In order to execute the research effectively, I knew I had to do away with any personal convictions, either way, about the law's existence or its myth. This meant doing away with the emotional or "sensuous" physical feelings often confused with making alleged connections to Truth or God or Divine inspiration or just wanting something to be right to the extent of creating delusion. I have to admit that at the time I researched the information, it was not difficult for me to deny the theory of the law of attraction, because my life as I knew it seemed to be crashing down all around me in spite of what I did *energetically* to prevent it. In all honesty, I desperately wanted to prove the concept simply does not exist.

And so, the search got deeper, and what I encountered when I researched the possible myths was an endless trail of metaphorical nonsense relayed by people who were clearly unaware of any real aspect of the law of attraction, and/or who had done little if any research on the subject, and/or who came to their conclusions due to their lack of success in manifesting their desires. A lack of success due to their confusion of how the law works, and a clear misunderstanding of what it means when it doesn't work. Even with my genuine commitment to find evidence to support the myth, I was able to effortlessly defuse any theory claiming the law did not exist. I do acknowledge that although I didn't find any such evidence, it doesn't imply such evidence doesn't exist, but what's more, in my search for the myth, I looked within and beyond, and it is then and there that I made some powerful discoveries.

Perhaps one of the greatest struggles most people face in understanding the law of attraction is that, like with the concept of infinite space, most of us come to understand the law of attraction as *all there is*, when in reality, the law of attraction is merely one law. It is one law which works in harmony with all laws; laws we understand and laws we don't understand. For example, the laws of perpetual transmutation, relativity, vibrations, cause and effect, polarity, rhythm, gender, and a plethora of laws of which we are currently unaware. The key to understanding the basics is to understand that the law of attraction is *A* law, not *THE* law. This law works in harmony with thoughts, feelings and actions, and with other laws. As I researched and found no sustainable theory to deny the law, I realized that the people relaying their theories were not necessarly negative – although the vast majority of them were – but most were merely not thinking deeply enough, or as I like to refer to it; not *thinking spherically*. Nor were they affirmatively dwelling within the realm of affirmative possibility; this oversight being one of humanity's biggest downfalls.

Of all the aspects of which I have come to recognize concerning the concept of the law of attraction, perhaps the most significant is the realization which actually contradicts that which most spiritual "gurus" are trying to sell us on the concept. Whereas we've been told time and again that the law of attraction is the *"most powerful force in the universe"*, I maintain that the law of attraction, although a profoundly powerful force, is merely *one* powerful force among *many* other *equally* powerful forces. Countless forces in fact that, without which, the law of attraction could not function nor could it even exist. It's like giving credit to our fingers for what we can accomplish with our hands, all the while overlooking the importance of the palm, the wrist, the arm, the elbow, the heart, the lungs, the brain, or even the electricity that makes it all work.

To state that the law of attraction is the most powerful force in the world, and that it is all we need to master in order to succeed in life, is arrogant beyond reproach, because, in order to make such a calculated deduction, we'd first need to recognize every single force in existence *(which we have not)*. We are a young species still discovering ourselves and everything around us, and there is no way to emphasize what little we truly know about anything.

To further underscore that the law of attraction is not alone entirely responsible for what goes on in our lives, consider the following (note: *this example is 'extremely' graphic and includes illustrations of a negative nature*): A seven year old boy who is being raised in a loving, balanced home by two loving parents, and who has never been introduced to violence, is being stalked, unbeknownst to him, by a child predator. The predator scopes out the boy for weeks, learning where the boy goes, when the parents are out, who the babysitter is and a surplus of other details which help the predator draw up the best plan of action for his undertaking. Before long, the boy is creatively persuaded away from safety and into the hands of the stalker. Soon thereafter, the boy is alone with the predator, at which point the predator violently performs his heinous acts and ultimately brings the boy's life to an end.

All those "gurus" who are selling the idea that *everything we think about, we bring about*, are implying that we must simply think of something in order to attract it. In the above example of the abducted boy, it would be impossible for the boy to have attracted such an event to himself for the mere reason that by virtue of his upbringing, he couldn't have even considered something so horrifyingly dreadful. All this to say, inasmuch as where we are now, and what we may go through, is habitually the result of our feelings, thoughts, words and actions, it should be understood that it takes more than a mere thought to realize something into actuality, and no matter where you're going, there's more at work than the law of attraction alone, for better and for worse.

Whereas most books on the topic of the law of attraction utilize hundreds of pages to explain the same process, the Bible advises on the law of attraction with one single sentence: *Whatsoever ye desire when ye pray, believe that ye receive them, and ye shall have them* (Mark 11:24). Books explaining the law of attraction, or any other one universal component, are definitely worth reading for more in-depth examinations and study of the subject; after all, understanding how a thing works generally improves one's ability to work that thing. Regardless of our beliefs, however, it is certain that limiting ourselves to the understanding of merely one component of the Divine process limits the extent to which we can manipulate that process.

Even as a regular dude whose convictions go well beyond the limitations of organized religion, I cannot deny the power and inspiration I've personally experienced as a result of consulting the Bible. This power and inspiration is available to everybody for the taking, without restricttions or conditions. Best of all, it's free! As a researcher, scientist and thinker, I must admit that it's possible that all I've encountered from the Bible has absolutely nothing to do with Truth and everything to do with perspective. I have to admit this because to do so is honest and logical. Logically speaking, however, as a person who supports people's rights to believe what they believe, and where it applies to spirituality, I must admit that it does seem absurd for anybody to commit their life to just one aspect of spiritual consciousness when there is so much more available. It's like trying to get around town on just a bicycle tire when you have access the entire bicycle.

I have come to understand that the law of attraction as it applies to spirituality is merely the process of prayer, and we know that prayer is merely one component of the complex mechanism that is spirituality. With all there is available to us, especially where it applies to achieving dreams, goals and living our best lives, why wouldn't we open ourselves to the greater picture? Why do we deny ourselves the whole mechanism in the name of one component? Is it because we're scared of discovering Truth, or that we may be wrong? Or do we think because we have some of the preliminary knowledge, we have *all* the knowledge? Maybe it's a mix of things, with just a pinch of laziness, a whisper of stubbornness and a whole lot of ignorance and ego.

While researching the myth theories, I was bombarded with questions like; if doctors are always around sickness, why aren't doctors always sick? Or, why do things, good or bad, for example winning a lottery or losing a loved-one, happen to us when we're *not* thinking on them? To respond to these questions, I just needed to think affirmatively, logically, and of course, *spherically*.

First off, although doctors are surrounded by sick people, a doctor's intentions, thoughts and actions fundamentally revolve around *healing* the body, and usually, so do those of the patients. Furthermore, a hospital is a lot more affirmative than people give it credit for. For example, most people go to a hospital with the idea to get well. Second, most hospitals have a cleanliness protocol beyond most other establishments, and if you don't believe me, compare microbes you'll find on hospital blankets, floors and even toilets compared to the basic surfaces within even some of the finest hotels anywhere around the world. As for attracting things we're not thinking about, this has as much to do with other laws and Divine purposes beyond our current comprehension, including lessons we need to learn, places we need to be, and experiences others need to go through in spite of the fact we're connected to them. Sometimes a fortunate or unfortunate event happens to people around us, but our attachment to the people and their lives and their experiences makes us believe the event is happening to us. Then there are the deep-rooted feelings and the beliefs we carry around. And, let's not forget karma (cause and effect).

Perhaps the most important thing all humans, religious and non-religious alike, must understand about the law of attraction is the law's basic nature and its reasons for being. What religious people must recognize is that the concept of the law of attraction as it is being introduced in current times is merely a scientific explanation of the prayer process delivered in laymen's terms; a process which is clearly outlined and entirely supported by the Bible. Therefore, those who are adamant to deny this law and its scientific explanation on religious grounds are doing themseves and their fellow man an immense dis-service. What non-religious people must recognize is that this *new-world* process is not at all *new*, and it is only one part of life in the same manner of which a thumb is only one part of the body. Therefore, again, to imply that the law of attraction is *all there is* or *the most powerful force* is to deny all that to which it is connected and ultimately deny the many reasons for its existence.

Many of us have a better than basic understanding of the law of attraction, yet we still seem to not have a firm grasp of how to put it to use. One day we seem to master how to manifest things into our lives, and the next day, we're back at square one. One major culprit behind in-effective manifesting is simply the lack of faith; this lack often rooted in the core misunderstanding of what faith actually is. Here I'll state it simply: *Faith is not belief alone. Faith is a balanced amalgamation of belief and trust.* Another culprit is in the application of actual faith only for the duration of a prayer when it should be for the duration of one's entire day. Then there are other culprits; how to visualize, when to think on it, when to let go, and how to handle doubt.

In short, what it all comes down to is practice and the learning process. One of the reasons for this is because, like it or not, life is a constant *learning/graduating* process. In school, we don't graduate from grade three to grade four only to sit at our desks for a year waiting around for grade five. We graduate at the height of one level of experience and then move up to the base beginnings of another level where we must learn and practice anew. And life, just like school, is about learning what we don't know, at every level. In my current grade, on my current level, the following is what I have come to understand...

Since the beginning of time the law of attraction has been part of all existence. It has forever been this way and forevermore will it be. Like with anything created by God, the law of attraction is inherently good. Like anything else however, once something has been recognized by humanity, what we choose to do with it; good or bad, or even acknowledge or deny it, is up to us. Regardless of how we choose to wield this tool; this divine power, its vital core essence remains inherently pure and good.

Since long before recorded time, the misinformed teachings of the law of attraction, well meaning as they are and may have been over the millennia, were and often still are more detrimental to people's consciousness, life and wellbeing than if people had never been introduced to the concept to begin with. In past times, misinformation often had to do with mere perspective of findings, and learning through trial and error. In current times, the danger is higher than ever because everyone and their mistress is a self-proclaimed avatar, teacher, healer or guru, and the miracle and plague that is technology is allowing these "teachers" to broadcast their compromised findings, non-factual conclusions and unsustainable theories as facts. These inaccurate findings, conclusions and theories are being fed to the ignorant by the ignorant and by individuals who want something from nothing, looking to sell nothing for something, and so the cycle continues.

Because for many it's easier to log on to the Internet for easy answers, or read book after book of some over-marketed self-help guru, than to go within their own minds and hearts, they are inundated with the same misinformation served by different looking people using different words and tactics yet in essence all selling the same empty lessons that at best keep us from committing suicide for at least one more day but which don't offer any real sustenance other than a proven marketing ploy which keeps us coming back for more inaccurate and incomplete information.

I made this discovery of the dangers of misinformation not only through erroneous literature and misinformed teachings of others, but also through prayer, meditation, immense deep thought, and of course through observation of what I, and others around me; whether it be a friend or a neighboring country, were manifesting into our lives. This discovery has served me well, for it consistently reminds me that no matter what I absorb, I must continue to seek well beyond whatever is said or written, regardless of where it is said or written.

I had been introduced to the basic concept of the law of attraction in the 80's with five magic words; *"You Reap What You Sow"*. From that day forth, I paid attention to what I was attracting into my life and how I attracted it. That fateful day kick-started my basic understanding of the law of attraction decades before I was to make friends with the overabundance of books available today on the subject. After some popular books about the law of attraction were published in recent years, I was thrilled that people came forth and brought the subject to light in terms which most people could easily comprehend. As excited as I was about the books, however, after reading them, I was equally concerned about the books' many contradictions, non-factual statements and obvious oversights. I personally believe that the books accomplished much more good than bad in the world, and as much as they certainly serve as excellent *introductions* on the subject of the law of attraction, in my view, they are perfect examples of how lessons on prosperity can be detrimental when the facts are not understood and then inappropriately transmitted to others.

For example, most books on the subject of the law of attraction refer to the theory of *what goes up must come down*, but said theory is applicable to the law of *gravity*, not the law of *attraction*. In space, what goes up stays up! Furthermore, the law of *cause and effect* is not the law of attraction. Whereas the law of attraction dictates that *like attracts like*, the law of cause and effect dictates that you cannot do something without causing something else to happen. These laws work together; one is as important as the other. If we're going to master just one law, however, we must understand what it is we're mastering. In short, most books on these subjects are helpful to humanity, but readers must stop using them as bibles or the final word, and they need to keep learning and thinking and searching beyond one overhyped book.

One of the biggest dangers I've witnessed in regards to the teachings of the law of attraction is in the teachings of one of the most powerful tools recommended to manipulate the law of attraction in one's favor, which is, *affirmations*. In book after book, and website after website offering instructional training pertaining to accurately performing affirmations, somewhere along the line, there always seems to be an element of contradiction or negativity which neutralizes, at best, any effort made in this powerful *thought exercise* process. In every book and video which I've ever researched, the problem wasn't so much in the teachings of the lessons (although most did contradict themselves at some point), but rather the detriments were found in the exercise examples; the *how to*.

Sometimes the misinformation is something as simple as watching a person offer online weight-loss solutions, and the person facilitating the lesson is grossly overweight. At other times, the facilitator is teaching a relaxation technique yet the facilitator is more uptight than the observer. Of course it could be argued that maybe the overweight facilitator was previously much larger and is sharing her knowledge through her personal experience, and who better to support proven relaxation techniques than a person who needs to relax? On the other hand, if you dig deeper than the visual obvious; dig deeper than the hearing and the feeling, right down to the intuition, you'll discover that weight and anger issues have nothing to do with merely fat or anger; they're both fear-related.

Just because a person learned to lose weight or they discovered a relaxation technique, does that qualify them to teach the technique? Does it qualify them to diagnose what is best for your ailment? At most, while one woman learned to meditate long enough to distract herself away from food, and the other learned to breathe away her momentary frustration, neither have necessarily truly dealt with their deep-rooted issues; the eating disorder and the rage *brought on by fear*. Otherwise why would they have these reoccurring issues? Everybody who has weight or anger or other issues needs to seek out the root cause of their personal issues, and because these would-be gurus don't recognize this inherent need, they are absolutely not qualified to eradicate the personal problems of others.

One person's anger is not rooted in the same area as another person's, and where one might be able to curb their anger with affirmations, another may require psychiatric care, medication and counseling. To look at this from a different angle, would you trust your dentist to diagnose you with pancreatic cancer? Of course you wouldn't, not any more than you'd entrust a car mechanic to perform a root-canal treatment on your tooth. When it comes to the important things, we place our trust in the experts who have the most knowledge and experience. The big question is, why don't we do this when it comes to the little things?

If we paid attention to all the little things; the things we eat, drink, think, say, do, and especially paid attention to the people we associate with, live with, make love with, and the places we go to and spend our time, energy and money, then all the big things would take care of themselves. If we gave all our attention to each moment, then each day, each month and each year would take care of themselves, because life is merely a series of moments, and they're all connected. If we put as much care in the advice we get for the little things as we do with the big things, as well as to whom we get this advice from, we'd rarely, if ever, have big things to deal with, or at least when the big things come up, we'd be well versed in dealing with them and finding reliable resources when it comes to figuring things out. Most importantly, if something is so important to us (like relationships, wealth or weight-loss), then why would we not invest time and money researching a true expert's advice rather than heeding free advice from someone who is clearly not an expert?

There are many sources which suggest that affirmations don't work, but the fact remains, they do work if carried out correctly. Implying affirmations don't work is like suggesting that surgery doesn't work. Naturally, if a surgeon is operating on a man's foot when it's his hand that needs the attention, the surgery won't be a success. Like surgery, correctly performing affirmations first requires an accurate diagnosis of the problem. This lack of correctly diagnosing the true, core, root problem of any ailment before proceeding with affirmations is a big reason why affirmations simply don't work – this and the fact that people place little time or faith in those affirmations; *faith being the major component.*

Take for example the following: If your intention is to use affirmations in conjunction with a weight-loss program, then stating that you are thin won't do much for your stubborn fat if anger is the root of the problem. Many people also use affirmations as a form of denial. Stating that you are a *confident winner* can only give you a false sense of self-assurance if you haven't figured out why you feel insecure. If you've got bad breath and you keep eating garlic sandwiches, affirming that your breath smells minty-fresh is not going to do away with the bad breath. The core problem in this case is garlic.

This isn't about being realistic, it's about being logical. For those of you who don't know the difference between reality and logic; reality dictates that you have only a one in ten million chance of winning the lottery, whereas logic dictates that you have just as much chance of winning as does anybody else (as long as you play). My point is; *be logical.* This same concept applies to emotional issues. If you affirm that you feel safe but haven't uncovered what it is that makes you feel unsafe, you will not be able to replace the instinctual thought pattern which reinforces the idea that you are not safe. Also, it's very possible that your intuition is trying to tell you that you aren't safe, and as such, affirming that you're safe when you're actually in danger is not going to keep you safe.

The practice of attempting affirmations, as with any form of self healing, without first knowing what you need help with is problematic not only because we don't know what we don't know, but also because we take this information from just about anybody who gives it to us without putting real thought into it, and they usually don't know any better than the rest of us. I remember watching a TV commercial with a gorgeous woman with a radiant smile, talking about a toothache remedy, raving about how it always gives her relief no matter where she goes, day or night. While watching this commercial, my friend yelled back at the television, *Go to the dentist, stupid!* Ah, spoken like a true guru! My point is, we've become accustomed to taking advice from pretty faces that know nothing but are always ready to share their vast bank of know-nothing-know-it-all wisdom, and I'm not just talking about a pretty face on a TV commercial, although that does go a long way in our society. Along with our willingness to take advice from just about anybody is our unwillingness to pay for advice, whether the advice is through a seminar or book or television program or a truly dedicated specialist.

Perhaps the biggest danger that lies in learning from misinformed *affirmation* teachers is in their instruction on using actual words. I've heard many instructors say things like, *"I am safe from sickness,"* or *"Nobody can harm me,"* or my personal favorite, *"Money is limitless and effortlessly flows into my life"*. The fact is, the subconscious mind is more literal than our conscious mind generally considers, and as every word is a prayer and a praise, the universe, or God, always responds affirmatively. Keeping in mind that the conscious mind understands words as symbols rather than as language, and keeping in mind that the response from the universe is always "yes", whatever word or thought or feeling we utter, think or feel is always affirmatively responded to.

When you affirm the following: *I am safe from sickness, nobody can harm me, money is limitless and effortlessly flows into my life*, along with the good thoughts, this is what the mind recognizes: NOBODY, SICKNESS, HARM, LIMIT, LESS, EFFORT, LESS. In the preceding affirmation, you've not only sent out a mixed message to the universe and your mind, but you've also emphasized the problem. And just read those seven words and pay attention to how you feel as you read them. When these same affirmations are done using only affirmative words: *I am happy and healthy, I am safe, money is abundant and easily flowing into my life*, the mind recognizes: HAPPY, HEALTHY, SAFE, MONEY, ABUNDANT, EASILY, FLOWS. Now read these seven words again and compare the feelings they encourage in contrast to the feelings evoked when reading the previous seven words. These words encourage affirmative feelings, and they do not emphasize the problems because they don't mention the problems.

When giving attention to the words we use to compose affirmative statements, it's important to recognize how the subconscious mind understands the words, but it is equally important to *not* use words which one might personally associate with negative connotations. For example, the affirmation *I operate with Divine purpose* for most people would be perfectly affirmative, but to someone who associates the word *operate* with images of surgical procedures, the affirmative statement is not inherently positive to their mind. In this case for example, it would be ideal to adjust the statement to read; *I act with Divine purpose* (substituting the word *operate* with the word *act*).

Perspective is everything, but when it comes to our senses, some things are what they are. For example, to our eyes, the word *"know"* basically means to acknowledge or to be aware, but the two center letters are clearly spelled *"no"* and make up the phonetic (sound) of the word, and it is therefore both visually and verbally recognized by the subconscious mind as "NO". To our eyes and ears and thus to our subconscious mind, the word *"know"* means "NO". If you have trouble accepting this theory, just take into consideration any parent's mounting frustration upon hearing their arguing teen say, "I know!" For this reason the phrase *I know* should always be replaced with *"I recognize"* or *"I am recognizing"*. On the surface, to anybody who's just grasping this concept, the whole process of affirmation exercises may seem agonizingly complex, but it's really as simple as black and white. It's either affirmative or it's not.

Whatever we wish to manifest into our lives, paying attention to *the manner* in which we perform our affirmations is just as important as *performing* the affirmations. Making affirmations *affirmative* sounds pretty simple, and it should be, but unlearning what we've learned and detaching ourselves from the detrimental misinformation fed by the misinformed is crucial to manifesting our best lives. I've encouraged countless people to make daily affirmations part of their regular daily routines, and not only am I amazed how little importance people place on incorporating such a valuable, simple and *proven* practice into their lives, but I'm just as amazed at how people expect to get so much from doing two minutes of affirmations yet continue to spend twelve to eighteen hours a day thinking and feeling miserable about everything. Affirmations don't work alone; they are one powerful process you do to support changes in your attitude and your actions.

An important thing to remember when we're looking to manifest anything is to take a look at the whole picture. There's no use affirming a *"plethora of money"* if you've not first imagined what a plethora of money looks like. Furthermore, we must pay attention to what we're commanding from universal law. If you're asking for a million dollars and peace of mind, you might as well be asking for heart-smart fat-free pork-chops, because not only does a million dollars *not* imply peace of mind, but it usually implies quite the contrary. Think of how your heart fluttered the day you found twenty dollars or the time you received a present you truly enjoyed. That's stress! If finding a twenty was exciting, imagine what receiving a million bucks would do to you! The other thing to remember is, the law of attraction is merely one law, and although you may think you know what would make you happiest in life, God and your subconscious *higher self* knows better. Although everyone imagines how happy they assume they'd be with a million dollars, very few people actually consider that they have enormous potential to be completely happy *without* a million dollars, and thus they don't focus on gratitude for being where they are in the present, or focus on being grateful for having what they have right here in the now.

Learning is an ongoing process in life, and this applies to learning more about what we already know. I have read many books and have seen many presentations about affirmative living and collective consciousness, but I have yet to read or hear anything or anybody that did not, in some way or another, contradict itself/themselves. It is with this observation that I realized that if I were to advance in deepening and widening my consciousness, and do my part to encourage the planet to do this as well, I'd have to think for myself. Ignorance is not a bad thing; ignorance simply doesn't know it exists, and where it applies to us as humans, we don't know what we don't know. That said, the miracle about ignorance is that *we* know it exists, and there's no excuse to remain ignorant. Releasing old patterns includes letting go of what we assume we know to be correct. This plays a huge role in how much of the ignorance we possess will be replaced with True knowledge.

In the process of bringing consciousness to the world, even the greatest minds made, and make, their mistakes in expressing themselves. A popular founder of a well known scientific/religious movement who published his book in the mid-1930's filled the pages of his book with information that by even today's standards is considered to be extreme forward thinking. Yet inasmuch as his book is filled with examples of affirmative prayer treat-ments and meditations, almost all of those examples completely contradict the message of the entire book.

Now, I personally know how challenging it is to compose a literary work about affirmative consciousness without using words and explanations that are contrary to being affirmative. Sometimes you just gotta say *God ain't bad* in order to make people understand *God is good*. In my opinion, contrary to the belief that the building of a boat does not arrive through the contemplation of the sinking of things, I believe that if you don't consider all the ways in which a boat may sink, you might make it float, but you won't keep it from sinking. That said, inasmuch as I believe that the aforementioned religious founder meant to use the vocabulary he did to explain his theories (all relayed in basic laymen's terms, which is remarkable considering the limited basic vocabulary laymen possessed at the time), I do believe he erred in the process of providing his examples.

For example, in his examples of meditation/prayer treatments for *abundance* and for *peace of mind*, his examples include the following negative words which, along with the affirmative words, are meant to be prayed and meditated upon; *long for, need, not, no, bondage, poverty, fear, fears, strain, coerce, limitation, doubt, gone, none, argue, uncertainty, worries, future, past*. These ideals and terms are precisely what the affirmer wants to do away with. In order to manifest the opposite, the affirmer must focus upon the opposite, and *only* upon the opposite; *all that is positive*. Furthermore, dwelling upon the future and the past removes us from the now, ultimately rendering us powerless in the present; the only place we ever do have power.

This same unfortunate negative concept applies to the Bible, making powerful scriptures which should be affirmatively empowering otherwise detrimental to one's faith and wellbeing. Take for example just a few excerpts from the Lord's Prayer: Thy kingdom come, thy **will** be done, forgive us our **trespasses** as we forgive those who **trespass against** us, lead us **not** into **temptation** but deliver us from **evil**. The bold print represents what you have fed your mind each time you recite this prayer; ILL, TRESSPASSES, AGAINST, NOT, TEMPTATION, EVIL.

I can appreciate that in ancient times there was little understanding about the subconscious mind and how damaging these words are, especially in prayer and meditation, but with our current understanding it is clear that the mind absorbs *everything*, and as such, we must be constantly vigilant of which words we use to pray and meditate upon, especially where manifesting our desires is concerned. Negative words said in prayer are what the subconscious mind goes forth to realize into your experiences and your reality. For the record, this is an example of the Lord's Prayer relayed affirmatively: *Our Father who art in heaven, hallowed be Thy Name. Thy Kingdom come, Thy Intention be done on Earth as it is in Heaven. Give us this day our daily bread and love as we love all others. Lead us always into righteousness and deliver us unto goodness, for Thine is the Kingdom, the power and the glory, for ever and ever.*

Religious or otherwise, understanding that employing something as powerful as the scriptures, especially during times of difficulty, makes it clear that we must revise scripture terminology; not in order to change the message but in order to ensure the message is inherently affirmative, because what we read, we affirm, and what we affirm we realize into our lives. I wonder how many soldiers in combat recited the 23rd Psalm (The Lord is my Shepard), and after repeatedly affirming *He maketh me to lie down in green pastures* were shipped home to rest six feet beneath those green pastures. For those adamant to apply scriptures to their lives, I present the following example of an affirmatively revised scripture:

The Lord is my Shepard and always provides. He maketh me to relax in green pastures; He leadeth me beside the calm waters. He restoreth my soul; He leadeth me in the paths of righteousness for His name's sake. Yea as I walk this journey, I walk in confidence with the Lord, for Thou art with me; Thy rod and Thy staff they comfort me. Thou preparest a table before me; Thou anointest my head with oil; my cup runneth over. Goodness and mercy follow me all the days of my life, and I dwell in the house of the Lord forever.

Perhaps one of my biggest pet-peeves about spiritual terminology is the imposition by *addicts* about how we must refer to God. As a youth at church, I was constantly reprimanded for using the word *God* (even during prayer) because according to some beliefs, the word *God* is so sacred that it shouldn't be uttered by our lips. This thinking goes beyond religion and into the *spiritual* movements and organizations as well. Time and again it's been suggested that I should utilize the word *Spirit* or *Universe* rather than *God*, for various reasons including but not limited to the ideal that many spiritual people are offended by the use of the term God.

Well, first off, I do employ these terms; often in fact, but the word *God* in every language is perhaps the most affirmatively powerful word in existence. This is perhaps the best reason to not take God's name in vain, but where it applies to empowering my prayers and meditations, no other word will do. Second, we're all talking about the same Almighty Creator, so whether I say *God* and another person says *Spirit* and another says *Universe*, we're all speaking the same language. Most people who are put off by the use of the term *God* are usually put off due to past religious experiences or because fanatics have ruined it for them. I, however, refuse to allow anybody or any opinion to come between me and God. In fact, I think the times that God has heard me the most is when I've addressed God as God. There's something to be said for simplicity.

The key to working with any teaching, whether it's taught by teachers, friends, mentors, science, religion or the Bible, is to move forth transforming all teachings into *affirmatives*. When we get to information or scriptures that are unclear, like plucking out eyes, cutting off limbs, or laws limiting anyone or anything from pure life expression, we must go within ourselves and seek out answers in prayer, meditation and deep thought. I've personally used science-based religious affirmations and prayers in combination with affirmations of my own, and they are profoundly effective, especially when incorporated with Bible study and meditation. Regardless of religion, if we'd each approach every thought, every feeling, every word and every action in a manner which is *inherently affirmative*, then all we we'd ever get back would be affirmative.

Since the beginning of recorded history, many Truths and untruths have been written. Many untruths were written over time, and continue to be written, to trick people and/or hold people back, for financial or political gain, or for some other form of power or control. On the other hand, many untruths were written as truths because according to personal or mass perspective at the time, it was understood to be the truth. As for the latter, when untruths are written as truths out of pure ignorance but with the intention of assisting humanity in expanding its consciousness, it is unacceptable to leave the untrue statements unchallenged. I believe that if the aforementioned well-meaning writer/religious founder were alive today, he'd correct his oversight. Since he's not here however, I believe it's up to us to make the adjustments in an effort to excel his teachings. I believe this applies to the discoveries of all great minds.

As I write these words, it is my sincerest hope that these pages be filled with the most affirmative of knowledge, and that my words are truthful, however, I am open to the idea that in the days to come, either tomorrow or in decades to follow, that affirmative thinkers and doers bring challenge to these ideals, convictions and theories, and accordingly correct them affirmatively, in the name of God, Truth and science, for the betterment of all humanity.

One final note, and perhaps the most important principle for those who truly are struggling with the law of attraction, or the prayer process: *It doesn't work without faith!* I have come to recognize that when it comes to prayer or manifesting anything, "faith is the prayer". When it comes to *putting it out there*, information relayed through affirmations and visuals are simply not enough. Anybody can do affirmations and stick pictures on a board and go window shopping for a luxury home or test drive a roadster, but faith, belief, conviction, or whatever you want to call it, is where most people struggle with the manifesting and prayer process. Faith is truly the key. Knowing without an iota of doubt that your prayer or intention is manifesting. Whereas affirmations and visualizations might be measurable, the major key component, which is faith, is not measurable. You either have it or you don't...

Here's to hoping you do!

CHAPTER V

=WhyBadThingsHappen=

Bad things happen because they *can* happen...

In our search for Truth, we ask a multitude of questions which ultimately lead to additional questions, yet in our search we tend to overlook the ultimate answer which is: *Question Everything!* Regardless of humanity's current level of consciousness – whether brilliant or archaic – we are guaranteed to ask questions, but there are no absolute guaranteed answers, or rather, there are very few; for few things are ever absolute. For the most part, we don't ask questions, and the reason for this is because we're either terrified of burning in hell for questioning authority, or we're terrified of change, or of what the answers may be, or we don't want to face facts about just how much of our misery we're directly responsible for creating. Either way, whatever our reasons for not questioning things, it typically all comes back to dwelling in fear.

Most of us are afraid of the truth, however, it's not the truth that hurts, but the stubborn beliefs and untruths we've become addicted to that are terrifying. It's also the thought of detaching ourselves from ideals that hurts. *The thought;* the one place where everything begins. Believing everything we read and hear, and swallowing it all as a result of not thinking for ourselves is one of our biggest downfalls. We need to have the courage to think for ourselves and ask honest questions, and only then will we get the honest answers.

One question that never seems to yield a satisfactory answer is *why do bad things happen?* Or, why do bad things *have* to happen? The answer is quite simple: Bad things happen because they *can* happen, and we *allow* them to happen, and bad things don't *have* to happen! Something that is rarely considered when bad things happen is that usually, what we get upset about is not really bad at all. For the majority of us, most bad things that happen are really not as bad as they *seem*, or rather as we *choose* to see them. Usually our pain is a result of our stubborn attachment to our perspective. I am not denying that dreadful things happen in the world, but for most of us, it's the little things we make big deals over which threaten to, and succeed at, destroying our happiness and our lives.

Humans are no different from any other species in that we are creatures of habit. How we do *anything* is generally how we do *everything*, so how we overreact to the bad things is the same way we overreact to the good things. For example, when we get an unexpected bill in the mail, we imagine going broke, getting other bills, not being able to pay our mortgage, and so it grows until we've imagined the end of the world. Conversely, when something good happens, like a phone call regarding a tax return, we get excited and think *jackpot!*, when in reality, at most, we're only able to buy an ice-cream cone.

Both situations are prime examples of what happens when we dwell in the realm of possibility. The difference is, in one case we're dwelling negatively, in the other we're dwelling affirmatively. In both cases, however, we are not dwelling on facts. In the case of the first example, we've merely received a piece of paper in the mail; no more, no less in the present. In the case of the second, we've only heard a voice over the phone, no more, no less, in the present. In both cases the responses are due to our perspective, and most of what is considered bad or good is merely an illusion.

As for the truly bad things that happen, yes, there are reasons as well. Most bad things not only happen because we allow them to happen, but also because we *invite* them to happen. There is a little quote that says; *"If God leads you to it, He'll lead you through it"*. This is a very inspiring ideal until you realize that most of the miserable places to where we've been led, we've led ourselves to, and God had nothing to do with it. In fact, in most cases, those negative places we arrive at in our lives are destinations reserved for those who don't dwell in Truth or in God, and we get there by doing exactly what we clearly know we should *not* be doing. Our greatest actions towards allowing and inviting bad things to happen in our lives and our world is not only by virtue of what we tolerate, abide by and stand for without giving any thought to the ultimate sacrifice our actions imply, but by virtue of the fact that in the face of the development of bad things, we do nothing about it and we never change our ways. Each of us do this personally, all of us do it collectively.

It would be inaccurate to imply that our complacency about the development of *bad things* is motivated by mere laziness. Everybody wants peace, at least for themselves and their loved ones, but I believe our biggest motive behind our complacency has more to do with fear than anything else, as well as our lack of understanding to what extent we're all connected. Of all the fears which keep us from *doing something*, our biggest fear lies in whom we might upset in the process, as well as who won't approve of us. Yet, by not upsetting one or two people, far more people are affected because nothing ever changes. We must recognize that anger is merely the result of unmet expectations and misunderstandings, and like every other emotion we experience, it exists to serve us. It's not a bad emotion; it's not a good emotion. It's just an emotion.

Concerning the anger of others in relation to stepping up and *doing something* or questioning their power; whether it's the power over the progress of one man or the power over the progress of a nation, we may have much to fear, but that fear is nothing compared to the catastrophic tragedy humanity experiences for every moment we stagnate as a result of not challenging authority. Lack of courage, remaining uneducated, imbalanced perspectives, lack of commitment, accountability and discipline, and not wanting to get involved, all fuel the fire of "bad things", but nothing feeds bad things more than does our negative mindset which, again, largely comes down to fear. Fear of being removed from our comfort zone, fear of not attaining the approval of others, and an epic fear of learning.

Life can be whatever we want it to be because *it is* what we want it to be. Whatever we willingly attract to ourselves has little if any bearing on what we unwillingly attract to ourselves, and has no bearing on the lessons life has in store for us. The lessons one learns if he is poor, he can also learn if he is rich. You provide the lifestyle; Divine Purpose provides the lessons, no matter what you do, no matter where you live, no matter what you drive. The life you create for yourself is your classroom, the lessons will be the same. The life, the environment, the people, all that you have created through words, thoughts, feelings and actions, is your classroom, but regardless of the classroom you've made for yourself, life provides the same lessons. If bad things are going to happen in order to teach us, we'll experience our perspective of what's bad. Regardless of the powers behind the law of attracttion, the immaculate beam of light that is Divine Purpose will always shine superior! In the same manner of which a child in a private school in Malibu learns 1+1=2, a child in an impoverished public school in Harlem will learn that same lesson. Yes, wealthy schools offer different opportunities, but a student who truly wants to learn will learn no matter where he is, and the general lessons we all must learn, whether they be 1+1=2 or *what goes around comes around,* will be taught.

Many of us are aware of rich families who live in colossal mansions designed to outdo the neighbors' alleged wealth, and how those families have lost touch with reality, with each other, and with what's truly important in life. In actuality, however, most poor and middleclass families are experiencing the same lessons as do the rich. They're all out of touch with each other, and their money – or lack thereof – has nothing to do with it. Whether you're in a palace or on the street, if your lesson is about loss, you will experience loss. Life uses what we have in our lives as tools to teach us, so whether a rich man loses his house, a poor man loses his shoes, an athlete loses a limb, or all three lose a child, the lesson will be the same for each man: Loss.

I use the example of finances to make my point, but this also applies to other areas of our lives. For example, often finances are not a problem for people, but their life-lessons come through other areas, like through relation-ships, experiences, and especially health. So, rich or poor, a saint will be a saint, and a jerk will be a jerk, and the lessons that are going to set him straight have nothing to do with his financial standing. Being a good dad or a deadbeat dad has nothing to do with wealth. Being honest or dishonest has nothing to do with wealth. Financial wealth is a mindset some of us will experience. Learning is something ALL of us will experience.

Financial wealth, like anything in life, is about attraction, not about merit; it's not about whether or not we deserve it. There are plenty of wealthy people who are arrogant nasty pieces of work, and they have more money than they can count. They usually have this money because they've *attracted* it to themselves, not because they deserve it. Yes, they may *believe* they deserve it, but when it comes to attraction, the universe remains unbiased to merit, and it responds to what we *believe*. Those born into wealth may maintain their wealth because if wealth is all they've ever known and it's never occurred to them to *not* be wealthy, they'll stay wealthy. The lessons they must learn however, will come to them through other areas of their lives. If the possibility of something good or bad occurs to us, we've planted the seed because we've given birth to the thought. The seed lies dormant unless we continually feed it with additional thoughts and feelings. Whether we attract wealth or we attract otherwise has nothing to do with whether or not we're a good person, just as learning has nothing to do with merit. We all have the right to attract wealth. Some of us do; some of us don't. We all have the obligation to learn things. Some of us do learn; some of us don't learn, but mark my words, eventually; *all of us will learn!*

It's vital to keep in mind that what we attract – good or bad – has largely to do with the more profound feelings we carry deep inside ourselves – guilt, fear, despair, insecurity, etc. – and it's simply impossible to attract beautiful manifestations when our demons make us doubtful. Sure, you might be a good person, but if you were abused as a child and told how useless you are, a part of you is programmed to believe this. Although you may imagine how it would feel to be wealthy, you don't feel as if you deserve it, so the wealth never arrives, or, on the off chance that it does arrive, it doesn't linger. This is why one mustn't dwell solely upon the concept of the law of attraction for complete sustenance, because the law of attraction, again, is really about the prayer process, and it alone cannot cater to the deep psychological issues which impair our perspectives and thus our lives.

Again, although financial wealth really has nothing to do with merit, it's how we *feel* about whether or not we merit wealth which attracts wealth, and it's that feeling *(along with taking affirmative action)* which dictates whether or not we'll maintain that wealth. Take for example the following: Three men each purchase a new convertible on the same day from the same dealer. Two men are honest, the third is a scoundrel. Of the two honest men; one bank executive and one entrepreneur, one drives off the lot feeling satisfied and rewarded for his hard work and determination, and he *feels* and *believes* he deserves the car, in the same manner which he *feels* and *believes* he deserves the house he bought with the garage to protect his new toy. The entrepreneur, however, drives off the lot feeling that although he worked hard and he truly deserves the car, subconscious flashbacks of his abusive father telling him how worthless he is can't be drowned out by the car's impressive sound system, and his feeling of unworthiness attracts an accident only days later. He didn't get into an accident because he didn't deserve the car, he got into the accident because his subconscious feelings were affirming what he is conditioned to believe, and the universe responded, like always, with a *YES!*

Now to the scoundrel; a man with no remorse for how he gets his money and what he does with it. He drives off in his new ride to his next crooked venture, never having car trouble or accidents because he has no remorse or guilt over his shady ways. But alas, the fact remains, he created deep personal misery for others, and as such, the law of *cause and effect;* a crucial component of the Divine Purpose process, dictates that what goes around comes around, and although the scoundrel gets to keep his car and will never experience jail, he instead comes home at the end of the day to discover that his beloved child is missing.

Of course this example does not imply that all people who've lost a child or experienced some other great loss or challenge actually warrant such an experience, because such personal loss entails individual meaning and lessons for all. The aforementioned example is meant to simply illustrate how consciously choosing to *do* bad things leads to *experiencing* bad things. The example also does not imply that all bad or challenging experiences are necessarily related to *karma*. Whereas many people have a challenging mission upon which they have consciously chosen to embark by virtue of their very conscious actions, so are there many people who are on *"unseen"* missions. Missions which involve experiencing great loss or challenges in the name of something we'll only ever come to wholly comprehend after our time here has passed. All this to say, if you've been jerk, chances are you'll reap the results of your actions where it matters to you most, and, it will be multiplied.

As a brief footnote, I have come to recognize that perhaps the most important reason for the challenging events and experiences in our lives is, if things were always right, rosy and perfect, we'd have little motive to search deeper and go beyond what we know and beyond who we are. Like it or not, when things are challenging, our intelligence, resilience, creative brilliance and strength rises to the top, and it strengthens and defines our character. That's always the time you get re-introduced to the real you!

As I look back upon my personal experiences – the bad and the good – I recognize that it was always during those challenging times that I grew and learned the most; about others, about my world, and especially about me. I also recognize that my growth and learning was always by choice; not by chance. When bad things happen, we might not have the immediate answers, but we have a choice about whether we're going to run away, or be brave and deal with it and seek out the affirmative perspectives that will make the journey worthwhile and turn those challenges into gold!

Universal Law is unbiased about what it gives. It has no interest in our material possessions. Like electricity flowing through an outlet, unbiased whether it powers a toaster or electrocutes a finger, its interest is purely energetic and giving, and it will balance energy with like-energy. This is its job. Regardless of what's happened in your life and where you may find yourself, whether your situation is out of your choices or out of Divine Purpose, one thing is certain: God, The Universe, The Divine Creator, will meet you where you are right now and will lead you where you to want to go. You need only to start walking, and Life will provide the direction.

All you gotta do is ask!

CHAPTER VI

=PrayersMeditationsTreatments=

OM...

Well before the concept of *affirmative action*, thoughts, words and feelings are conclusively the top driving forces behind everything we experience. Reversing the power of all the damaging day to day, moment to moment thought patterns which reinforce the negative programming we experience during our lives is the most powerful action every human can and should take to improve their lives. The best way to reverse negative patterns is to abandon attention to them while planting and reinforcing new affirmative patterns. When these actions are coupled with a *commitment to faith* and emphasized with taking *affirmative action*, the results are astounding, especially when applied in harmony with affirmatively approaching traditional religious rituals.

Consider for a moment the following: As you visualize a monkey in a zoo wearing a red baseball cap enjoying a fresh banana, did you notice how miraculous it was that as you visualized a monkey in a zoo wearing a red baseball cap enjoying a fresh banana, you gave no consideration whatsoever to a toothbrush? The reason you didn't consider the toothbrush while visualizing the monkey scenario is because I didn't mention the toothbrush. This is the power of suggestion. It's the very same reason that until I mentioned it just now, you gave no thought to a nun wearing a pink sombrero while riding on the back of a penguin. Now that you have that image, I command you to NOT think of a nun wearing a pink sombrero while riding on the back of a penguin! Not so easy, right?

Simply stated, if you want the mind to consider and dwell upon something, you must suggest something. If you want the mind to ignore something, then you don't suggest that the mind ignore something; you just don't suggest it at all.

The following pages consist of examples of affirmative mind techniques which are proven to yield results in every aspect of our lives. These affirmations and treatments are *inherently affirmative*, which means that every word used to create each statement is affirmative to the conscious and subconscious minds, and, they are affirmative *visually* and *auditorily* as well. The final ten pages of affirmations entitled *Ten for Twenty* consist of a mind conditioning technique developed to replace the negative ideas we carry since birth as a result of all we've ever heard, thought, said and felt. For those who read aloud all ten pages for the duration of twenty consecutive days, the results will speak for themselves.

(Please Note: Affirmations are not designed to replace necessary medical procedures or therapies. If you are currently under the supervision of a doctor, please consult your doctor before doing these exercises. Affirmations are also not designed to replace taking responsibility for our lives; they are merely a thought-pattern altering exercise. More will be explained when you reach the *Ten for Twenty* section.)

The following *affirmative mind technique* can be used with and altered around any spiritual or religious rituals, or it can be used as it is presented here. Keeping in mind the most powerful words you can use are the word *God*, the word *I*, and the word *AM*, the statement *I am God* appears in the following exercise. If the statement does not appeal to you or offends your current belief, simply substitute *I am God* with *I am a child of God,* or forego the statement altogether. Remember, this exercise is meant to recondition your mind's thought pattern and is not an act of worship, so God won't be upset if you imply you're God.

It is my sincere hope that these exercises assist in bringing you closer to Truth and to God, and/or lead you to your ideal life where peace will be your reality.

Namaste

=Affirmative Prayer=

There is One absolute divine source, One infinite power, One universal law, One complete whole energy. I call this energy God. I recognize that God is all aware and perceptive, all loving and powerful, all peaceful and healing, all giving and forgiving, all abundant and prosperous, all pleasant and compassionate. As a reflection of God, as a reflection of God energy, and as God myself, I recognize and accept that I am all aware and perceptive, all loving and powerful, all giving and forgiving, all peaceful and healing, all abundant and prosperous, all pleasant and compassionate. In this moment of sincere grace and solemn gratitude, I declare God as the foundation and structure of my very being. I recognize that I am an expression of God and I am part of God's Supreme Universal Plan. I am grateful that I am Divinely provided for and protected and surrounded with Love. I am grateful that clarity surrounds and indwells me always, and I am immensely grateful that the collective that is my spirit, soul, body and mind recognizes my connection to the One Omnipotent Source which created me and loves me in this moment and forevermore. I recognize that God loves me and provides for me always. I am grateful for abundance, wealth, health, prosperity, joy and ease on all levels in and around my life. I am easily flowing, moving and changing with Divine Purpose, and I move forth with grace, gratitude and faith, to make the world and the Universe a better place. All this I declare in the name of all that is Divine and Good and Just and True. With a grateful and humble heart, I release these thoughts and ideals to the Universe, and the Universe responds with a resounding and absolute *YES! It is done!* I let go and let God. All is well, and so It Is…

=Ten pages for twenty days=

The final ten pages of this section consist of affirmative phrases designed to replace old thought patterns; non-factual beliefs and ill perspectives which keep us from achieving our greatest potential.

I don't deny that this is a brainwashing exercise. In fact, brainwashing is exactly what it is. This process is no different than what we encounter on a daily basis each time we turn on the television or radio or surf the Net, however, it's different because it's condensed, intense and involves intentional discipline. The content is also *entirely affirmative,* and it is as much an exercise for the brain's physical neurological components as it is for its mental components. The idea of this exercise is to read all ten pages daily for twenty uninterrupted days. For those up to the challenge, more than once a day would be a definite asset, however, once a day will suffice.

The point of brainwashing is to *persuade completely* the mind into believing something. We commonly associate brainwashing with evil doings, however, brainwashing is merely a tool, and like with any tool, how we wield it is how we'll benefit from it. When brainwashing is used to persuade the mind to do bad things, no effort is made to erase old ideas of remorse or guilt; all effort is made in planting, dwelling upon and reinforcing the new idea until it is seen as *absolute truth.* Conversely, when brainwashing the mind to do good, the same actions are applied. Therefore, when you plant these thoughts in your mind, your subconscious mind believes what you've stated and seeks to convince you of this same truth. When you repeat these ideas over the span of twenty days, you reinforce the ideas until you willingly believe them. That is when things truly begin to change. If this process can affect you in just twenty days *(or less, which is habitually reported)*, imagine what will become of your life after doing it daily over six months. Imagine a year. Imagine ten years!

In considering that the mind applies everything into our life all that which it absorbs, I recognized the importance of conscientiously developing affirmations that are *entirely affirmative* to the subconscious mind, ensuring that every word is of an *inherently affirmative* nature, but also ensuring that words composed of other *negative* words were excluded. For example, because the word *NO* is interlaced within their composition, the words **no**tice, **no**urish, k**no**w, k**no**wledge, ack**no**wledge, e**no**ugh, and even the word **no**w were all excluded because they're not *inherently affirmative*. This also applies to the words *fill, filled* and *still*. The words **harm**ony, **harm**onious and be**lie**ve have also been excluded because they are not *inherently affirmative*. To better understand the reasoning, consider the following:

When you read: *I am filled with knowledge. I am still and at peace knowing my needs are harmoniously met. I am nourished and noticed. I believe I am enough,* your mind reads: I am **fill**ed with k**no**wledge. I am st**ill** and at peace k**no**wing my **need**s are **harm**oniously met. I am **no**urished and **no**ticed. I be**lie**ve I am e**no**ugh. This statement is detrimental to any possible success because the mind recognizes *all* commands; even the interlaced commands. Also, this statement has more negative than positive commands. This unfortunate process is the manner in which most humans function by virtue of not being conscious of one's basic vocabulary, as much in thought as in conversation.

Beyond this, much consideration was given to ensuring that all affirmations give attention to the *immediate*; not the future nor to the past. Stating *I am going to succeed* places potential success in the future thus leaving you powerless in the immediate. Stating *I release the past* also removes you from the moment and brings attention to the past. Words are sustenance to the mind. What you say is what you feed the mind; every word and every *interlaced* word. If you want something to die off, you must stop feeding it.

This process of eliminating negative terminology applies as much to painful memories as it does to anything requiring sustenance for survival. Yes, it's vital to speak your mind and express your hurts, wounds, pain and frustrations, but just not during the affirmation process. Consider psychotherapy like surgery for the mind; a time to focus on the ailment, to go in and find the problem, yank it out, and prepare the body for healing. Performing affirmations is more akin to physiotherapy after surgery. It's the time to focus on the mind's health, and focus on what the mind can do and to help it regain its strength. It's not a time to reopen the old wound and operate again. Yes, affirmations can and should be used during the psychotherapy *(as long as it's not used as a tool for denial)*, but during the affirmation process it absolutely must be affirmative, or it's simply ineffective.

It's been said that the proper way to do affirmations is by saying *I am* rather than just *I*. Although I agree that it is a powerful method, this is not the only manner in which people think, and as long as it's affirmative, *I* is powerful. For this reason, these affirmations are presented in ways that can be absorbed by, and benefit, everybody. To get the most from this exercise, it is crucial to respect a few guidelines, otherwise, it's pointless. For one, whether you do this morning or evening matters not, although before bed is ideal because what you take to your sleep generally becomes part of your sleep. What does matter is that you do the exercise around the same time each day; early or mid-day or in the evening. The more disciplined you are about this exercise, the more your mind will comply. If you choose to do this more than once a day, stay with the exact routine for the entire twenty days, otherwise, just keep it basic and stick with once a day. If you choose to do affirmations before bed and happen to fall asleep, that's fine because, again, the last thing on your mind before you sleep is what you dwell on during sleep and into the next day.

The twenty days must be *uninterrupted*. If you miss a day, start anew. No matter how you proceed, affirmations are useful, but to truly get the most from the exercise, follow the guidelines. If you practice religious rituals, perform the rituals around this process; your rituals will reinforce the ideals not only because you are including God in the process, but also because you are approaching it with faith. Also, go through the pages at least once before you begin. If you associate any terms with negativity or find them offensive, replace them with affirmative substitutes.

Most individuals who do this exercise feel immediate change. Others feel change in a day or two. The changes you may feel; mental and physical, aren't imagined but are feedback from your subconscious mind which is responding to what you are feeding it. As the process continues, it is likely you will experience a lull or a desire to quit, and that's absolutely normal for two main reasons. For one, that's the point when you've reached the boundaries of your comfort zone. When this happens, remember that getting out of your comfort zone is the point of the exercise; *when you expand your comfort zone, you expand your life!* Your comfort zone includes inaccurate thoughts about limitations. This is what you're working to change. The other reason is that your mind is trying to resist the new ideas; and so it should in light of the practice it's had over time. When the mind resists, it's important to remember that you are in control of your thoughts and you will no longer allow your thoughts to control you.

Believing what you're reading isn't essential. It's not you who will make the beliefs stick; it is the exercise which feeds the subconscious mind which in turn works from the inside to make *you* believe, so just go with the flow. Obviously, the more feeling and belief you put into the process, the more effective it will be, but belief is in no way essential. On one hand, this conditioning process may seem a little too easy, but the work is not in the reading as much as it is in the commitment to follow through for twenty days. Finally, this exercise is as much of a physical workout as it is a mental workout, so stay well hydrated. As this exercise actually stimulates the physical components of the brain and its circulation, you'll want to drink some water before, during and after the process.

10 for 20 Affirmations

I trust the process of life and I am safe. I am completely at ease with all of life. I am wealthy and prosperous and I am always attracting and inviting my rightful abundance. I am rejoicing in this moment and I am happily at peace. I am lovingly allowing joy to flow into my life. I am creating affirmative new feelings and thought patterns and I am at peace. I am worthwhile and appreciated. I am easily inviting wealth in all forms into my experience in this moment and forevermore. I love and approve of myself and I approve of my body and my mind. I am loving and loveable. Happiness and grace flow easily into and around my life. I am a divine expression of life always flowing with ease and joy. I am loving and accepting myself at this moment and forevermore. I am completely grateful for my abundant financial wealth. I am always discovering how wonderful I am. I am choosing to love and enjoy myself right here in this present moment. I am choosing abundance and prosperity and success in everything I do. I am lovingly caring for my mind, my body and my emotions. I am always welcomed and deeply loved by all. I am being provided for always throughout my life. I love and approve of myself inside and out. It is safe to care for myself. I love and accept myself at every moment and at every age. I experience joy and grace in all of my relationships. Each moment in life is perfect. I am always healthy, wealthy, abundant and joyous. I am important because I am part of the universal plan. I am important and I am loved and appreciated by life itself. I am powerful, able and capable. I love and appreciate all of myself, at all times in my life. I am inviting joyous experiences as I read these words. I am joyfully living in this eternal moment with ease and with grace. All of my experiences are wonderful and beautiful. I am choosing to see my self worth. I love and approve of myself and all is well. My world is beautiful, safe and friendly. I am always safe. I am at peace with myself and with my life. It is safe to be happy and I deserve to be happy. There is always a new and better way for me to experience my wonderful life. I am moving deeper into joy with each new day. I am worthy of being successful and I am rejoicing in all that I am and all that I am becoming. I am safe and secure at all times and I trust the universal flow of life. I am a magnificent expression of life flowing perfectly in all manners and at all times. I am allowing financial freedom to abundantly flow throughout my life. I am safely experiencing joy in all of my experiences and in every area of my life. I forgive and move delightfully into joy and bliss. I love my wonderful life. I joyfully recognize and accept my intelligence, my courage, my magnificence and my self worth. It is safe for me to be alive and joyous. I love my wealthy abundant prosperous life. I am recognizing that I am important and worthwhile. It is safe for me to succeed because life loves me and I love life. I am joyfully allowing abundance, wealth and prosperity into my life. I deserve to celebrate and rejoice in life. I am enthusiastically accepting all the joy and delight life is offering me. I am rejoicing in contentment in all areas of my life. I completely trust the process of life to bring all good into my experience. Divine right and good action is always taking place in my life. I am grateful for being rich in all the areas of life which are important to me. I am always safe being me and I am wonderful as I am. I am joyously choosing absolute confidence and self acceptance. Wealth and prosperity abundantly indwell and surround me always. I am easily and comfortably moving on to the supreme essentials which are rightfully mine. I always allow joy into my life. It is safe for me to joyfully move on to the new. I welcome, invite and allow new thought, new ideas, new brilliance to bless my life and bless me. I am moving forth to the new, with love and contentment, and I am always free. I am love. I am abundant and prosperous. I am lovingly forgiving myself and I am lovingly forgiving others, and I feel lighthearted and liberated. I am lovingly welcoming the new and the wonderful into my life. I am choosing to love and approve of myself here in this moment and forevermore. I am gratefully accepting my good fortune. I love and approve of myself and I trust the process of life, and I am safe. I lovingly accept my divine rightful abundance. I am confidently being wise at all times. It is safe to feel and I am happily opening myself to new life experiences. I am prepared to be abundant and prosperous. I am safe and I am relaxing and I am letting life flow joyously to me, through me, and around me. I am so very happy and very grateful for all of my wonderful relationships. I am safe to be, to feel and to live at all times in my life. It is always safe for me to be happy and joyous, and I am feeling rich and abundant and wealthy and prosperous. I am honestly loving and approving of myself in this moment and forevermore. I am attracting divine abundance in all areas of my life and I am lovingly embracing each new experience with ease and with joy. I am being blessed with joy, and joy is flowing through me with every thought and with every beat of my heart. I am joyous and grateful as I accept my wealth. I am completely open to life's many gifts and life's many joys. I am choosing to see with divine love and with compassion. I am choosing to be abundant and prosperous, and I see everything and everybody with love, patience and compassion. I am loved, I am loving, I am loveable, and, I am love. I am choosing to absolutely love and approve of myself, and I approve of my beautiful life. I am always seeing others with love, with compassion and with joy. I am seeing a rich life inundated with joy and love and health and abundance and beautiful friendships. It is safe to be decisive and take charge of my life. The world is safe and I am safe. I am lovingly accepting my divine good fortune, riches, wealth and abundance. It is safe for me to take charge of my life. I am completely accepting my abundant divine good. I am choosing to be free and liberated. I am financially free, financially abundant, financially wealthy, and I am financially secure. I am always perfectly safe, and I happily recognize that I am loved and I am loveable. I am always welcomed, appreciated and cherished. I am welcoming divine abundance at this present moment and forevermore. I love and approve of myself and I am giving myself permission to move ahead and succeed with my dreams and my goals. It is always safe for me to move forth, and I joyfully move forth towards abundance and prosperity. I am recognizing that life is always supporting me in every way. I am lovingly accepting and welcoming my life of divine abundant wealth, blissful prosperity, excellent health and blessed relationships. I trust the process of life in this moment and forevermore. I am accepting that all that is essential for my ideal life is always provided, and I am confident that all my dreams are coming true. I am safe and I am moving forth towards goodness and joy. I am free to move forward with love in my mind and in my heart. I am always moving towards my superior good. I love and approve of myself in this eternal moment and forevermore. Life is supporting and loving me and I accept and welcome my divine gifts. I am easily moving into the present with love and I am happily dwelling upon this moment. I am voicing love and joy and compassion. I am grateful for my good and I am confidently centering myself in divine goodness and divine love, and all is well.

100

I am gratefully accepting the perfection of my beautiful and wonderful life, and I am at peace with my heart and my mind. I am perfectly wealthy, abundant, prosperous and joyous, and I am safe at all times and in all places. I love and approve of myself in this moment and forevermore, and I am confidently trusting life. I welcome and accept my beautiful life, and I am feeling and thinking thoughts of gratitude. I am seen with love and joy and I see with love and joy. I am seen with compassion and consideration, and I see with compassion and consideration. I am safe and all is well in this present moment and forevermore. Abundance and prosperity surround me always. I am completely at peace and it is safe for me to express my feelings. I forgive myself and I forgive all others and I claim my peace of mind. Financial wealth in all forms is attracted to me, and I invite it into my life from all good sources. At this moment I am beginning a joyous and wonderful and prosperous new life, and all is well. I am always being provided for, and every experience is perfect for my mind, my body, and my growth process. I am at perfect peace. I forgive myself and I love myself in this current moment and forevermore. I am recognizing that omnipotent wealth is my birthright, and I am always successful. I am always content and joyous. I am free and happy and all is well. I am financially secure, financially abundant, financially prosperous and financially free. I am gently calming my heart, my mind, my thoughts and my feelings, and I am at peace. I am comfortably and easily moving forth to welcome wonderful new experiences into my life, and I am safe. I am gratefully receiving my rightful divine gifts of abundance. I am completely trusting that right action is always taking place in my life and I am at peace. I am so very happy and very grateful for joy and contentment. I am gracefully flowing with life and with each new day and with each new experience, and all is well. My life is always abundant and prosperous. I am the perfection of joy and grace expressing and receiving perfectly in this moment and forevermore. I am joyously and easily moving into this moment and I am blissfully at peace. I am joyously welcoming wonderful new relationships into my life, and I am happily living in this present moment. I am at peace. I am happily accepting the wonder and joy that life is providing for me, and I am blissfully moving towards my rightful abundance. Joyous new thoughts, ideas and inspirations are circulating freely within me and around me. I recognize that all is well, and that I am always safe.

I am grateful that divine wealth flows into my life every day. I am consciously awakening new ideas and new life within me and within others. I am allowing and inviting all forms of abundance into my life from all good sources, and I am grateful for all good sources. I love and approve of myself in this moment and I am safe. I am easily expressing love and joy and I am at peace with all people and with all of life. Abundance in all forms is constantly attracted to me and I use my abundance wisely. I am recognizing that omnipotent good is the structure of my being and of my life, and I am safe and loved and totally supported forevermore. Universal law supplies me with abundant prosperity and I gratefully rejoice in this divine gift. I am gladly breathing in life completely, fully and freely, and I am relaxed. I absolutely trust in the process of life. Joyous experiences are flowing throughout my life easily, frequently and abundantly. My attention is always on the present moment and I accept my wonderful new experiences with joy and grace. I am easily accepting new experiences and welcoming new joy into my life. I am freely and easily moving into this current moment, space and time, and I joyously embrace my life. I am grateful that financial abundance comes to me in many forms and from many good sources. I accept and rejoice in my richness and wealth. I am healthy, happy, abundant and prosperous. I am embracing and expressing divine sustenance in perfect balance. I am grateful that I am abundant and prosperous. I am important and I always care for and nurture myself with love, with happiness and with joy. I am allowing others the freedom to be who they are and I am allowing myself the freedom to be who I am. I am happy, healthy, joyous and wise, and I feel liberated. I love life and I am perfectly safe to live and experience my wonderful experiences. I rejoice in my cheerful lifestyle. It is my birthright to live life fully, happily and freely. I am worthwhile and I accept and approve of myself in this moment and forevermore. I am choosing to live my life fully, happily and freely, and I move forth with grace and gratitude. I am always inviting divine abundance into my life. I am loving and approving of myself in this moment and forevermore. I care for me and I am totally adequate, worthy and wonderful at all times. I am happily living my absolute best life and I am declaring peace within me and around me. I am accepting my divine birthright to be free to live the life of my dreams. I am safe and I love and cherish myself. I am filled with joy and peace of mind, and my life is good.

I am being kind, compassionate and gentle with myself and with all others in my life, and all is well. I am being generous and giving with myself and with all others. I am loved, appreciated, cared for and provided for, and supported by life itself. It is safe for me to be alive and happy and joyous. I am abundantly prosperous and blissfully happy. I am joyously moving ahead to welcome my wonderful new experiences. I am always creating peace of mind within myself, within my relationships and within my environment. Prosperity is all around me and within me. I am intelligent and powerful and I am using my intelligence and my power wisely. I am strong and I am safe, and all is good and well in this moment and forevermore. It is safe to see, hear and experience new thoughts and ideas in brand new ways. I have an abundance of divine gifts and I am using my gifts wisely. I am lovingly forgiving myself and all others, and I am choosing to bless my family, my friends and my neighbors with joy. I love and approve of myself and I am safe at all times and in all places. I rejoice in being abundantly satisfied and prosperous. I am giving myself permission to obtain my goals and achieve my dreams because I deserve the best in life. I love and appreciate myself and others. I deserve to be happy therefore I am happy. I am always creating wonderful experiences in my life and in the life of others. I am creating all forms of wealth for me and for others. I am moving forth with ease and grace through time and space and my life is truly wonderful. Love and beauty always surround and indwell me and my life. I love all those who surround me, and they love me, too. I am joyfully moving on to magnificent new levels of living. I am in my perfect place and time. I am allowing the blessing of time to heal every part of my life. I allow true happiness into my life. I always choose to create a life that is joyous and abundant, and I am at ease and at peace. I love and appreciate my job and I receive excellent compensation, praise and appreciation for my work. My life is overflowing with immense joy and I blissfully look forward to every beautiful moment. I am healthy, happy, joyous and wise. I forgive others and I forgive myself. I am free to love and enjoy my life. I am free to be profoundly happy, abundant and prosperous. I am contributing to a united, loving, peaceful family life. Money, wealth, prosperity, health and wisdom always flow easily within my life. I am divinely protected and I am completely surrounded with love. I am always safe and secure and protected, and I am at peace. All is truly well.

Joy is always attracted to me and I am grateful for my many joyous experiences. I am always choosing to love my life. It is safe to receive prosperity and abundance, and I am always accepting and inviting prosperity and abundance into my life. I am happily changing and growing and moving forward in life. I am always creating a safe new future filled with wonderful new experiences. I am recognizing that divine blessings and gifts are my birthright. I love my wonderful life and my wonderful experiences. I am always creating peaceful experiences for myself and for others in my life. All is well and I am allowing my mind be perfectly relaxed and at peace. Clarity is always within and around me at all times, in this moment and forevermore. I respond to loving thoughts and loving actions and I express loving thoughts and loving actions. All is peaceful and all is well. All is flowing perfectly, peacefully and wonderfully. I am easily moving into this current moment and this present time. I forgive myself, I forgive all others, and I am free. I am deeply grateful for the financial freedom that is my reality. I am totally surrounded by love and I am totally loving. I am allowing time and space to heal and to grow. I am loved and I am loving. I am happy, healthy, wealthy, abundant and prosperous. I am calming my thoughts and feelings, and I am calm, peaceful and serene. I love and approve of my beautiful life and my joyous experiences. I am seeing with eyes of love and I am seeing all the good that is rightfully mine. I am always looking at the affirmative aspects of my wonderful life. There is always an easy and better way to handle everything and I accept it at this present moment and forevermore. Joy flows to me and through me at all times. I allow happiness to flow through me, and I am expressing my blissful joy. I am rejoicing in my magnificent life. I am moving freely forward and I am safe and all is well. I am liberated and free. I am safe and perfectly happy and healthy. I am joyously choosing absolute confidence and self acceptance. Wealth abundantly indwells and surrounds me always. I am easily and comfortably moving on to the supreme essentials which are rightfully mine. I always allow new and happy experiences into my life. It is safe for me to joyfully move on to the new. I welcome, invite and allow new thought, new ideas and new affirmative feelings to bless my life and bless me. I am moving on to the new, with love and contentment, and I am free. I am love. I am abundant and prosperous. I am lovingly forgiving myself and I am lovingly forgiving others, and all is well.

I feel lighthearted and liberated. I am lovingly welcoming the new and the wonderful into my life. I am choosing to love and approve of myself here in this moment and forevermore. I am gratefully accepting my good fortune. I love and approve of myself and I trust the process of life, and I am safe. I lovingly accept divine guidance in everything that I do, and I am always making good decisions. I am confidently being wise at all times. It is safe to feel, and I am happily opening myself to new life experiences. I am safe and I am relaxing and letting the brilliance of life flow joyously to me, through me and around me. I am so very happy and grateful that I am healthy, strong and well. I am safe to be, to feel and to live at all times in my life. It is always safe for me to be happy and joyous, and I am feeling abundant and prosperous. I am honestly loving and approving of myself in this moment and forevermore. I am attracting and inviting divine abundance in all areas of my life and I am lovingly embracing each new experience with ease and with joy. I am being blessed with joy, and joy is flowing though me with every thought and with every beat of my heart. I am joyous and grateful as I accept my wealth. I am completely open to life's many gifts and life's many blessings. I am choosing to see with divine love and with compassion. I am choosing to be abundant and prosperous, and I see everything and everybody with love, patience and compassion. I am loved, I am loving, I am loveable, and I am love. I am choosing to absolutely love and approve of myself, and I approve of my beautiful life. I am always seeing others with love, with compassion and with joy. I am seeing a rich life inundated with joy and love and wealth and abundance. I am joyously loving and approving of myself and my wonderful life. It is safe to be decisive and take charge of my life. The world is safe and I am safe. I am lovingly accepting my divine good fortune, riches, wealth and abundance. It is safe for me to take charge of my life. I am completely accepting my abundant divine good. I am choosing to be free and liberated. I am financially free, financially abundant, financially wealthy and financially secure. I am always perfectly safe, and I happily recognize that I am loved and I am loveable. I am always welcomed, appreciated and cherished. I am welcoming divine abundance and blessings in this present moment and forevermore. I love and approve of myself and I am giving myself permission to move ahead and succeed with my dreams. I am feeling fulfilled and happy about my life and I am truly content.

It is always safe for me to move forth, and I joyfully move forth towards abundance and prosperity. I am recognizing that life is always supporting me in every way. I am lovingly accepting and welcoming my life of divine abundant joy, blissful prosperity, excellent health and blessed relationships. I trust the process of life in this moment and forevermore. I am accepting that all that is essential for a joyous ideal life is always being provided. I am confident that all my dreams are coming true. I am safe and I am moving forth towards goodness and abundance. I am free to move forward with love in my mind and in my heart. I am always moving towards my superior good. I love and approve of myself in this eternal moment and forevermore. Life is supporting and loving me and I accept and welcome my divine good. I am easily moving into the present with love, and I am happily dwelling upon this eternal moment. I am voicing love and joy and compassion. I am grateful for my family and friends. I am confidently centering myself in divine goodness and divine love. I am gratefully accepting the perfection of my beautiful and wonderful life, and I am at peace with my heart and my mind. I am safe at all times and in all places. I love and approve of myself in this moment and forevermore, and I am confidently trusting life. I am always expressing feelings of gratitude. I am seen with love and joy, and I see with love and joy. I am seen with compassion and consideration, and I see with compassion and consideration. I am safe and all is well in this present moment and forevermore. Abundance, prosperity and an overall sense of wellbeing and contentment surround me always. I am completely at peace, and it is safe for me to express my feelings. I forgive myself and I forgive all others. I am claiming my peace of mind. At this moment I am beginning a joyous and wonderful and prosperous new life, and all is well. I am one with all of life. Life completely and absolutely supports me. I am being recognized and praised, and I am appreciated in the most affirmative of ways by everybody. I am relaxing and allowing my mind to be at peace. I am accepting all the good that life is offering me. I am grateful that wealth flows freely to and through my life. I am always peaceful with all of my emotions and I allow my thoughts and feelings to be at peace. I love and approve of myself and I am lovingly balancing my mind, my body and my spirit. I am choosing thoughts that make me feel good here in this moment and forevermore. I am always creating a life blessed with wonderfully miraculous rewards.

I am eternally wealthy and always provided for in the most wonderful of ways, and I am welcoming continual wealth into my experience. Life loves me and I love life. I am always choosing to blissfully take in life fully and freely. I am listening to divine wisdom, and I am one with all. I am joyfully moving on to magnificent new levels of life and living. I am in my perfect place and time. I am always moving into the realm of affirmative possibility to create my abundantly beautiful life. This moment is happy, joyous and blissful. It is safe for me to take charge of my life, and I am confident with all of my decisions. I am choosing to be free and liberated. I am always perfectly safe, and I happily recognize that I am loved and I am loveable. I am always welcomed, appreciated and cherished. I am welcoming divine abundance at this present moment and forevermore. I love and approve of myself and I am giving myself permission to move ahead and succeed with my dreams. It is always safe for me to move forth, and I joyfully move forth towards a blissful reality. I am recognizing that life is always supporting me in every way. I am lovingly accepting and welcoming my life of divine abundant joy, blissful prosperity, excellent health and blessed relationships. I trust the process of life in this moment and forevermore. I am safe and I am moving forth towards goodness and abundance. I am free to move forward with love in my mind and in my heart. I am at peace with myself and with all others. I am at peace with all of life and I am deeply centered and serene. I am safe, alive and joyous. Wealth in all forms flows easily into my life frequently and abundantly. I love and approve of myself inside and out. It is safe to care for myself. I love and accept myself at every moment and at every age. I experience joy and grace in all of my relationships. Each moment in life is perfect. I am one with all and I joyfully accept my rightful good. I am blissfully moving on to wonderful new levels of joy. I am thinking and feeling and acting in the realm of affirmative possibility. I am creating abundant and blissful life experiences in this moment and forevermore. I am profoundly enthusiastic about life and living. Joy, bliss, contentment and overall happiness surround and indwell me. I am joyously living with divine energy and passionate enthusiasm. My awareness is perfectly clear. All this I declare in the name of all that is divine and good and true and honest and right and just and of good rapport. It is done. All is well, and so It Is...

CHAPTER VII

=DreamsGoalsSuccess=

Success isn't about *beating* the competition,
Success is about *outperforming* the competition.
You do this by outperforming *yourself*...

Subsequent to my extensive research into Heditniemi's Conjecture, which states that the chromatic number of product of two graphs is at least half the minimum of the fractional chromatic numbers of the factors, I've concluded that mathematics is not my forté and that I should stick to what I know, which, after said research confirms that what I know isn't all that much!

What I do know is that successful people, regardless of what they know – or don't know – all have one thing in common: They affirmatively dwell within, upon and beyond the realm of affirmative possibility. In fact, the only negative involvement in their process is to remove any ideals of what is *not* possible. This allows them to dwell only on the possible, the probable and the affirmative. Most successful people also focus on what they do best. Although there are some people out there who have succeeded at something by accident, without planning, those people are not necessarily as successful as they are lucky. Truly successful people are the ones who set out to do something, whether or not they know how they're going to do it, and they actually *do it*.

Their commitment to their goal takes precedence over their concern for the alleged obstacles which threaten their imminent victory. Where others stop to consider why they shouldn't do something, successful people continue full speed ahead, motivated by the many reasons why they *should* do something. It would be incorrect to imply that successful people, while on their journey towards their goal, never think about quitting or never give any thought to the hurdles they may have to overcome in the process, but they don't see these hurdles as limitations to what they can accomplish, but rather, they see the hurdles as opportunities, and in many cases, guidelines which in the long run prove to be valuable stepping stones on their journey towards, and maintenance of, their ultimate success.

An important and severely overlooked reason why most of us are not successful in life is because we let others dictate what success looks like and what our dreams should involve. A great example of this is when wealth-promoting self-help gurus use examples of "menial" jobs and how degrading it is to do those jobs. I recently watched a program where one popular *wealth guru* gave a talk about how he flies to his Arizona office, and when he gets there, he can barely handle the heat, and he feels sorry for the guys working construction in that heat, with tools and jackhammers and such, and he mentions that we don't have to do those *menial* jobs. First of all, every job needs to be done by somebody, and second, as a person who is in the business of inspiring people, I am troubled by those damaging words, and I'm insulted on behalf of every single person who ever worked on all the roads and highways I've ever driven upon, and who enjoyed the process.

This *guru* goes on to suggest (as do most wealth-gurus) that we should all fly *first class* as much as possible, explaining that that's where the rich people are. First of all, seeing things from my perspective, I figure that if I can get to Phoenix by air, I *am* traveling *first class!* Second, these days, most of the people who you see traveling first class are not the wealthy on leisurely vacations but rather are usually people who travel so frequently for business that the airlines automatically bump them up to first class as both a thank you for their business and an incentive to keep flying with them. I know this because I was such a working traveler for many years, and I was constantly bumped up to first class, and I rarely sat next to wealthy vacationers in first class. In fact, many a time while occupying a first class seat, I've found myself envious of the sounds coming from back in the coach section of the plane where vacationing families just relaxed and where wealthy folks who know the value of a buck snuggled up with a good book instead of thinking about a boardroom meeting awaiting them at touchdown. As for the super rich who can afford first class, trust me, they're not flying with the masses; they're in their own private airplanes.

When it comes to those so-called *menial* jobs, here's a newsflash: There are no menial jobs! Not everybody hates their job, and not everybody *can't* take the heat of working in a hot climate. For one thing, bodies adjust to temperature changes and people become acclimatized to different environments. Where one hundred degrees is unbearable to one person, it may only feel like eighty degrees to another. The thing about *menial* jobs is, whereas one public motivational speaker can't imagine the joys of breaking up a roadway with a jackhammer on a scorching hot day, a construction worker doing just that couldn't imagine trading in his dream job of being paid to demolish things with big machines, in exchange for a job talking to crowds about what they already know they should be doing. Furthermore, he might be unable to imagine being capable of living with himself for selling compromised, off-the-cuff recycled poppycock that we've all heard before. He might also be someone who previously took that advice and is now doing precisely what he always dreamed of doing and quit his job in medicine or law or as a motivational speaker.

Again, there are no menial jobs. All jobs need to be done by somebody. I hold as much respect for a person who works at fast-food joints, following their dream to one day own the place, as I hold gratitude for them when I'm on the road at four in the morning and they are the only people available to feed me. Incidentally, whenever I've hired people, especially where filling a position where consistency, accuracy, speed, quality control and efficient customer service are required, if a candidate doesn't have some kind of fast-food work experience, I rarely bother reading the rest of the resume. Places like Wendy's and McDonald's, if they're being managed according to strict corporate protocol, have stringent training procedures which most employees carry with them throughout their careers. Like brainwashing, once you're trained and have done a task a few thousand times, you never forget how to do it, whether it is covering the whole burger with condiments to ensure consistent taste with every bite rather than just randomly squirting mustard on a portion of it, or referring to everyone who enters the establishment as *guests* rather than *customers*, or satisfying a disgruntled guest enough to make him want to come back again.

Of course it's okay to seek advice on success from all possible sources, but we need to stop approaching wealth *gurus* and their books from the perspective that we know nothing, and understand that we are merely adding to our own massive body of knowledge. We're all intelligent beings with immense life experience, and we need to bring forth that intelligence upon opening each book or listening to every speech, and use our logic, intuition and common sense. The meaning of success is different to each of us, and it should never be dictated by anybody else, whether they are our parents, our teachers, or some overinflated stuffed-shirt who thinks the value of one's success is measured by the class of an airline ticket.

There are so many books out there on the subject of success, and for the most part, they're all correct about the various paths towards success. The problem is that most people who read those books simply don't want to do the work. Most folks are looking for a quick-fix/get-rich-now program, but if the experts are all saying *work is what success takes*, chances are, *success takes work*! Praying, meditating, chanting, doing affirmations; they're all important components of the wealth-attraction process, but nothing will make a greater impact on our success than the actual physical actions we take when pursuing our goals.

For anybody who has ever wanted to achieve anything in life, whether it's to become president of a country or a corporation, or to become the greatest sewage treatment plant floor sweeper, or the greatest homemaker, or the greatest doctor, or the greatest whatever they can possibly imagine, undeniably, there is work to be done. With growing knowledge of the law of attraction, not to mention the compromised teachings on the subject, there are millions upon millions of people who think they are going to *affirm* their way to the top. Yet, while most people are doing their affirmations, and more still doing them incurrectly, the few people who will actually make it to the top are *working* their way to the top, and the blood, sweat and tears shed in the name of their calling, and every challenging step along their journey is as much their reward and their success as is the destination itself. A reward only those who continue to learn and who have given their *all* will ever come to know. Furthermore, affirmations might possibly get you to the top, but it's the experience of the *climb* that will keep you there.

Giving one's all isn't just about selling someone on our knowledge; it's about adding to and improving upon our knowledge. Ideals surrounding affirmative reinforcements apply to just about everything, especially learning. We all first learned to read by reading and re-reading the same few lines of a child's book, and we did this until the sentence "see the dog run" was not something we read but something we recognized. The process of re-reading non-academic data is rarely practiced by most of us because either it seems like a waste of time or we assume that reading something once is enough to make it stick. For example, this book you're now reading contains over one hundred thousand words, yet most people who read it once will come away remembering a minute portion of the book's ideals. When I purchase a book, especially one about self-empowerment, I make sure to read it a minimum of two times. If it's really good, I'll read it five times or more. This results in actually *learning* the principles instead of just *considering* them, and it sure gives me a bang for my buck!

If you buy a book for $21 and read it just once, you're pretty sure to recall between one and ten percent of the books data. If you read that same book twice, you've gone beyond considering mere data and have absorbed its ideals, and the book has now cost you only $10.50 because you got two reads for the price of one. By the time you've read the book three times, the ideals are now possessed knowledge, and your book has only cost you $7. If you actually read a book five times, you're pretty much an expert and your price drops to just slightly over four dollars. How incredible is that, especially when you consider that university students often pay over one hundred dollars for a single textbook? This process is called study. If you're not going to study your books, then save your money, because merely considering ideals does not get you places; studying, absorbing and putting them into practice does. Countless people have shared with me some great books they've read – books which they claim have changed their lives – but they never go back to those books. When a book changes my life, however, I go back to it because I want to get into that zone and stay there. I want it to become my reality.

There are many books out there on the topic of success, and I've read many of them, and quite honestly, almost all the books I've read had some kind of useful proven for-mula for success; especially the books written by people who share their *unique* formula for how they succeeded in spite of the fact they didn't know how they were going to do it. There are plenty of writers who have published great works, and it's always good to continue absorbing great ideas from every perspective, even if we've heard it all before, because you can never have too much affirmative knowledge, or ever hear it repeated often enough. The key, however, is to not just read and re-read; the key is to keep moving, keep working, keep doing, keep thinking and not just sit around waiting for success to find us. Ideas are just ideas. Without action, ideas are merely data. That said, here is some of my own data, ideas and information which I've implemented and which have helped me realize many of my personal and professional goals.

I believe that the very first step towards any success is to take full *responsibility* for everything around you. All success in life is about management. If you're not ready to take responsibility for what happens in your life, your relationships, your profession, for any reason, then you're not management material and you're not going to succeed. I don't only mean management material as represented in the corporate world, I mean managing yourself and your life.

I learned this fact long ago when my own world was seemingly crumbling around me and I had the choice to legitimately cast the blame, or I could work at fixing, saving and salvaging what was left of my world. I did not cause all the problems that had arisen at the time, but I knew that taking responsibility to change what was going on was key, so I took what was left of my crumbling pit of hell, built myself a ladder, climbed towards the sun, prayed like I never prayed before, and I even wrote a book along the way. What was then a terrifying reality is now a fond memory of the most exhilarating challenge of a lifetime because what I see when I look back on it is my shining resilience, creativity, strength, courage and faith, not to mention the faces of the friends and family who stood by me during that time and who consequently have my loyal devotion forever. I also recall the compassionate voice of my sister cheering me on along the way.

Time and energy wasted on blaming and looking for fault in others is time and energy that should be used constructively. When things get messy in our lives, it doesn't matter who made the mess, it's up to us to clean it up if we want things to be different. There is no time for blame. Just take responsibility for making things better, regardless of how impossible the task may seem, and ignore anybody who stands in your way. People are imperfect and they won't always have your drive or your vision, and as much as there are some people out there with bad intentions, the truth of the matter is, there are far more people around with good intentions than bad. The problem is, those good intentions are not always coupled with the same passion and integrity and motivation that you may come to the table with, so don't waste precious energy on getting angry with people when you should be putting that energy towards repairing things and appreciating your new lessons which are guaranteed to see you through life's next hurdles, and believe me, there will be other hurdles.

Taking responsibility doesn't mean you blame yourself if things go wrong. It means there is no blame, and that you're committed to making things right no matter what happens or who makes it happen, and that you're committed to keeping things moving. Taking responsibility is the biggest commitment that yields the greatest rewards because it's the very first step before anything else. No other action can teach you more as you go along, about yourself, about what you know, and ultimately if you are on the right track. Furthermore, assuming responsibility is the most mature thing you can do in any situation; personally, professionally and otherwise.

A close second step towards success is *decisiveness*. Too many lives are wasted because people are indecisive about what they want to do or where they want to go in life. Sometimes destinations and directions are not clear, but doing *nothing* should never be an option. Doing something will always lead to the discovery of where to go and what to do next. Indecision is worse than making a bad decision because making a bad decision still takes courage and risk, and there's always a valuable constructive lesson to be learned when the results of a bad decision arise, whereas indecision is just plain destructive. In short, indecision is actually the decision to let someone or something else decide what's going to happen. When this route is taken, nothing happens, or worse happens.

Prioritizing from the very first step is crucial to any success. Whether it's money, time, practice or anything else, your goal is only as attainable as the priority in which you place it. This is very important to remember especially during those times where you reach a plateau and things get boring, or during those times when all seems hopeless. During the difficult, challenging or boring moments, give your goal more of your time, energy, passion and love. Breathe life into your dreams especially during difficult times, because that's where most people give up. It's the time when your consciousness is the most vulnerable, and it's where your convictions and intentions weaken or strengthen, depending on what you're doing.

Taking *action* is *THE* essential part of each step towards success right from the word *GO*, because every step along the way requires action. Even the greatest of intentions will mean nothing if action in some form is not taken. For those sailing uncharted waters towards a unique goal, your next step is not always obvious, but that should never be an excuse to stop moving forward. There is always action to take, even if it's just actively reminding people of what you're intending on accomplishing.

This next step seems almost a little too obvious, and perhaps that's why people rarely or ever do it. Either way, it bears mentioning: *Always know what you're going to do the next day.* Keeping in mind that every day can bring unexpected changes, always plan your day the night before so there is very little time wasted. The more strict you are about adhering to your schedule, the more committed you'll be to accomplishing things within your set timelines. As you discover more efficient ways to accomplish those scheduled tasks, you'll make more room in your schedule to accomplish other important tasks. This process may seem menial at times, but anybody who applies this action to their daily lives will not only discover how quickly they can get things accomplished, but will also discover the true abundance of time that actually does exist in a day.

Within this ideal of scheduling and planning, it's very important to understand how to delegate. If you don't know how to delegate, *learn!* When business gets big, you won't be able to accomplish everything on your own, and knowing the difference between what you should do yourself and what you should pass on to another could mean the difference between *all* and *nothing.* If you're the pie-baker and business is growing, pass on to another the responsibility of washing dishes and delivering pies, and you focus on what you do best.

When it comes to "walking the walk", *label yourself!* Take every opportunity to *tell the world what you're doing,* and don't be shy about it. By this, of course I mean keep your secret if it's a process which requires confidentiality, but if you're writing a book, or training for the Olympics, or wanting to own a car dealership, then tell people you're a writer or athlete or car dealer. Labeling yourself is a great way to feel you've already attained your success. Those around you will also inquire regularly about your progress *(a great way to be held accountable)*, and you just never know where you'll find your first customer or greatest supporter.

When I began writing my first book, LoveDare, I told everybody; friends, family and strangers, about what I was doing. It was a long process, and although some ridiculed or didn't believe me, most people were completely supportive, especially those who know that when I say I'm going to do something, I'm going to do it! Most people inquired about my progress, and before I knew it, the book was being printed and I was selling books before they were off the press. Since then, I've developed an avid following. I've also given countless talks, seminars and lectures to various organizations consisting of writers, physicians, psychologists, scientists, adoption agencies, and corporate and charitable organizations. All this because I said, *I am a writer!* If you don't believe in the power of labeling yourself per your goal, just think of the power that labels have when used negatively; *crippled, stupid, retarded.* Compare how a cashier who says she's a writer might be inspired as opposed to a woman who says she's a cashier who writes. Good or bad, labels are powerful, so use them wisely.

My disclaimer to the above, however, is that although you want to share where you're headed, you want nobody to discourage you, so unless a person has hands-on experience in the area of where you're headed, or you know they want to see you succeed: *Ignore Everybody!*

The point in sharing your goal is to be motivated on a daily basis, as much by your own words as by the words of others. If anybody even hints about how or why you shouldn't or can't achieve your goal, or discourages you in any way, get away from that person at all costs and never let them near you again, and leave the guilt out of it no matter who they are. As for business advice, this may seem somewhat superficial, but before you place any stock into anybody's negative feedback, take a look at what they're driving, or the state of their home, or the friends they keep. Someone relayed this suggestion to me quite some time ago, and it never fails that whenever a person tries to dissuade me from my endeavors, they almost always have a junky car, or a messy house, or bad finances, or miserable friends, if they're lucky enough to have friends. Incidentally, this concept is supported by the scripture, *By their fruits you shall know them* (Matt 7:20). I'm not suggesting that all business minds must drive posh cars and live in mansions, I'm merely suggesting that when advice is negative, look at what they've produced for themselves before you let them tell you how to go about producing your thing, or dissuading you altogether.

A funny thing you'll notice about those negative people is that they're the same people who benefit from and rave about innovations and inventions (light bulbs, telephones, cars, airplanes, medications, etc.) which were created by the kind of people to whom they would have said: *That's impossible; don't waste your time.* They're also the people who'll boast about knowing you once you've made it in spite of their discouraging words. These are the ingrates of the planet, and although they deserve (and need) your forgiveness, they do not deserve a moment more of your time or your consideration; at least not where your dreams and goals are concerned.

Whether we have good fortune or bad fortune, we tend to ask, "Why me?" This also applies to the process of imagining the fruition of our dreams. Why would I become a world renowned *fill in the blank* and why would anybody buy my *fill in the blank?* Yes, following our dreams is difficult enough when coupled with our doubts and lack of support from others, but there is no reason why you cannot or should not succeed. Imagine the doubts experienced by the likes of Winston Churchill or Mother Teresa or the Wright Bothers or Thomas Edison or Isaac Newton. On one hand, you might say *"But I'm not them, I'm me."* And I would reply; *You're right, you're not them; you're you, and they're dead and you're alive which means you have all the power to accomplish your dreams.* Thank God that, where it came to their dreams and ideals, none of the aforementioned people ever listened to the nay-sayers and dream-crushers of their time. Here's to hoping you don't listen, either. As for the magnitude of your goal, large or small, rest assured that any endeavor of an affirmative nature will change the world for the better. So go and become an astronaut or ballerina or thimble museum curator or dishwasher or mom or dad or whatever it is you want to do. Yes, I promise you, that pursuing your dream will in fact make the world a better place, but it will also make your life-journey worthwhile. Don't die wondering, *"What if I'd have...?"* That would be sad for all of us!

Anyone familiar with concept of the law of attraction may have already heard the term *live as if.* Living *as if* is a powerful *action* tool which affects all of our senses and works exceptionally well in manifesting our goals. For example, imagine you would like a new luxury car. For many it's easy enough to imagine ourselves in that car, but we wouldn't dare set foot in the dealership. The reason for this is very logical; you don't have the money to buy the car, you've never been in that showroom, you don't know where the showroom is, you don't know what to say to the salesperson, you don't know how to deal with pressure sales, etc. When it comes to these excuses, it's important to acknowledge them as just that; excuses. They are not reasons. On one hand, if you'd like to get into that car, you really should *get into* that car, and where better to do this than at a place where you're invited to do so. Conversely, if you can't find it in yourself to go to a dealership, which is really nothing more than a glorified parking garage, how will you ever get into that car?

Now, before I proceed with a personal example, I'd like to reiterate that before anything else, I am a scientist, and as such, I'm not a fan of hearsay, and I like to have proof that something actually works. As such, I researched this phenomenon before, during and after attempting this exercise, and what I discovered is that this "as if" phenomenon exists as much in the body, brain and mind as it does in the *universal quantum realm*. It's a factual, scientifically proven phenomenon that is now becoming common knowledge among the general populace. In brief, we know that when we're feeling happy, we smile. This is a natural reaction. But, the opposite action also provokes a natural reaction. It's now well recognized that when we're down and want to feel good, we simply need to smile, and we'll start to feel happy. Seriously, as you're reading this, just smile *(for real)* and try *not* to feel better.

This also applies to taking power-poses *(superhero stance)* which raise testosterone levels and lower cortisol levels *(in both men and women of any ethnicity)*. Taking power-poses, while standing or seated – prior to performing – increases confidence and enthusiasm and lowers awkwardness and unease prior to, and during, performances such as job interviews, public speaking, sales pitches, preaching, teaching, negotiating, dating, and pretty much any realm in which one wishes to perform. As a smile is a natural response to the mind's happiness, so is it natural for the body to react confidently when the mind is confident. And, where the mind will switch into happy mode in response to a smile, it's also a natural reaction for the mind to perform confidently when the body is acting *as if* it is confident. Fortunately, this process is a universal phenomenon which applies to all that we experience, and all that we wish to experience.

It's the same idea as *the clothes make the man*. This isn't just about how we perceive a man according on his attire, but also how a man perceives himself according to his attire. What man *(in general)* doesn't feel a certain feeling of distinction or power or intrigue while wearing a top-notch suit and brand new shoes as opposed to sporting jeans and a t-shirt? And what woman *(in general)* doesn't feel one or all of those same feelings when wearing her favorite ensemble and best shoes on a good hair day? Anyone who's delved into the world of Feng-Shui knows firsthand the importance of dressing one's best, never wearing clothes with rips, tears or holes, or clothing to which negative thoughts or memories are attached. This is because what one wears – whether it's a suit, a smile, or a superhero stance – is what one intends for one's day, and ultimately, for one's life.

As for one of my own experiences: For an entire year previous to purchasing my first fully equipped, top of the line luxury car, I visited a dealership and made a good acquaintance with a salesperson with whom I was completely honest from the beginning. When I first went in, I said I wanted to see their full line of cars and learn about their up and coming models. I also made it clear that I wouldn't be purchasing a car that day. He appreciated the honesty, didn't waste time trying to qualify the sale, and he concerned himself with ensuring I had received a cup of coffee by the time his colleague brought me a list of *in stock* models. A year later, after several visits, I had the money to purchase my car, and it was him I went to see.

It's been my experience that wherever I've shopped, the establishments which offer minimal sales pressures are the upscale establishments. I've never been pressured into buying a high-priced item in the same manner as I have experienced from establishments selling merchandise of compromised value. I guess if an item or a service is so good, its value speaks for itself. If a person really likes and wants an item or service, if he's got the money, he'll buy it. If he doesn't, there's no point in pressuring him.

Although the whole point of the *"live as if"* exercise is to *fake it til you make it*, you'll want to be real with people. On one hand, you don't have to say you're broke and can't afford the car, but you most certainly don't want to tell lies, so keep it on a need-to-know basis. Don't fake it to the point of telling lies because lying is not affirmative, and if you lie about being rich when you're not, they'll know anyway, and when the time comes that you do have the money to buy that car, you'll have no leverage to get a better deal. One thing that most high-end merchandise sales professionals understand is that most wealthy people are wealthy because they make good decisions about money and they make no excuses for why they're not buying right now. So when you start shopping, leave the excuses and explanations behind and let them know you're doing your homework before committing to anything.

Living *as if* is something we all do anyway, we're just not really aware of it when we're doing it. When we're down and out, things always seem worse than they truly are. As a result, we attract more of how bad things are because we are constantly living *as if* things are so bad. The same applies to when things are good. A phone call, a job prospect, a kiss; they all represent potential but are not more than what they are. Regardless of what we see or what we think we see – good or bad – how we feel is always communicating with and through our mind, brain and body, and thus communicating with and through our life, but it's also communicating with and through the law of attraction, the law of cause and effect, and all other governing universal laws, and those laws always respond with, YES! So, watch what you're feeling, thinking, saying, doing and yes, even wearing, and pay attention to how you're treating people and how you're treating yourself. This is all attracting something; at all times!

Because materiel possessions for many people represent that they have *arrived*, when I speak with people about what they want out of life, the popular response is, *I want the best of everything!* This statement is usually followed up by a restrained or embarrassed giggle; their hesitation usually due to shame for having uttered something so seemingly superficial. In all honesty, however, there is nothing superficial about wanting the best of everything. If you were planning a dinner and God was the guest of honor, and you had the choice between regular dishes and the very best dishes, would you not want to use the very best? That said, if it's not good enough for God, why should it be good enough for God's children? I realize I'm taking this to the extreme, but in actuality, we don't have any reason to settle for anything that's second best. The reason why we settle is because we *choose* to settle!

Accepting only *the best* has perks beyond what we see. It's one thing to own a sofa that makes your home feel like a palace, but it's another thing when only the best products were used to make it and the people who constructed and upholstered that sofa enjoyed every minute of making it because it's their passion and it brings them joy and they're well paid for doing what they love to do. Compare that energy to a cheap mass-manufactured sofa that spent six months in a musty warehouse with a bunch of disgruntled employees, and was built by twenty different guys who wish they were somewhere else and who put little, if any, love into what they're doing if for no other reason than for the fact they're getting paid pennies to do that job. Furthermore, the chances of you loving your high-end sofa to the extent of keeping it for the next thirty years are pretty good, whereas you might go through five cheap sofas in the same period, sending each old sofa to landfills. Energy is in everything, and the way you feel about your *best* possessions will be dictated as much by the quality of the workmanship as by the energy left there by the ones who did that work.

A surefire way to have the best of everything within the next twenty-four hours is to consider the following: As an exercise for people who want the best of everything, I suggest that they go to their house or room, or wherever their *stuff* is, and do away with anything that is not entirely *the best;* furniture, clothes, electronics and so forth. By *the best,* of course I am referring to everything that is made with quality materials and workmanship. Anything you decide to keep that is not made with the best of quality should have a completely affirmative meaning to you; Grandma's chair, Aunt Dorothy's painting, your original wedding ring made of aluminum. These are *the best* because of what they represent. By ridding your life of anything that is not the best, you make room for the best to enter your life, and you make a very clear statement to yourself, to others, and to the universe, that only the best will do. By settling for second-best, you're sending the message that second-best is good enough for you. In the event that you need to keep items until you can afford to replace them with the best – computer, TV, car – make sure that when the time comes to replace them, you don't settle for anything less than *the best*. This practice ensures that only *the best*, regardless of how much or little you possess surrounds you. And, because it's constantly on your mind, you are sure to attract it.

When it comes to language, if there is only one word you will ever banish from your vocabulary, do yourself a favor and banish the word *try*, especially when pursuing dreams. Some would argue this point and suggest that we remove the word *no*, but much of what we go through in life is because we don't say *no* when the need arises. So, if someone asks what you're doing, don't say *I'm trying to realize my dream*, instead, say *I am realizing my dream*.

To give you an idea of how powerful the word *try* is, consider this: When a hypnotist comes to the end of a therapy session with a patient, he'll tell the patient that he's going to count to three, and when he does, he wants the patient to *try as hard as possible* to wake up. The reason for this is because the subconscious understands the word *try* as a command to *struggle*. Couple that with *as hard as possible,* and the mind focuses its attention on *trying* to awaken. In the process the mind forgets what went on during hypnosis. Forgetting the session details is an integral part of hypnotherapy, so in this case, the word *try* is used as an affirmative tool. Every time you say you're trying something, *"okay (sigh) I'll try"*, you've set yourself up for immense difficulty in the task, if not for complete failure.

Commitment is mentioned here again because it's actually the key element that brings our efforts and success together, and it falls under the category of *decisiveness* because commitment is really nothing more than a series of decisions – a decision to carry on. Committing to one's goal moment by moment is essential to achieving the goal. Commitment is a promise in action, and when it gets difficult to keep that promise, I find the best way to keep on track is to pledge that commitment; that promise, to the one you love the most, whether it be to yourself, your inner-child, your spouse, your children, or to God. If that doesn't work, commit it to all of them, and let them know it, and let them hold you accountable. Believe me, this works!

In the process of working towards our goals, thinking for one's self is a key principle to any success, and it's most certainly a major key factor in achieving the greatest things. Everything begins with a thought. All the greatest people in the world knew this (and know this), and had to (and have to) think for themselves because if they subscribed to thinking like the rest of society, they would have succumbed to society's basic reality. On the surface, thinking for one's self in our current *reality* might seem difficult. If it were so easy, everyone would be doing it, right? In actuality, however, the greatest advancements humanity has ever known only ever came to be because somebody somewhere thought beyond the limitations enforced by ideals of mediocre thinkers. The greatest advancements came to be because some people thought for themselves and thus, it is clear, the forthcoming great advancements in the history of humanity will come to be because somebody somewhere thinks beyond that place where most of us stop thinking. But what are we supposed to do when we don't know what it is we want to do in life, or what it is we should be doing?

There comes a time in almost everyone's life when we find ourselves sitting in traffic, or at our desk, or in the laundry room curled up in the fetal position between the washer and dryer, clutching a bottle of bleach in one hand and a Martini in the other *(not that I've ever personally been in such an unfortunate position; I'm more of a chocolate-milk man myself)*, and frustrated over our current circumstances, and we find ourselves asking God, *"What do you want from me!?"* while all along God is asking us: *"What do you want, my child?"* While we're too busy wallowing in the illusion that is our misery to hear God bounce that question back at us, we're also not hearing; *"This is your life, it's your decision, it's your time to shine!"*

All kidding and Martinis aside, this really is our time to shine, regardless of age or health or marital status or financial standing or the fact that we might not be able to squeeze our huge butt into last year's jeans. Now is our time... *"Now"* is all we have! Contrary to popular belief, the reason that most of us don't have what we want in our lives is not because we're lazy or dumb or insecure. The main reason is because we simply don't know what it is that we truly want. Yes laziness, ignorance and insecurity play a huge role in not achieving success for those who do know what they want, but most people, and by this I truthfully mean *most of the people in the entire world*, sincerely don't know what they truly want in life. I'm not talking about the generic ideals of being rich or wanting a hot partner or a fancy house and car. I'm talking about that thing that occupies and sustains us; the thing that has the power to catapult us towards our ideal selves: *Your Dream!*

At the risk of sounding all religious-like, it astounds me when I see something as effective as the power of prayer being so blatantly overlooked when it comes to pursuing our dreams and goals, and especially when it comes to discovering the path of our life's journey. I don't think people are as much put off by the idea of prayer because they're offended by its connection to religion as much as they're simply too impatient to take the time it takes to pray, and too impatient to await the results. Once again, I'm just a regular guy, but I'm living a highly irregular life (in a good way) and none of it has come to be without prayer. What impresses me the most about prayer is that it is the one solitary thing about religion that has been proven effective as much by science as by religion. Of course there are the basic components of prayer which bring power to the process; faith and intention, but the mere thought that we each have a direct line to the Almighty Creator never ceases to impress me beyond anything else I have encountered. The fact that it is *scientifically proven* to work impresses me that much more. The mere concept of prayer's simplicity should mean the world to all of us to the point of making prayer our global pastime, but somehow, even in the face of this undeniably miraculous concept that anyone can master, it's the most important tool we utilize the least.

Prayer aside, truly achieving something of real *worth* takes more than just saying you're going to do it. Whether our dreams involve art, academics, athletics, law, medicine, homemaking or otherwise, or we're on the search for what it is we want to do, it's not enough to just think about it; you truly have to *want it*. You have to convince yourself you want it. In fact, you have to convince yourself you want it before you can convince anybody else, including God. You do this by planting the seed.

One cannot expect to yield one thing if the seed of another thing has been planted. You cannot excel in figure skating by giving all your time to your terrible job and then to the television anymore than you can get the car clean by washing the dishes. If you want bananas, don't plant cucumber seeds! Conversely, if you do know what you want and you've planted the idea that you *don't have a chance*, then that is what will come to be; *no chance!* Waiting for something to grow or to happen on its own doesn't work. One must plant the seed and nurture it in order for it to grow. Prayer, if we employ it and allow it to do its thing, can play an immense role in getting us to a place where we can get to do what we want to do and be who we want to be, but it can also help us *discover* what it is we want and are meant to do and be.

Prayer makes things clear and makes things possible. Just because we might have been forced to go to church as a child, and maybe we had religion crammed down our throats or were taught to pray out of fear rather than out of the perspective that God really *is* waiting in the wings to give us direction and cheer us on, should not be reason enough to deny ourselves this incredibly powerful process.

As with all the important things in life, there is an overabundance of questions we need to ask ourselves when embarking upon our pursuit of success. Questions like, *Does this reflect my values? Is it good for me?* and so forth. As this isn't a psychology book, I'll leave to the experts the questions we should be asking. I will say, however, that coupled with the aforementioned ideals, I always ask myself this question: *And then what?* Visualize your dream accomplished; finally being where you want to be, and then ask yourself the golden question: *And then what?* Upon asking this question, if you're happy with your response, then you're on the right track. On the other hand, if you can't imagine your dream, you have to ask yourself if it really is your dream, or merely somebody else's dream imposed upon you. You also have to ask yourself: *Do I want it bad enough?*

The other thing about the *Then What* question is that it allows you to envision your dream and ask yourself what's stopping you from living that dream right now? If you'd like to get an education to become a pediatrician because you dream of taking care of babies, why not become a nanny, or become a volunteer in a hospital, or go to work for a daycare center, or have a few of your own babies, or adopt babies. If, on the other hand, all you want is a doctor's salary, then marry a doctor!

Ultimately, your success should never be defined by others, because as previously mentioned, this is your life. This is your time to shine, it is your time to live, and it is your time to experience all the success you could ever imagine. Most of us know that anything is *possible*, but what most of us don't know is how to make it *probable*. You make it probable by deciding that *it is* probable, then you pray, and then you take it from there...

CHAPTER VIII

=Money=

Money, finances and economics are largely individual topics having little to do with each other.

The advancement of humanity and human consciousness clearly advocates that eventually humans will move on from working for *money* and *things*, to working towards bettering ourselves and our world. The reality remains, however, that money in our current reality is necessary. Inasmuch as most of us are attached to ideals of money for relatively superficial reasons, money nonetheless remains a spiritual ideal, and as such, it requires of us discipline and respect in order to get the most good out of money, and to do the most good with money. Whatever your monetary intentions; pure or superficial, this chapter serves as a basic crash-course in finances, economics, and money. Its ideals are proven. One only need put the ideals into practice.

Before I proceed with ideals about what causes money woes, and with ideals on attracting wealth, the first thing I wish to do is bust a few myths about money, if for no other reason than to make people feel better about money, feel better about having money, and feel better about their relationship with money regardless of how dysfunctional that relationship may seem.

The first myth about money is an outright lie; the popular, erroneous, over the hill quote that says *Money is the root of all evil.* First of all, the quote is actually from a misinterpreted scripture, yet ironically, religions still want your money – but that's another issue altogether. At any rate, the actual scripture says that it is the *love* of money that is the root of all evil; not money itself. The second myth is about the love of money. It's not the *love* of money but rather the *attachment* to money that is *a* root of evil. I came to this conclusion when I realized that *love* is inherently good and therefore cannot in any way be evil.

When a person uses money in any manner which is unharmonious, it is always out of attachment to an idea, and as such, is not an act of love. Attachment flows against universal law and therefore is not an act of love if for no other reason than attachment limits change, and change is to life as what oxygen is to the lungs. As for Matt 19:24 *"It is easier for a camel to go through the eye of a needle than for a man to enter into the kingdom of God"*, note: It is not implied that a rich man *"cannot"* enter the kingdom.

Money is about *exchange* and consequently about *change.* In actuality, money is merely a manifestation of energy and is nothing more than a bartering tool, therefore it's as preposterous to consider money as the root of all evil as it would be preposterous to sentence to death a baseball bat which was used to bludgeon someone to death. If a bat was used to kill a person, we wouldn't accuse the bat; we would accuse the person who *wielded* the bat. Conversely, when a ball player hits a home run, we cheer the player, we don't cheer the bat. The bat is a bat just as money is money. They are both merely tools. How we wield them has very little to do with the tools and everything to do with intention, action, and perspective.

Consider for a moment what would happen if we eliminated baseball because a bat was used in an evil manner. Imagine a world without baseball practice, little-league and even the World Series. It would negatively affect the economy, not to mention make for a planet full of unhappy little boys, husbands, buddies, dads, sons, nephews, grandsons, great grandsons, grandfathers, great grandfathers, boyfriends, uncles, brothers...and that's just the men (who account for just barely half of the population). I won't even get onto the subject of what would happen if crayons, Hot-Wheels, Lego, make-up, clothes, automobiles, hockey, the Internet, the Bible, or anything else that brings us joy and stimulates the economy, were to be considered the *root of all evil* because someone used them in an evil way.

If after considering this perspective you still think that money is the root of all evil, perhaps you can explain it to the single mom who can feed her children today because people donated to a charitable organization. Explain it to a quadruple amputee who can run, ski, bike, dance, hold his child, and then brush his own teeth at the end of the day because someone gave money to War-Amps. Explain it to the retired veterans who have a roof to sleep under in July because someone gave money for a poppy in November. Explain this to the millions of working people whose income depends on people *buying something*. Beyond this, explain it to yourself the next time you receive a bill in the mail, or maybe a cheque.

In the grand scheme of all things, money isn't everything, but then again, in the grand scheme of all things, neither is oxygen. Actually, in the grand scheme of all things, universally speaking, oxygen is pretty insignificant, but where it applies to humans, it comes in handy! What's interesting is that I have yet to meet a person who is wealthy say, *money isn't everything*. In fact, I do believe that the only people who I've ever heard say those words to me were either people who tried to hide their attachment to money, or were jealous of others with money, or were people who just plain gave up. Sure, in the grand scheme of all things, money isn't everything, but in the grand scheme of all things, money isn't *nothing*, and money can and does work towards good and towards joy.

Where money applies to religion, in spite of many religious views, joy is a virtuous state. Joy is something we're all meant to aspire to, and most people would agree that lack of money almost always implies lack of joy on some level. Lack of money implies limitation, and limitation is not what life is about. When we lose a job, it's generally not the job-loss that troubles us but rather the money-loss and the consequential ramifications of which it implies. All religious traditions suggest that life is meant to be prosperous. In most religions, abundance is a reward for loving God and for living a good, clean, honest and disciplined life. It is a reward we are to aspire to. Even the most extreme religious radicals, terrorists for example, do what they do out of the promise of a reward of abundance.

Religious or not, there is no glory in being poor. The world is not better off if you're poor, and no one is admired for being poor. Some deny this theory, suggesting for example that Mother Teresa was poor, but Mother Teresa was not poor; she *chose* to go without. In fact, Mother Teresa was worth as much money in her time as most millionaires will ever be in theirs, if for no other reason than for the generosity she encouraged worldwide during her lifetime. In fact, millionaires who give of their wealth are often inspired by the likes of individuals such as Mother Teresa. Her PR/media value was of such unprecedented worth in itself that it would be interesting to see how well advertisers in Time Magazine did when she graced its cover. I also wonder about the influx of church attendance, memberships and tithing revenue during that same era.

Choosing to *go without* is not poverty. Being poor, however, has always been a burden on society. A burden in the realm of welfare, of unemployment insurance, and especially of the healthcare system in light of the fact that poor people cannot afford nourishing food and are generally highly stressed which wreaks havoc on the body's ability to heal itself. They also cannot participate in paying taxes or in anything else which helps the local or national, and thus global economy. The lack of academic education is generally much higher among the poor as well, which also contributes to the continuance of poverty. Regardless of why poverty still exists – whether it's through laziness or the by virtue of the lack of community exhibited by most all humans; rich or poor – the fact remains that poverty is a burden on society and on humanity, and especially on the planet.

When it comes to desiring joy, there is no shame in wanting to be happy. No one wants to be miserable or depressed or poor and unable to provide for themselves. When we're depressed, we want to be happy. When we're happy, we don't want to be depressed, we want to stay happy. The same goes for finances. We want this because financial stability is part of a divinely favorable state. Even a wealthy *sick* person will tell you that it's better to be wealthy than poor. For example, if a poor person is home sick with the flu, they might not be able to afford medication and food. And if they can afford medical care, chances are they have to go to the doctor rather than have the doctor come to them. Conversely, if a wealthy person is home in bed with the flu, he can afford medication and food, and he can afford to pay for a good doctor who will make a house-call. The difference in stress levels between these two experiences as a result of finances alone could mean the difference between a speedy recovery and being sick for many more days, and in some cases, even death.

Everything we experience in life, including the process of death, is part of our life experience. Having financial wealth is conducive to a greater life experience no matter how you slice it. For example, the advantages to being wealthy are: You have access to more resources, the pricier items you consume are generally better made and create better paying jobs for others, they help the economy, and when you're done with them, they're less likely to find their way to landfills. By being wealthy you can afford healthier foods, better supplements and better quality of everything. You also contribute more to your government at tax time than you would if you were poor. Furthermore, the best way to teach is by example, and what better way to encourage others to create wealth for themselves than by showing others that it's possible?

For the record, I am not necessarily referring to wealth in terms of dollars, but rather to whatever harmonious wealth means to each of us personally. For some it does mean millions of dollars; for others, it means having a good job that provides the essentials. Attracting wealth is like attracting everything else in life. You've got to be clear about your desires and your intentions. This is where things might again start sounding familiar to those of you who are familiar with the concept of the law of attraction. That said, here are observations I've made about people in general and the mixed messages they send out to the universe with their actions:

If you're going to consciously attract money into your life, you've got to commit to it. I've seen many people go at it whole-heartedly for a few weeks and then they fizzle out because they don't see results, but if they knew why the results weren't happening, they'd stay the course. For most people, negative thoughts have been part of their everyday lives for many years, so it's important to take this process not *day by day*, but rather, *moment by moment*. I use the term *moment by moment* because life is just that; a series of moments. Not minutes or seconds, not days or weeks, but truly moments. Moments are not measured by time as much as they are measured by experiences, and you can no more measure a moment than you can measure faith or catch a shadow. So, most of us go through our lives with incorrect belief systems and programing, and then we read about the law of attraction and we expect that we'll get it all in one day, and that's where the problem lies.

Being affirmative every moment of the day takes practice. Yes, some days you'll attract money, and other days you'll be tempted to throw in the towel, but the key is perseverance. Each thought, each feeling, each word and each action must be accounted for. It may sound tedious, but humans are designed for this kind of programming. The fact that we're unconscious of our thoughts implies just that; *unconsciousness*. It does not imply that we *cannot* become aware of our thoughts every moment of the day; it merely implies we're *choosing* to be unaware.

As previously mentioned, it's been suggested by researchers that it would be impossible to gauge all of our thoughts, but in fact, if we were in touch with ourselves and completely conscious, we would control our thoughts instead of having our thoughts control us. To imply that we cannot control our thoughts is like saying we cannot control our words. Although we don't usually remember exactly what we've said all day long, much less five minutes ago, the fact remains, we are absolutely capable of controlling everything we say. The same goes for what we think and feel. If we truly got in touch with ourselves and took control of our thoughts in the manner of which we are predisposed, our thoughts would not be so scattered and on constant auto-pilot. It's really all about practice and mastery of the self.

This concept may seem implausible to many, especially to those who've been taught that the mind is limited, but just because you were taught that the mind is limited doesn't make it so. Yes, we use a limited amount of our mind, but to imply what percentage we use of the mind in its entirety; conscious *and* subconscious, is to imply there is a limitation to the mind in its entirety. What I do know is that the mind is *omnipotent*, and as the alleged five or ten percent of the mind we are said to be using may have to do with measuring the *conscious* mind, I would never be so arrogant as to suggest to what percentage we're using, or not using, our mind in its entirety. To anybody who does provide such an absurd notion as a limitation of the mind, I would just like to inform them that Earth is not flat!

A huge barrier we set up for ourselves in achieving our financial goals through *law of attraction* endeavors is our lack of patience. Whatever we desire will come to us, if we let it. The timeline is different for each of us, and it arrives not only when we completely surrender and allow it, but it manifests in harmony with other laws, with timing, and with what greater Divine Purpose God has in store for us. Oh, yeah, and it helps to get off our butt and work for it, too! Also, what most people don't realize when attempting to manifest something into their lives is that they've been psychologically walking a certain direction all their lives; a direction that may have been keeping them from their goal. When they finally do change their direction, universal law acknowledges that shift, and it shifts accordingly. It is during that shift that most people give up. For example, according to the law of gravity, when something goes up, it must slow down and stop before it can come back down. It is that *slow* and *stop* period that I refer to as a *shift*. This is otherwise known as the gestation period. It's during this crucial period where people lose faith and give up. When people give up and return to an old direction, the progress is reversed to the previous direction of failure.

To some people, introducing *quantum physics* into their finances may seem downright silly, but in actuality, what has anyone got to lose by attempting it? Most individuals have already done the worry/anxiety method, and to be perfectly honest, how far has it gotten them? The thing is, one must truly commit to this process in order to get the results. Incidentally, for those who are religious and are concerned about this practice possibly being blasphemous to their current faith, I'll say it again; this process is accepted by virtually all religions and is absolutely supported by the Bible.

When dealing with the power of intention, it's important to realize that making adjustments to thought, important as it may be, is not enough. Dwelling uniquely within and upon the *affirmative* is imperative. One cannot be in a state of mind to create wealth when thinking upon a level of poverty. Thoughts must be completely and wholly affirmative. This means thoughts shouldn't be on bills or debts but rather on abundant success, money, cheques, bank drafts and other monetary implements. Furthermore, all thoughts should be supported by visualizing financial wealth in every aspect of your *ideal* life; the car you'll drive, the house you'll live in, the place you'll work, the places you'll travel to, what you plan to do to attract that money, and the people you plan to share it with, because as your life changes, so will the people who surround you.

It's important to recognize that wealth arrives in many forms. Sometimes we want the money to purchase something, but instead of receiving the money, we may receive the thing we desire as a gift. Other times we don't have quite enough money to get what we're saving for, and miraculously, the item goes on sale. This also applies to things beyond merchandise. For example, when I was a child, I wanted to go to Arizona. It was a dream of mine which I always kept in my heart right into adulthood.

Amazingly, when I was an adult and unsure about how I could swing the finances of spending time in Arizona and maintaining a home in Canada, I was offered an on-going contract which lasted about eight years, permitting me to spend as much time there as I wanted and included airfare, a car and a terrific condominium in a gated community with a gym, a hot tub, and two pools (one heated and one cool). The best part is, I was paid to go there! Yes, I worked hard, but I always work hard anyway, and the organization which hired me wouldn't have kept me working with them if I hadn't. They were people of integrity and they associated with such, and to work *with* them required that I worked *like* them, and so I did. The extras that came with my experience and hard work; things like friends, professional connections, and an education in business that money cannot buy, were all bonuses for the extra effort I put into my work; extra effort that was rarely noticed because much of my work was done on my own and nobody saw those efforts.

In the process of changing thoughts and feelings, it's important to support your endeavors with immaculate speech. Yes, there are plenty of people with lots of money who use foul language, but those are not happy people, and no matter how much money you have, if you're not happy, then you're not wealthy or successful, so what's the point? Remember the character Rose in the hit-movie Titanic, and how unhappy she was with the pointless parties, endless gossip and the rich fiancé who had no compassion or morals? Aside from the money, where was the wealth in that situation? When it comes to foul language; if you swear, it's important to change your language. The same applies to gossip. *Gossip is poison!* Be done with gossip, even at the risk of being ousted from the "club". Learn to say what you mean and mean what you say. There is no better way to show yourself and the world where your mind is and what you're thinking than by the words you use to express yourself.

Many people claim to aspire to wealth, but their actions clearly tell another story. For example, some say they really want money, but what they clearly want is the lifestyle that money can buy. It's important to be clear on these things because if you want to have money to buy a luxury car for example, you might receive that car, but receive nothing with which to maintain, insure and fuel that car. If you see yourself living in a big house with servants, be clear that you own that house, or you might end up living in a mansion as one of those servants. That's alright if that is what you want, but if your idea is to be waited on in a large mansion, be as specific as possible, because the universe is as literal as a five year old, and just as determined to play.

Over time I've asked many people with money problems a powerful question: *If you want money, why is it that when you get it, you're so quick to trade it in for something else?* The response is usually something along the line of, *"There's not enough money for..."* In actuality, the reason we have little or no money has nothing to do with the lack of money and more to do with our lack of discipline, commitment and creativity, coupled with our unwillingness to work for what we desire, and very little, if any, faith. The results of an unfortunate financial standing have nothing to do with money and all to do with the absence of honesty, integrity and discipline and the presence of fear, blame, laziness, addiction, ego, and our need for approval, to name just some basic detrimental factors. Whatever their motive, financially strapped people tend to spend everything they get, thereby consistently nickeling and diming themselves into debt, yet they don't have the patience to nickel and dime themselves into wealth – a process by which many people do get rich – they literally watch and build upon every single penny. If you really want money, hang on to it when you get it. That will make your intention VERY clear to everybody, especially and most importantly, to yourself!

What's interesting about our desire to attract money is, we so much want something we know so little about, so the question remains: *How exactly can we attract something we know so little about?* Over the years most people have taken time to study their debts, invoices and bills, but not study money. Most people know their credit limit, their credit card company's logo and so forth, but very few people have actually taken the time to acquaint themselves with the one thing they allegedly so much desire.

For an interesting *attraction* exercise, think about your country's currency. Now, think about the highest denomination; a one hundred or a one thousand dollar note or otherwise, according to your country. Now ask yourself whose picture is on that note? Whose signatures are on the note? How many signatures are there, and what are or were the positions of the people who signed that note? How many digits make up the serial number? What year was it printed, and who designed it? My point with this exercise is, if you can't imagine a one thousand dollar bill in its entirety, how exactly can you attract it? Furthermore, have you actually taken the time to imagine what your wealth in its entirety looks like? If you are adamant about attracting money, it's a good time to start considering the details. Most people don't know what a million dollars looks like, what they'd do with it, how they'd handle the details, or how long a million dollars would last. In the very same manner, most people haven't given this same consideration to one hundred dollars.

Along with thoughts, feelings, words and actions, there's a powerful attraction tool called affirmations. Affirmations, as described in detail in a previous chapter, are affirmative words that are stated repeatedly in the present tense which suggest the way things are in your ideal world. For example, *I am wealthy, I am healthy, all is well.* Affirmations are a great tool, and they work, especially when it comes to changing the damaging thought patterns which can wreak havoc on one's life. Then there's the affirmative prayer; a combination of prayer, meditation and affirmations. It's a super powerful tool that's only made more powerful by following up with actions which support your declarations. These other actions go beyond thoughts, words and feelings. They are the actual changes we make in our day to day routines. Things like changing our vocabulary, being kinder to others and making changes to the customs, habits and actions we consistently carry out and which work against our goals. Things like impulse shopping, complaining, gossiping, smoking, laziness and dishonesty in any form, to name only some.

As for smoking, whenever I meet anybody with financial woes who also smokes, my compassion for their financial dilemma has little to do with their finances and everything to do with the self-imposed plague that is their stupidity. You may think my perspective is harsh, especially if you are a smoker, but before you jump to that conclusion, I invite you to consider the following:

A household which smokes two packs of cigarettes per day at ten dollars per package spends as follows:

$20.00 daily

$140.00 weekly *(assuming not more on weekends)*

$7300.00 yearly *(assuming not more on holidays)*

$36,900 over a five year period *(assuming you haven't died from a nicotine related illness)*

When you include additional costs incurred through extra heating in winter and air conditioning in summer each time someone goes in and out of the house for a smoke, coupled with the cost of matches, lighters, lighter-fluid, burnt cloths and furniture, dry cleaning, and medication when your common cold turn into bronchitis, pneumonia, emphysema and cancer because of smoking, you get to a grand total of at least forty thousand dollars over a five year period.

To put these numbers into perspective, over a five year period, you can use that money to buy a forty thousand dollar car, which by today's standards easily buys a brand new Lincoln or Cadillac, or even the introductory level models of BMW, Mercedes and Jaguar, or for those of you with simpler tastes, a small fleet of Toyotas. An even more interesting perspective is, over a twenty-five year period, you could actually purchase a house priced at $200,000.00, or a $100,000.00 house, and a Cadillac, and a small fleet of Toyotas. That's just the financial aspects of smoking. The real senselessness is in continuing to smoke when it's overwhelmingly clear what cigarettes do to the body, but since this chapter is about money, I'll move on.

We all know that not all smokers are in debt, and all people who are in debt are not necessarily smokers, which brings me to a huge culprit in our financial issues, which is the *would-be* monster that is Credit and Credit Cards. I say *would-be* monster because actually, the monster is our own lack of accountability, responsibility and discipline.

With everything from health to finances, we are a society which needs somebody to blame. In this process, many people blame the credit card companies for keeping them in debt with ludicrous interest rates of 18% and 29% and so forth. However, if you ask anybody, while remembering when they first applied for those cards, if they can recall having a gun held to their head, of course the answer will always be, *no*. The bottom line is, we are the ones who are responsible for our finances. Credit card companies are free to charge what they charge. We're free to deal with them, and we're free to *not* deal with them. This is just one of the numerous advantages of living in a free society. We have no problem accepting the terms at signing, but when it comes to being responsible and accountable, we place the blame squarely on the credit card company, when instead, we should be examining our spending habits.

In actuality, shopping is a necessity, and it is something that has been since long ago a part of humanity, and I suspect always will be. The problem is, we've turned a basic necessity into a sickness, and it's getting the better of us. The problem with the pleasure of shopping is that like with any kind of pleasure, it doesn't last, because pleasure is fleeting. Sure there are a lot of self-help gurus telling us to do what brings us pleasure, but the key is not to pursue what brings us pleasure, but rather, pursue what brings us joy.

The difference between pleasure and joy is, pleasure is fleeting, whereas joy is a state of being. Pleasure is what a person might get from eating a greasy hamburger every day, but that pleasure doesn't last, and it usually leads to other problems like weight gain, health issues and other reasons to be insecure. Joy, on the other hand, is what a person might feel after they've passed that hamburger stand for the 30th time in a month and can now fit into a favorite outfit, or never again need insulin, or can play baseball with their child. Joy is something that stays with us. Joy is always worth pursuing. Pleasure is something we deliver to our weaknesses. Joy is something we deliver to the God within us.

A big part of attracting wealth is starting anew. We must take manageable, moment by moment steps, starting by acknowledging where our life is; the good and the bad, and making sure to *acknowledge* and not *dwell*. We must acknowledge negative habits and actions that were used to create this current reality, and in the process, remember to be honest and forgiving. This is very empowering for someone taking on a new path in their life. We must acknowledge what we *can* and *will* commit to doing to create a better life, and stick with the plan and be patient.

It's also important to develop new habits. For example, we must learn to free ourselves from self-imposed ideas regardless of whoever fed them to us. This includes ideals about religious limitations and any negative thing we've ever heard about ourselves. We should pursue the job we want and do what we love. Working at our ideal job is not the only key to happiness; most of us know at least one person who's good at what they do and may be making much money from it, but they're miserable with everything else. That said, where money is concerned, doing what we love makes the good times great and the lean times bearable.

We've got to commit to being immaculate with our vocabulary. Again; say what we mean and mean what we say. If we stumble and utter words contrary to our intentions, we must correct ourselves. Also, it's important to be ambitious in our endeavors. Ambition is what separates the successful from the unsuccessful. Celine Dion, Barak Obama, Oprah Winfrey; these people – whether or not they were talented – were ambitious enough to make it; something that others – whether or not they are talented – were or are not. We've got to want the prize profoundly enough, otherwise the prize goes to somebody else, regardless of talent.

Another seemingly silly action is to take a *loving approach* towards money, like raising a child or growing a garden or building a hot-rod. Also, take a *holistic approach*. This means incorporating a little of (or lot of) *everything*. Be positive, believe in your goal, be patient, work well, visualize, pray, save, take action, believe you're worthy, stay the course, eat well, and especially take care of your health. It's not in just one thing you do; it's in *everything* you do.

When it comes to manifesting things with prayer and affirmations, it's important to release and let God do His job, but in the process, we've also got to do our part. Many people confuse patience with passiveness, and this is often the deal-breaker. Patience is action, whereas passiveness is laziness. While we're being patient for God to do His thing, we need to keep moving because we never know *when* or *how* God will provide, and usually things happen while we're busy with something other than sitting around waiting for opportunity to knock.

I realize it sounds somewhat redundant to mention this but I cannot stress enough the importance of breaking bad habits and eliminating addictions. Smoking, drinking, gambling, unnecessary spending and shopping...it's all gotta stop! This all costs money. In the process, while shopping for necessary items, it helps to go as far as clipping coupons and looking for deals, but it's a waste of time if we're just going to throw the money away elsewhere. Saving money is the best way to make money, so when you have to shop, shop close to home. You'll save money on gas and you'll keep your money in your community. Another thing I strongly suggest, especially for those who like to run around to many places to save a buck is, don't spend twenty dollars on gas to save twenty cents on soup! Instead, spend the extra pennies at one store and save the gas money, spare the car unnecessary wear and tear maintenance costs, and get some exercise while doing your part to protect the environment.

An important note to consider when looking for deals and pinching pennies is to pay close attention to your intentions. If you're saving because you feel like you can't afford things, you're dwelling in feelings of poverty, so feel good about your *financial project*. When you shop, keep value in mind, remembering that if you settle for less, you'll usually get less than what you settle for. This idea may sound confusing, but to keep it simple, just remember to stay affirmative every step of the way.

As you move forth to change things for the better, it's crucial that you *decide* to feel good about your circumstances. *Decide* to see the good side of everything, and always feel gratitude for that good. *Decide* to be done with dwelling on the negative aspects of your life, and focus on the affirmative. *Decide* what to change and make a commitment to that change. Be honest with yourself, take responsibility, be accountable, and be disciplined.

Review all of your relationships. Focus on the positive ones and do away with the negative ones, keeping in mind the golden rule in relationships: *You become what you hang around*. Hang around down and out folks, and they'll take you there. Hang around supportive people who encourage and believe in you, and you'll be better equipped to reach your goals. Make no mistake; we are all a product of our environment. When looking to make a change for the better, develop new friendships, find people smarter and more successful than yourself, and learn from them. If you're a complainer, stop complaining, or at least complain to someone who can do something about your complaint.

Join a success team or mastermind group, or get an achievement partner and commit to encouraging each other. If you're a jealous person, learn to be happy for what others have and be thankful for seeing it's possible to achieve goals. As things change, place yourself in the position to get the things you really want, regardless of whether it's a house, a car, a partner, better health or all of the above. Get out there, browse, window-shop, visualize, tell God you're ready, feel *as if*, act *as if*, believe, work, etc.

To get something *from* the world, give the very best of yourself *to* the world. Giving the best of yourself means giving your employer the best, most proficient, most honest day's work you can give. This means offering value to the company for what you are paid. It means working smarter and better. It also means putting an end to personal emails, personal telephone calls and especially personal texting during work hours. And contrary to the popular belief that we should promise less and deliver more; we need to *promise more* and *deliver beyond* those promises. If after all this, for some reason your workplace doesn't recognize you, God will, and your promotion will be forthcoming (keep in mind my Arizona experience), whether within your present company or within another company.

Lastly, if you're looking to acquire merchandise such as what your company produces or distributes, then buy the company's products. If you work for Chrysler, then buy Chrysler! If you work for a store, shop there. Nothing tells God that you appreciate what supports you better than when *you* support what supports you. This action also indicates the extent to which you approve of what you are doing with your life. Incidentally, if you work for a company which provides products you don't require; flight simulators or fire trucks or train engines for example, you can support them by working meticulously and conscientiously.

So what's the point of working for wealth if we can't take it with us? Well, here's some food for thought: We do take it with us! Wealth is a mindset; an affirmative state of consciousness. Human life is about experiences, and experiences create energies which become part of us. When we're successful *(whatever success means to you)*, when there are no limitations, our consciousness is dwelling in an affirmative state. No, we don't take money with us when we leave, nor would we want to; once we see the other side of this spectrum, we'd never want to limit it with material energy. All the ease and joy that comes with affirmative wealth is a mindset, and our mindset dictates where we've been and where we're going. The higher our conscious frequency, the deeper within God we will go after this experience. Consciously choosing to go without is not poverty, and, *choosing* to go without can be as liberating as winning the lottery, but, lack and limitation out of poverty leads to misery and a state of mind that does not lead to a heavenly place.

When it all comes down to the essentials, we must not be fooled for a second with the idea that we'd be a better person if we were richer or poorer than we are right now. In actuality, we'd be exactly who we are today regardless of our money, and we'd be learning the same lessons. Yes, money does make people do bad things, but the same is true for the lack of money; that's why when times are tough crime goes up. Ultimately, whatever road you choose to take on your journey towards your idea of financial success, one thing is certain; your current life, where you are right now, is the result of all your past thoughts, words, feelings and actions. What you did in the past created today's circumstances just as what you do today will create tomorrow's circumstances. Furthermore, as hokey as it may sound, what goes around truly does come around, so give the best of yourself to the world, and the world will give the best to you, monetarily and otherwise. This is a promise...This is the law!

CHAPTER IX

=Religion=

A beautiful concept, an ugly subject...

Before proceeding further, I wish yet again to reiterate that I have come to recognize that every religion is, in one way or another, *connected* to Truth. I also believe that if we were to approach religion *affirmatively*, we'd get far more from its many gifts, especially where it applies to living for God and loving our fellow man. Sadly, because of the manner in which people wield religion – which is meant to be a gift to humanity – religion has become a weapon *against* humanity. For humanity to evolve to its ultimate Divine potential, our perspective of religion, and how it is wielded by those who practice it, must change.

Perhaps the most significant discovery I've made about religion – about why religion is *seemingly* ineffective and *seems* to have exhausted its usefulness, and why religion as it's wielded today can't possibly lead us towards progress – is because religion itself doesn't progress. Religion itself doesn't subscribe to the law of *perpetual transmutation*. An all-encompassing, all-inclusive, omnipotent universal law applicable to all that exists. Our understanding of everything has changed over countless centuries; science, medicine, arts, academics and so forth, yet religion remains the same. Any religious process that claims imperviousness to change is purely arrogant and is simply a dead-end road to nowhere.

Perpetual transmutation means constant change; continual transformation. This law applies to everything that exists, including the concept of perfection and of God. By virtue of the very fact that religion does not change, religion is thus by definition not a process, and in fact, religion cannot even exist. At best, in its current capacity, religion can only do what it is currently doing; *it's dying,* and because humanity is so attached to its ideals, religion is taking the greatness of humanity with it.

There is only one way to save religion and the inherent greatness within, and that's to breathe life back into it by making it subscribe to change. The law of perpetual transmutation works in harmony with everything because it is part of everything; all animals, minerals, elements, space, processes and all consciousness. All is touched by change, and nothing is impervious. This law works in absolute harmony with the laws of attraction, cause and effect, and with all other laws. In this discovery lies the fundamental reality that religion must change, otherwise, any endeavor to affirmatively advance humanity under religious guidance is a fruitless endeavor.

It goes without saying that as a person who is on a constant search for Truth, I have been around many religious people and many different religions, and I've endured what I'd consider to be beyond my fair share of bible-thumping religious *addicts* who have tried to show me *"the way"* (or at least, *their* way). Although I've had countless fascinating discussions with these *addicts,* as well as with people who are less addicted to their beliefs, I admit that I've observed much of the same characteristics coming from all of them. What's fascinating about most religious people is that no matter how different a religion is, its followers seem to speak the same language. They all believe that their religion is the one true religion, and that they are the *chosen* people, and that only they will be saved, and they're willing to defend it to extremes beyond reason. Yet observe how they're living their lives personally, whether in regards to their tithing or their divorce or their judgments about how their fellow man is living, and that's when they usually drop the *"I'm not a fanatic"* bomb. Perhaps my own perspective is myopic when it comes to religious convictions, but, if you're founding your entire existence on a belief of any kind, shouldn't you be a fanatic? This is where the confusion about religious fanatics comes into play. Humanity is not being held back by religion or even religious fanatics, it is being held back by radical religious *addicts*.

Now, I know there are many people who really do live according to their gospel, and I'm not disputing that, but I do wonder about the man who lives *"by the book"* and about the consciousness which motivates him. I wonder who fed him his first helping of *spiritual nourishment*, and if he actually thinks for himself. And if he does think for himself, how can he possibly live *by the book?* Throughout my travels and studies, I've met countless addicts who preach the alleged *"Word of God"*, but I have yet to meet anyone who has ever plucked out their own eye or cut off their own hand because said organ or limb offended them. If we're supposed to take the Bible so literally, and if your eye does offend you, how does one go about plucking out the eye, thereby mutilating the body, while at the same time respect the body temple? I've also observed that addicts will jump to a religion that suits their life rather than live their life to suit their religion, which somehow seems too convenient, especially when it comes to the oppression of others and of life in general. Then there are those who claim they're ready to give their life; to actually die for God, but can't find it in their heart to forgive their neighbor or resist gossip or file an accurate tax return. In my estimation, before being willing to die for God, we should be willing to first *live* for God, or just drop the charade altogether.

I've met many people who claim to be living *by the book,* whether it's the Bible or another religious book, and there has yet to be a time when discussing their "truth" that they didn't use the phrase "Because the Bible (or their religious book) says..." One thing I'd like to clarify is that this book you are reading wasn't written to dispute the Bible or other religious books, or to discourage religious beliefs, but it will challenge perspectives, and as previously mentioned, it was written to encourage people to *think*. That said, here are some of my thoughts on the Bible:

Imagine for a moment you've been medically diagnosed with an ailment; something curable like a minor bacterial infection on your big toe, and you go to a doctor to treat the infection. When you arrive at the doctor's office, you observe instruments reminiscent of saws and pliers and a surplus of books including medical journals and encyclopedias dating back to two hundred years ago, and then you discover that all of the doctor's medical knowledge is based solely upon those books. Then, upon seeing your infected toe, the doctor says that the toe must come off, but to be really sure to get all of the infection, he'll need to amputate your entire leg from the knee down. What would you do?

I'll tell you what you'd do; you'd run for the hills! You'd run because it's a no-brainer. You'd run because even with your personal lack of medical expertise, you know there's a simple antibiotic that can be administered to heal the infection. You'd run because even without possessing extensive medical knowledge, you know that medical books from two hundred years ago – as advanced and informative as they were for their day – are now considered archaic, erroneous and obsolete, and if a doctor today were to practice medicine based solely upon such outdated information, he'd probably kill more people than he'd save (at best), and he'd be considered a quack (at best), not to mention be imprisoned (at best). I present this analogy in order to make a point: If it's a preposterous idea for a doctor to found his knowledge, thus compromising life, based on information from a book that's two hundred years old, shouldn't it be considered preposterous for a society to found their knowledge, thus compromising life, based on writings that are two *thousand* (or more) years old? How about two thousand year old book that's had its Divine essence perversely translated and hacked to death in order to control, instill fear and make our Divine Creator into some kind of monster?

To place this question into both greater and simpler perspectives, imagine trying to program your new computer using a program from only five years ago. Now go back twenty years. Now go back thirty! Those old computer programs may have served their purpose in their day, but the level of that technology was in direct proportion to the level of knowledge possessed by its developers back then – a level of knowledge that by today's standards is considered painfully obsolete (at any time, our knowledge is rarely, if ever, in proportion to our intelligence; what we *do* conceive of is nothing compared to what we *can* conceive of). As miraculous as those programs were for their day, they were developed for computers which are now considered obsolete, and if you want to challenge me on this, just try to download anything from the Internet using a Commodore Vic-20, if you even know what a Vic-20 is!

I've often asked friends, family, acquaintances and spiritual leaders; all of whom have different belief systems, the same question about comparing a two hundred year old medical reference to the current standard editions of the Bible. The only people who seem to entirely disagree with my theory have been the religious addicts *(in my experience, people who don't generally think for themselves)* who usually respond with, *because the Bible says (insert archaic law here)*. Then they feed me facts based on the same hearsay as religion itself is based, and then they say they'll pray for my soul! I'm not questioning if the Bible is Truth, I'm merely suggesting that much of its content may be Truths which were applicable to a previous time, much like amputating a limb to save the body was at one time standard procedure for what we today consider basic curable infections.

Although much of the basic principles in the Bible provided guidance which was clearly instrumental to survival at the time, most of the laws and ideas in the Bible were about then, not about now, much like the ideals of today would have been ridiculed in the past, and will surely be ridiculed hundreds of years from now; if they're even a notion by then. Furthermore, I do believe that the many prophecies recorded in the Bible are actually true prophecies about the future, but about a future which has since already come and gone. I also have come to recognize that the warnings in the Bible about perverse changes in religion are speaking about the current oppressive and violent manner religion is being wielded, and are not applicable to spirituality and current new age consciousness thinking.

As for living according to the Bible as it's presented in our day, extensive research carried out by renowned theologians, anthropologists, philanthropists and scientists worldwide has revealed the absence of many books in the Bible and possess overwhelming evidence; *actual authentic proof* which supports their findings. However, even with these rock-solid findings, the addicts don't want to hear it. And why would any religious addict not want to hear they've been wrong all this time? For the same reason any substance addict wouldn't want to become sober. They'd have to face the truth, accept that they might be wrong, take responsibility for themselves, discover there's work to be done, stop blaming and judging others, and stop hiding from whatever it is they're hiding from.

As a result of religious impositions and archaic thinking, we're going about our lives walking a destructive path, and our fear of reaching beyond ourselves and what we know, or what others have convinced us they know, keeps us in our stagnancy. Parents beat their children as a result of what is understood to be written about discipline in the Bible. Two thousand years ago, humans had very little knowledge of childrearing, and even less knowledge about the permanent effects of childhood trauma brought on by archaic correctional practices such as corporal punishment. Centuries later, we have a surplus of psychologists, psychiatrists, pediatricians, therapists and other professionals all confirming the negative ramifications of corporal punishment, yet because we're not clever enough to figure out how to get through to our children without raising a hand to them, or we're too scared and lazy to think for ourselves, or we can't control our anger and use the Bible as a crutch, we continue to discipline our children based upon archaic concepts created at a time we deemed fit to nail a man to a cross for speaking consciousness, logic and love.

We're founding our existence, raising our children, running governments, creating laws, and compromising our very lives and the lives of others, and all of humanity and its great potential, all based on words written thousands of years ago. Words written by people under questionable circumstances and questionable conditions, with questionable perspectives in questionable states of minds during questionable times, translated by questionable individuals with questionable literary skills and a questionable understanding of a work written at a time when we just barely stopped walking like apes. With all of these questionable details, the problem is that we don't ask questions, and we don't think for ourselves, and these actions are the very first steps towards our demise no matter how you slice it.

When I ponder this, the questions that stand out in my mind concern the motives behind the Bible's compromised changes, translations and omissions. Who commanded such changes and translations? Who were these people, what kind of power did they possess, how did they attain that power, what were their motives and why? What were they trying to hide by commanding the omissions of passages and even entire books? The answers to these questions are not always clear, but each answer has one common thread. They all involve disempowering humanity, inciting fear, and keeping people from Truth.

I mentioned religious addicts earlier and how they don't think for themselves, and in this group I include *spiritual* addicts (yes, the ones who claim to be spiritual but not religious), because they do the exact same thing as the religious addicts. They take what's written, preach it as their own revelation, hide behind it, live it where it's convenient for them, change churches *(or spiritual centers)* when it gets too tough, turn single Truth components into their complete religion, all the while acquiring none of their knowledge by meditating on, praying about, or thinking for themselves, and committing to nothing in the process. I believe in essence these people mean well, and their reluctance to think for themselves is not necessarily out of laziness (although that accounts for a big chunk of the reason) but that they feel they have no right to search and think for themselves. This doubt in our right to ask questions and look beyond the written word has been fed to us as much by the current translations of the Bible as by those who have heeded the same advice out of nothing other than fear. Whether out of fear or out of laziness, humanity's reluctance to go *beyond* and *within* is unfortunate, because we could definitely use revelations that are applicable to our time.

As for religious revelations, why are Matthew's, John's or anyone else's words, revelations and stories more important than yours? Who decided that although every single thing in the world changes and evolves, that spirituality must remain the same? Who decided that no other ideals could be written, revered, praised or feared, thought of, prayed about or meditated upon, than those misconstrued, miscommunicated, uber-manipulated words of so long ago? The answer is, we all did, and we all do! We all do because those of us who believe there's something more are not searching deeply enough, or at all, and those who are searching and who are having the revelations and epiphanies and are finding the answers, or at the very least the questions we need to be asking, are not expressing them in some form or another, and when we don't share our wisdom, nothing changes and humanity stagnates.

The detrimental ramifications bestowed upon humanity as a result of limitations imposed on society by religion, or rather, by religious addicts, have not only slowed down the progress of society, but the progress of all of humanity, and ultimately, all that to which we are connected. These limitations set by extreme religious applications are designed to keep us from change, to keep us scared and to keep us under control, and to keep us from Truth. We learn this programming day after day, generation after generation, and we carry it in our hearts and minds; everything we say, think, feel and do, and it holds us down and holds us back, and it does nothing more, nothing less, than keep us from Truth. If you come away from reading this book with only one message, make it this one:

Anything which keeps us from discovering, knowing and advancing towards Truth, is an inherently evil thing!

Perhaps the most ludicrous reality in society today is how we continue to allow religion to control our governments. What astonishes me about this process is how governments protect the rights of the religious, but the religious have license to express their blatant disregard for humans, human rights and basic human expression. I am a spiritual man with great faith, however, I am also a logical man, and I can see that running government based on biased heretical ethics before running it based on what is best for *everybody*, is not the way to succeed at advancing humanity. Society, like humanity, is unlimited, and no other thing has held society and thus humanity back from its greatest potential more than has religious involvement in governmental affairs.

In an ideal world, here's how government would function: Everybody pays taxes, everybody works, everybody obeys the law, everybody respects everybody else's right to believe what they believe, and if you don't like the way someone looks, prays, believes, or dresses, just don't look at them, and if you don't believe in gay marriage, marry a straight person. If you become rich through working hard or you are poor from being a lazy slob, you are taxed at the same rate. Above all, religion should be protected but should have little, if any, business in governmental affairs.

I'm all for everybody having the right to practice their religion as long as their process causes absolutely no harm to anybody, and as long as it does not infringe upon basic human rights. By this, I mean, pray to whom you want to, but allow others the right to do the same, and the right not to. Unfortunately, religious rights are placed above all other basic human rights, and things are getting messy everywhere in the world, including North America. For example, it is illegal for a taxi-driver in Canada to refuse a ride to a person because of race, however, if the driver's religion dictates that he mustn't pick up a person based on racial background, gender or orientation, then this practice is legal. So, basically, as long as you're religious, you can discriminate because your religion turns your hate-crime into a basic human right! One has to wonder what this practice will mean the next time a murderer says *"God told me to do it"*. To some who read this, it might seem I'm exaggerating, but if we're protecting someone's right to be racist based on his faith, why shouldn't we protect another man's right to kill somebody based on his faith? Whether we refuse somebody a ride in a taxi based on their racial background or we take their life, we're compromising their life experience, and one act is as evil as the other.

The oppression of life based on religious convictions is the ultimate transgression to all of humanity. In actuality, religion is largely without grounds. There is barely any indisputable proof anywhere that anything in the Bible, or any other religious volume, ever took place in all of history. There are only stories, anecdotes and heaps of hearsay, but there is hardly any truly indisputable evidence; just books filled with more stories of violence, turmoil, tales, and well-meaning parables than anything else. As for possible proof, there is only scientific evidence of "some" events, origins, and sources. Even with our intelligent minds – our logical, rational, lucid, practical, sensible, and reasonable conscious and subconscious minds – we consistently extend to the religious the absurd, illogical, irrational, unreasonable, insane license to deny and prevent humans their right to their life experience and life expression – Life which is one hundred percent, absolutely and completely evident, logical, and grounded.

I realize that by stating religion's lack of grounds, I risk compromising my whole point on religion and the important role religion plays, or should be playing, within humanity, and I risk defeating the purpose of this chapter, which is actually to encourage unity between all religions. My point here is, we need to bring religion into the light. If we're going to wield religion, we need to exercise it in a manner which is conducive to the benefit of all humanity. No exceptions! As a citizen of many countries, one can face persecution for relaying antireligious remarks, yet religious addicts can impose their belief-based actions without facing persecution. This is simply unfair and unjust, but as unfair as it is, it's up to each and every one of us to take a stand and stop accepting that things be run as they are run today, keeping in mind that religion is about belief; not about fact, and that the government works for us.

To underscore this point, let's move from racism, sex, religion and otherwise and into the wonderful world of taxes! As I write this, Canada has a GST *(goods and services tax)*. In most of the provinces the GST and the PST *(provincial sales tax)* are calculated separately. In the province of Quebec, however, one tax is calculated after the other tax is added to the total. In other words, people in Quebec are paying tax on a tax they've paid. Although almost all those in Quebec realize this process is unethical and illegal, for some reason, everybody puts up with it. On one level, it seems like such a little thing, but on another level, this is how bigger things get started; absurd laws are introduced, everyone complains, then becomes complacent, and eventually they just live with it. While this is going on, the government makes millions of dollars from a fraction-of-a-cent discrepancy and the issue itself serves as an excellent distraction from the larger illegal acts in which governments participate. Ultimately, if the government is not honest, how can it truly expect honesty of its citizens? Conversely, if the citizens are not holding their government accountable, you have to wonder if they don't deserve exactly what they're getting, including what is imposed upon them by the involvement of religion in government. I use this example to bring home my point that this illegal and unethical tax system is in place because people have decided to live with it. It is this same manner in which we accept the illogical, illegal, immoral fashion in which religion continues to be permitted to control political decisions. In this thinker's humble opinion, it's time for citizens to get a backbone when it comes to government, especially when it comes to continuing to allow religion to decide how government is run.

Again, where religion hurts humanity the most is when it comes to oppressing basic human rights. Many countries around the world are finally changing to accommodate same-sex marriage, and although marriage is a basic human right, for centuries, governments worldwide have denied this right to same-gender couples based on religious grounds. What's absurd about this form of oppression is that it is done in the name of something that only allegedly exists; God and historic Bible tales, yet millions of gays worldwide are real, they exist, and their rights have been neglected and denied, and so has the benefit to humanity that is homosexuality *(I'll touch on this in a forthcoming chapter)*. These benefits are denied to humanity by religious and nonreligious alike, again, in the name of something that only allegedly exists.

Much of the way the planet is run is based on religious and biblical views, including women's place in the world; women as lesser, lower order of the human race, and in some cases considered lower than *anything*. If truth came down to perspective, if everything we think we know about Jesus is true, and if God really felt this way about women, wouldn't His only begotten son not have been gifted to humanity through a man rather than through a being of the lowest order? In this thinker's opinion, it would seem that, based on Jesus' birth, along with the birth of every single human being, God regards women in a slightly different manner than most of us did at the time of Christ, and in many cases, more than we still do today.

We all have theories based on how we think, but those theories are not necessarily Truths. For example, I have a theory that when it comes to human conception, it is not the sperm that fertilizes the egg, but rather, the other way around. The very nature of the egg is to nurture, nourish and protect. Fertilization implies nourishment, and nourishment is inherently a female trait. On their own, the sperm gets nowhere without the egg, and the egg gets nowhere without the sperm, but this does not imply that when it comes down to survival, one couldn't find a way to survive without the other. If there is one thing I've come to understand about life, it's that there is always a way to survive, and if there's a way, nature will find it, or it will create a way. When it comes to nature as it applies to humans, scientific technology is one of *nature's ways*.

Upon sharing with others the theory that the egg fertilizes the sperm, some women *(note: some)* not only strongly disagreed with this theory, but displayed disapproval of my even suggesting it as a possibility. Their disapproval stemmed from their idea that I was implying that men carry the life and women merely carry the nourishment, but this suggestion couldn't be farther from the truth. To the egg, the sperm means life; to the sperm, the egg means life. As a researcher/thinker, I must acknowledge that this theory is possibly erroneous, however, in this same capacity I must also admit that the theory *is* possible, and *is*

171

probable, and it deserves consideration. I must also insist that in order to make the kinds of breakthrough discoveries which lead us to Truth in the grand scheme of all things, we must take our ego and religious limitations out of the equation. Truth is Truth whether we want to believe it or not, whether it shocks us or not, or whether or not it momentarily makes us feel like we're beneath an opposing gender.

Acceptance of this theory doesn't imply that men are above women or otherwise. It merely reinforces the ideal that both genders are equally important to all human life. On the other hand, the ramifications implied by our mere understanding of the possibility of this concept have the potential to catapult us to an immensely broadened understanding of human survival and what we are capable of doing to ensure its continuance.

To place into perspective what we are capable of currently, technologically speaking, if we were to dwell uniquely within the realm of affirmative possibility, and utilize our Divine innate ingenuity; our *creativity*, and then group these actions with the most advanced means of our technological capabilities, it would be entirely feasible to develop a synthetic nourishment-filled egg for which to house and nourish an *organic* sperm cell. In this same manner, we could develop a synthetic sperm cell which could be housed and nourished within an *organic* egg. In doing so, not only could the sperm survive without an *organic* egg, but the *organic* egg could nourish a synthetic sperm cell. Of course, this would mean humans would cease to exist *organically*. My point is, regardless of religious convictions, one way or another, nature finds a way.

With certain animal species, nature breaks through gender barriers by changing the sex of the animals in order to accommodate reproduction in a single-sex environment. Humans might not change sex to accommodate reproduction in such a manner (although this might be where hermaphrodites naturally come into play) but our minds, through technology, may find a way. This is not out of immorality or unethical *mad science*, but out of our basic nature to find a way to survive at all costs. I bring this ideal to light to make a point not only about humanity's capabilities within the realm of affirmative possibility, but also to suggest how, in the grand scheme of all things, nature will find a way to survive, and it is our minds that will take us there. Limiting our minds because of what we *assume* the Bible says is not conducive to our growth or to our survival.

With all that said, there is always the looming question about whether or not we should do something just because we can. It's no secret that scientific research is vastly held back due to religious morals, and in all fairness, as much as religion tends to take things too far, science is guilty of the same in its own rite. However, when it comes down to comparing the stagnation of humanity based on the *limitation of religion* as opposed to the advancements of humanity through the *endeavor of science*, religion is clearly the ultimate *life-suppressant*. Science may be agonizing at times, but true science is honest, and honesty leads to Truth.

Moving on now to the psychology of the religious masses: Because I'm a firm believer of *you become what you hang around*, I've become more vigilant of the people I spend time with, especially large groups, and especially where it applies to their religious or spiritual consciousness. I genuinely enjoy attending church, if for no other reason than to keep up on the progress of where most traditional churches are going, or not going, but mostly I attend to worship amongst other believers. That said, I increasingly find that along with the smell of old wood and candle wax, most churches smell like guilt, and that stench is to human spirit what sulfuric acid is to, well, most anything precious.

Who we hang around is hugely linked to whether or not we'll succeed in life, and this applies as much to who we pray with as it does to who we live with, who we study with and who we argue with. Because the energy of each one person's vibrational frequencies fills an entire room, when two people are present, their energy is mixed. When you go into a room filled with others, you bring your energy, and in the process, you join their energy and *they join yours*. A space containing 100 people with a scared and guilty conscience is not usually a breeding ground for affirmative, creative thought, and as such, does not bring you closer to success or to God. Ideally, church should be a place where we come to worship God, not bring our fears, shame and alleged sins, and it certainly should not be a place where we feel obligated to attend. It should be a place we feel honored to attend and worship and rejoice, with affirmative thoughts, words and feelings. Yes, we should feel comfortable enough to wear jeans, and we should not be judged if we choose to do so, however, there is something to be said for what we bring to a sacred place when we look and feel our best while delivering gratitude to the source which gives us life.

Ultimately, religion, or rather how we view, approach and wield religion, desperately needs to be healed. This *healing* can take place immediately, without revising or overhauling a single word or document which supports religion. The key to approaching the True Word of God in any and all religion is to speak God's language. When we understand that God is *inherently affirmative*, then we understand that we as creators need only be *inherently affirmative* in order to communicate with God. If while living our religion we are concerned that the Bible may have been compromised over time, we need only seek out all those biblical ideals which are affirmative, and then proceed to affirmatively pray and meditate and speak and do and feel and think on those affirmative ideals. Furthermore, we can forget about the "wrath of God" and God being a "jealous god", because those ideals are human ideals and have nothing to do with love, and anything that has nothing to do with love has nothing to do with God

You won't often find a book of this nature in the hands of avid religious devotees, mostly because books of this nature usually attempt to dissuade people from religion. I recognized, however, that it was important to do the contrary; to remind people of faith to get back to church, get back to praying, get back to the Bible or other sacred volume, and in the process, dwell on the affirmative Truths, love thy neighbor, live for God, and keep searching, learning and questioning. In the process of affirmatively exercising religion, we must do away with believing our religion is the only religion, or that we are of the chosen people or that we are saints or that only we will inherit the Earth or that we speak for God. These ideals separate us all and create war between families and nations. They are also the very foundations and indisputable hallmarks of every terrorist organization worldwide. Dwelling upon boundaries about what everyone is *not* does not bring us closer to God. Affirming that God is in everything and everybody does.

* * *

Walking the Walk...Together.

As previously mentioned, the time has come for all those who practice ANY religion to work together to dissolve the barriers which separate us all. This is the only way the religious process can ever ignite the beacon of consciousness which people of faith allegedly seek to ignite. This key is vital to creating peace between all religions. Working together doesn't mean supporting beliefs of others. It means supporting and respecting people's right to believe what they believe, and extending to them the same courtesies we'd appreciate having extended to us.

The following applies to every religion, so whatever your faith, just apply God or Allah or Buddha or Krishna or Jehovah or Universe or Spirit or Perspective or whatever your "God" may be, and as you read, dwell only on the *inherent affirmative*, dissolving all forms of judgment, while not hurting, killing, sacrificing or oppressing any living creature, while at the same time placing yourself in the shoes of all those whom you observe, without denial of the life-expression of anybody, and take it from there.

The greatest observation about religion is that, when affirmatively wielded; *and only when affirmatively wielded,* religion is a *process,* just like love and like life. As with love and life, religion *must be lived*, and living it requires *action.* Without action, religion is just a theory. At best, religion without *inherent affirmative action (walking the walk)* is merely a roadblock of heretical doctrine obstructing the path to the betterment of the human condition. At worst, without *inherent affirmative action,* religion leads to what the world at large is today, or worse; for we have not yet arrived at tomorrow to meet the residual of yesterday and today.

The pure motive of religion ideally is to set humanity on a Divine path; a blueprint to help us get the absolute best out of life. The areas where religion goes wrong have little to do with religion itself and all to do with those who put the process into action with little or no integrity, and who approach it without complete commitment, discipline and understanding of the importance of applying *inherent affirmative action* to the process. And then there are those with hidden agendas and other *evil* intentions.

The problems surrounding religion happen largely when those who lead are not true followers themselves. On one level, this lack of complete devotion seems pretty harmless, but approaching a religious process in a half-baked manner is done to the detriment of not only the one who walks without true devotion, but also to the detriment of the goodness of religion itself. It's fine to say "I'm not a fanatic", but in actuality, if you're going to do it, shouldn't you really *do it?* Let's face it, if you are a Christian and you understand that Jesus was committed and disciplined, and yes, clearly a fanatic on your behalf, shouldn't you be a bit of a fanatic on his behalf? I'm not suggesting getting crucified and taking on the sins of the world, but it might be considerate to repay the favor by obliterating any form of judgment from this day forth, to name just one thing you could do on the behalf of Jesus. According to Christianity, Jesus died for humanity, and he did this by courageously submitting to crucifixion. The greatest courage a Christian can offer up in return is to simply live for God, love his fellow man and submit all judgment to Christ and walk with him.

What's interesting about committing oneself to one single task like just removing judgment, or just never lying again, or just changing one's vocabulary to accommodate inherently affirmative terminology is that, even without changing any other thing one does, it's impossible for a single positive change to not affirmatively affect every other aspect of one's life. Committing to changing everything at once is where we fail because there are so many facets to our personalities and convictions – we might be honest in our marriage but not with our job, or we might not swear among the church congregation but swear around *the guys*. Anyone who's ever tried to stop smoking, or tried to diet, or tried to break any habit will tell you how hard it is to overcome just one vice, so it stands to reason, if we lie *(which most of us do)* or we judge *(which most of us do)* or we're less than affirmative with our vocabulary *(which most of...well, you get the idea)*, and then we try to change everything else all at once, we're pretty much destined to fail because we're creatures of habit and we're constantly on auto-pilot. This is not to say that one cannot change everything all at once, but for most of us, our day-to-day lives leave us little time to pay attention to our every thought and action. Therefore, for two reasons it is advisable to just commit to changing just one thing at a time.

For one, committing to just one change is manageable no matter how busy and hectic our lives are, and two, that one change will take care of kick-starting other changes because *everything* is connected. If you stop lying, it makes you conscious of why you're lying and what you're scared of. If you stop swearing, it makes you conscious of what you're thinking and why you're thinking it, and to what your deep-rooted anger is linked. As it's impossible for one negative change to not affect other areas of your life, it's also impossible for one *affirmative* change to not spill into other areas of your life, and it's impossible for it to not propel and deepen your religious and spiritual convictions and faith when you commit to just one aspect of your faith. It also helps you recognize your motives for believing in what you believe.

With so many religions to connect with, and so much to say to each of them, my message is for all the *would-be* religious people, which make up an incredibly large portion of the planet's population, to either *walk the walk,* or please drop the charade and give the world a break already! The world needs its believers now more than ever, and by believers, I mean *true faithful believers.* The world needs their commitment, devotion and compassion, and it needs this now; not when it's *convenient* and not when it *feels right.* For those who are waiting for a more convenient time, I can assure you, *this* is it right now. There never will be a more convenient time. This is as good as it gets! As a matter of fact, I can guarantee you that from this day forth, it will only become more *inconvenient,* so now really is the best time to start.

This message goes well beyond the realm of religion and applies to all the things we *plan* to do to make the world a better place. Everything from conserving electricity, to forgiving our transgressors, to not crossing the street at a red light, to being polite when we're telling the telemarketer that we're not interested in what they're selling. It applies to everything and everybody we are connected to, moment to moment. Kindness, forgiveness, compassion and love go a long way when approaching everything we do in life, but nothing fans sparks of conviction into flames of truth better than when kindness and compassion are fueled by true devotion to one's faith.

As much as I don't personally subscribe to organized religion, I do recognize that religion is very powerful and good, but one must always bear in mind that *true religion* is constructive only when it's *conscientiously* and *affirmatively* employed, and it is only destructive when we misuse it. Religion is like an exercise program. Having a gym membership is not enough; you've gotta show up and do the work! Religion is not an exercise until it is *exercised*. It is not a process unless it is *processed*.

Affirmatively exercising religion means speaking *truths* in such a manner that doesn't make God look like a heartless bully who's just out to torment the planet. For the record, to those of you who preach of God in such a manner, I ask you: When was the last time you worshipped a bully? Yes, the Bible clearly makes mention of God's wrath and hatred, and that he's a jealous god, but those are words which were translated from language to language over countless centuries. In other languages, such as ancient Hebrew, Greek and Latin, words like *jealousy* and *wrath* and *hate* don't have the direct meaning as we understand them according to our society in current times. As such, current interpretations of the scriptures are saying the exact opposite of the original messages, and the results are making God look horrifying, and are tearing humanity apart, and are destroying our world.

I believe that this is why there is so much confusion with the word *pride*. On one hand we're told how pride is a bad thing, while on the other hand we're told to take pride in what we do whether it's with our work or raising our children or with other worthwhile endeavors. Contrary to what we've heard, pride is actually a good thing, whereas *arrogance* is the problem. The ideal that we should be *pleased; not proud*, is more of a play on words than anything, because being *pleased* is an egotistical endeavor, whereas pride is integrity in action. When we work with pride, we serve God. This is why no matter what language we may read the scriptures, reading is not enough. Merely reciting words and imposing their misinterpreted translations on others and ourselves is meaningless and in no way serves God or humanity. Scriptures require affirmative thought, prayer, meditation and loving, affirmative, compassionate action on our part to bring their Truth to life.

Where translation is concerned, it's no wonder we all think God is angry and vengeful and capable of hating, but this is where *studying* and *meditating* on the scriptures truly comes into play. We must recognize that the scriptures were translated from one language to another and back again; this over generations of different comprehensions of words and languages. At a time when there was no affirmative term to imply the opposite of love, it made sense to imply that *"God hates"* rather than say *"God other-than-loves"*. Actually, there is no affirmative way to say *God doesn't love*, because love is what God does, but for the sake of relaying the message in translation, saying *"God hates sin"*, inexact as it may be, is blunt and direct and implies that sin is not the path to a great life experience or to God.

So what's wrong with religion and why is everyone offended whenever the subject of religion arises? How is it possible that people are offended by the very mention of the word God? Just this very day before I sat down to write, I ended a nice conversation with a new acquaintance by saying *God bless you*, and the expression on her face looked like I had just told her to go jump off a bridge. Her reply was; *Oh, god, you're not religious, are you?* It's a pretty sad state when one of the nicest things you can wish somebody is considered offensive, but, people have come to associate God with religious addicts and their compromised convictions, judgments and actions. Now anything to do with them, including the word *God*, is a red flag.

Something I discovered during my search is, not only have I been correct in my deduction that there is much evil surrounding religion, but also, that this evil is fueled and fed by many who consider themselves *religious*. These allegedly righteous self-proclaimed wannabe *saints* are the culprits; not religion. In a nutshell, if religion was preached in a manner which was loving, compassionate, affirmative and truly without judgment, whether preached in a church to the masses, or preached in a gutter among an assembly of two souls, far more people would become religious. That said, too much of the *preaching* is based on the *fear* of God rather than the *love* of God; this largely having to do with misunderstandings related, again, to translation, and too many self-proclaimed prophets have ruined it for the rest of us. Sure, perhaps those self-proclaimed prophets of the past who misled us are now burning in hell, but while they're burning, we're still following their teachings because we continuously refuse to think for ourselves and embark upon our journey with an affirmative, loving God, and we're terrified to question the authority of those would-be prophets, and as a result, many of us are living in hell right here on Earth.

For those who approach the Bible in an inherently affirmative manner, it goes without saying that the Bible truly does provide all we need to know about living rightly, however, living rightly in our time requires that we examine other ideals and perspectives which both challenge and support the Bible, if for no other reason than to widen, deepen and ultimately strengthen our faith, vindicate our convictions and expand our consciousness.

In a book I read recently by a respected and justifiably reputable Christian pastor, a chapter explains how the Holy Scriptures will provide all the answers we could ever need about God and life and our reasons for being. Although I'm inclined to agree with the pastor's estimation, I am as concerned with the expression of *his* ideals in the same manner of which he is concerned with the views of others which he summarizes as a fresh and skeptically easy manner of finding truth, meaning and purpose without working for it with their airbrushing of the Word of God.

Although I completely agree that the Bible potentially holds everything we could ever want to or need to know about God *(I say potentially because to imply that the extent of my knowledge is in direct proportion to the vast depth of my faith would be arrogant, to say the least)*, the question remains; if the Bible possesses all the answers, are we to completely disregard what others have to say about God? On one hand, the pastor makes mention of the *airbrushed Word of God*, but isn't that exactly the point of *his* book as well? Isn't the point of all these books to say *"in other words..."*? Furthermore, are we to imply that only Christians have the right to attempt clarifying the Bible?

The pastor makes mention of the countless books that ride the best-seller list; books having to do with spiritual content yet allegedly containing no sustenance; books, for example, which discuss ideals surrounding the law of attraction, cause and effect, and general aspects of quantum physics. As I mentioned in a previous chapter, whereas on one hand books based on spiritual science are viewed by some religious folk as blasphemous, I maintain that the concept of the law of attraction as it applies to spirituality is fundamentally a technical explanation of the prayer process expressed in laymen's terms. Yes, some may read such scientific books and decide they hold all the answers to life's fulfillment, but for many people, including devout Christians, these spiritual-science books clarify the prayer process; *ask, see it as done and believe; as ye see it, so shall it be.* I realize some people come away from reading science books with inaccurate perspectives, but in fairness to these books and to the Bible; if people don't know how to utilize a book's tools, this doesn't make the book bad.

I admit that the pastor's book is one of the more inspirational pieces of literature about religious conviction I've ever read, however, the book is not without its contradictions. On one hand, the book denies religious science, yet it proceeds to marvel about the story of a holocaust survivor who, during his captivity, kept his mind focused on his absent wife's smile which went on to inspire him to survive his agonizing ordeal. On the other hand, this *mind conditioning* process the pastor is praising is exactly what religious science is all about, and it is a concept that's completely supported by the Bible. This *visualizing* concept is also supported by most religions beyond Christianity, and it is basically understood that this is an actual way to improve our lives, empower ourselves, expand our consciousness, and bring ourselves closer to God. In fact, *visualizing* and *faith* "IS" prayer!

I recall quite some time ago Oprah Winfrey being accused of being the *antichrist* because she was said to have denied Christ. What sparked this controversy was that Oprah said that there are many ways to God. What's interesting is that many people who had abandoned Christ long ago came back to their beliefs as a result of religious science books and because of people like Oprah. Whether a person comes to God through the Bible, or through a twelve-step program or through a realization that prayer works because this understanding was relayed in a book which was written in the language of our times, matters not to God. What matters to God is that His children find their way back home to Him, not just when they die, but in the here and now. To place this into perspective; if you gave your child directions as to which bus to take home from school, and she missed the bus, would you reject her because she found another way home? Would you prefer she went missing, or would you be content that she somehow got home safely? The ideal that the only way to God is through Christ is a Christian ideal, just as Buddhism is a Buddhist ideal, and Judaism is a Jewish ideal. The ideal that Christ is the only way to God is according to Christians and is not a proven fact. It is an opinion. This is something one *chooses* to believe. Religion, like hate or addiction or love, are all choices.

One constant with almost all religions is that we are told not to question the authority of their source, for example, the Bible. However, if we are not to question the authority of the source, including how the source came to be, then how are we to discover Truth? Of all the gifts we squander, our intelligent sense of logic and our right to put it to use are clearly near the top of the list. Logic is a gift, and when properly employed, it helps us figure things out. For instance, questioning implies search, and search leads to answers, and answers lead to Truth.

I have read the Bible and have come to understand the basic teachings of Christ, and contrary to what many and most Christians have stated about humans, I believe that we *are* absolutely capable of living in a manner of complete righteousness without sin. I have had countless discussions with devout Christians who have all reminded me that, even in the midst of preaching their faith, that God doesn't expect us to *not* sin because he knows he set the bar just high enough for us to not be able to achieve that kind of righteousness. If this were true, then it would mean that it's not worth trying, because first of all, whether the sin is great or small, it is a sin, and in that sin is our ticket to hell. Second, if Christ died for all our sins, it makes no sense to bother living righteously, because we are forgiven before our sins are carried out. Third, if we're doomed from the get-go, then God is playing us for a bunch of chumps, and I in particular do not buy any of those explanations. The ideal that we are limited and are really just sinners and can only be sinners is in no way instrumental to our growth or to even wanting to grow. Yes we are imperfect, but we're not meant to be perfect, and imperfection and sin are completely different concepts and have nothing to do with each other. A mistake is not a sin; sin is about intentions. Imperfection is the basis of why we're here (see chapter 1 for a reminder) and imperfect beings make mistakes.

Yes, we're only human, but if we'd stop emphasizing on our limitations long enough to recognize that the religious ideals regarding our limitations are merely hearsay, we'd see that we are more than capable of *walking the walk.* Just because the *spirit is willing but the flesh is weak* doesn't mean the flesh is *incapable*, or that there is no other way. This is where the conditioning properties of exercising the process of religion in an *inherently affirmative manner* come into play. The point of Christianity is to *live in Christ* moment to moment, not only during sprinkles of moments throughout our lifetime. Moment to moment does not mean just on Sunday when we've made it to church either out of guilt or out of not being too tired from the previous night's bender or whatever excuse we have for not bringing our alleged faith to the one in which we have this faith, to church on Sunday. Moment to moment means *perpetually*.

Perhaps one of my biggest disappointments in the masses who claim themselves Christians is the self-righteous judgment in which they preach their alleged *Word of God*. On one hand, most any Christian will tell you that God knows that it's impossible for you not to sin and therefore God is all-forgiving, but Christians who realize this in the midst of their own transgressions fail to extend this same courtesy to everybody else, including other Christians. Like cops setting up cops, Christians are not supporting their own, thereby not strengthening the Christian process. So let me see if I get this; some people are allowed to sin, free of judgment, but others aren't? I personally don't buy this. I tend to look at God's mercy like welfare. It's available to all, but not all of us need it. Many abuse it for various reasons; laziness, self-entitlement, addiction, dishonesty, to name just some, but unlike welfare programs where the government doesn't always know who's really in need of it, we know, and so does God!

Regarding the quote that says *if God leads you to it, he'll lead you through it*, the problem is that what most of us face in life is not something that God has led us to; it's usually something we've led ourselves to. God does not control our finances, our addictions, our eating habits, how we run government or how the air is filled with cancer-causing particles. We are in charge of all of that. We are the cause of all these things. It is our choice to dwell on these things and their consequential residuals and continue to do nothing about it. This is our playground and this is our game. God is powerless to go against what we choose to do because he gave us the right to choose and do what we will. God's doing His part. Now it's time for us to do ours. For those needing reminders on how to proceed in their faith, here are some tips from perhaps one of the greatest books on sustaining one's faith. The Book of Job:

Job 16:34 *The congregation of hypocrites shall be desolate.*

Is there any wonder why religion is in such disarray or why attendance is dwindling or why there are more churches being made into houses than houses being made into churches? Sure, attendance is rising as world morality is plummeting, but attending church out of fear does not a faithful follower make, and, a church filled with hypocrites is a church filled with people who will find no sustenance. For true religious devotees, church should be about gathering to worship and praise and rejoice. It is time for devotees to come together, to strengthen themselves and each other, and to come away encouraged, refueled and revitalized in order to go forth and spread the gospel, and spread it with not just words, but with every single action at every single moment of every single day of their lives. This is True religious consciousness!

Job 40:10 *Deck thyself now with majesty and excellency; and array thyself with glory and beauty.*

I recognize this scripture to be less about wearing clothing and more about *expressing, being, doing* and *embodying* the majesty, excellency, glory and beauty which is the God in all of us, and surrounding ourselves with those who do the same. That said, I also really appreciate this ideal when it comes to the attire in which one chooses to attend not only worship meetings, but also attends *every single day*. There used to be a time when everybody got into their *Sunday best* to go worship, but it's clear to many that God doesn't care what we wear as long as we show up. That said, there's something to be said about the way one feels when donning proper attire for the occasion. The term *clothes make the man* is truthful in that the way a man dresses affects the way he feels, and the way he feels dictates what he attracts and becomes. Any man who wears a suit all day will tell you just how wonderful it is to throw on a pair of jeans and a t-shirt when he gets home, but he will also tell you that wearing a fine suit has far more impact than jeans and a t-shirt when it comes to the way he feels as he delivers a presentation to shareholders whose respect he's come to earn as a result of looking as integrous as his performance demonstrates. Sure, we can go to church in jeans, and God won't mind one bit, but worshipping is not about God, it's about what we bring to God. When you get down to it, once you understand that worshipping means bringing the best of yourself to God, shouldn't you be presenting and representing yourself in the absolute best manner possible?

Job 13:15 *I will maintain mine own ways before Christ.*

This is as much applicable to the person who worships God as it is applicable to the person(s) to whom they're supposed to preach the gospel. If you're a Christian, for example, then your job as a Christian is to live for God, to love your fellow man, and to preach the gospel. Your view of anybody's lifestyle, race, religion, marital status, sexual orientation, transgressions and so forth has nothing to do with your job as a Christian, and as such, when you resort to such acts of judgment and oppression, you cease to be a Christian. If you know of a prisoner on death row, his reason for being in jail is not your concern; that he knows that Christ loves him is your only concern. This also applies to the neighbor who works as a call-girl, the friend who's scamming the government, the cousin who schemes illegal deals and even the upright, upstanding, righteous person who may or may not need reminding that there is always room for improvement.

* * *

A Need For Tolerance...On All Sides!

In 2009 a gay couple was violently removed from the grounds of the Mormon Temple in Utah after they were asked to leave the grounds after sharing a kiss on temple property and then refused to leave. One thing led to another and the men were soon brought to the ground, handcuffed and arrested. On one hand, I agree that this treatment of the couple was completely uncalled for, ungodly and un-Christ-like, especially since it was merely a kiss and not a case of public fornication. Furthermore, I don't understand how so much planning can go into designing, building and sustaining a structure such as the Mormon Temple, and into the organization which it represents, yet no thought was placed into developing a peaceful resolution protocol for just such an incident. On the other hand, the property does belong to a private organization, and as such, the organization has the right to request that people respect certain rules of conduct in order to enter their property.

Although I admit that the couple were completely out of line with their conduct, I can't help but acknowledge that this would have been a perfect opportunity for the religious organization to have invited the two men to speak calmly with missionaries, not only to peacefully explain the reasons for the rule, but to encourage them to be baptized, thus spreading the Gospel to the tens of millions of gay men and women worldwide who had heard the story, and bring them home to the Lord. Furthermore, out of everybody present at the temple that day, it's clear that the two people who needed to be there the most, and who required the church's compassion and tolerance, were those two men. Isn't this the whole point of having missionaries and preaching the gospel and inviting people to places of worship? As much as the couple failed their community, the church undeniably failed their own purpose, and they failed God.

Basic rules of conduct apply to almost all establishments and organizations, private and public alike, and they are usually respected because not only are they reasonable, but they do serve a purpose. The Royal Canadian Legion requests that all who enter their buildings remove their hats and other headgear. This is done to show respect for those soldiers who have died and continue to die in defense of their country. As accidents happen and people sometimes forget, when someone fails to remove their hat, no one is violently arrested; they are merely reminded to remove their hat, and it usually results in the *culprit* buying a round for the gang. Many retail stores request that patrons leave bags and knapsacks at the counter, or patrons are denied entry. This discourages shoplifting thus keeping stores in business and especially assists in doing away with the alleged targeting when someone is erroneously suspected of shoplifting. Some night-clubs impose specific dress codes whereas others won't let you past the coat-check until you've removed all your clothing. This is to ensure that those night-owls who want to meet other night-owls are made to feel comfortable in the company of like-minded individuals.

The beautiful thing about private organizations in a free country is that you get to find the group that appeals to you, join in what they do, and enjoy the benefits that come with ensuring certain rules are respected. In the process of exercising our rights, however, we often forget to allow others the freedom to exercise their rights to do what they want to do within the confines of their own organizations and policies. Admittedly, I fail to see the problem with public displays of affection such as holding hands, sharing a kiss or even giving a hug; especially in the presence of God. The *no public display of affection* policy, enforced by the Mormon temple, however, is there to remind attendees to be reverent and pure of heart, but, I don't imagine that had a child hugged or kissed her parents on the grounds, that she would have been asked to leave, and as such, it does make one ask: Where do we draw the line? The answer is quite simply, we draw the line with troublemakers!

Without a doubt, what the couple in question did on the temple grounds was exceptionally disrespectful. For many who make the pilgrimage to the Mormon Temple, regardless of spiritual convictions, their visit is a sacred one, and the reverence by which all are requested to abide and respect plays a huge role in what others experience upon that pilgrimage. The request that public displays of affecttion not be executed on the private property is a request to *all* who enter the grounds, not just to gays. That said, there are harmonious ways of defusing situations when misconduct arises, and although taking down two guys because they shared a kiss is not what I would call godly or Christ-like, it goes without saying that what that couple did was nothing short of a hate-crime rooted in unjust intolerance, and, to those who go to that temple for spiritual assurance and to worship in peace, it was on every level an act of terrorism. When people are deprived of their right to worship in a place they've prepared for themselves, and violence and uncertainty ensue as a result of deprivation of one's right to peacefully worship, what else do you call it?

To underscore the malevolent intentions of these two men, on the following day, they returned to the temple property with a group of people, and all of them proceeded to kiss and *make out* in protest to the mess they themselves the previous day had created by not respecting the rights and freedoms of their fellow human beings. What's worse is, not only did these men make a mockery of people's basic rights on sacred grounds, but in the midst of all that gays have strived for in their struggle for humanitarian recognition and equality, these two men set the accomplishments of gay activism back fifty years, and that's just in Hollywood. In Utah, I would imagine it set them back about a millennium.

I have spoken with several gay Mormons, and their devotion to the teachings of Christ and Joseph Smith is as deep as any straight elder, bishop or Relief Society president I've ever met. Sadly, we've yet to arrive at the time when sexual orientation is completely exempt from judgment within the confines of most organized religions, but, the wheels are in motion, and the price gays are paying for equality is only set higher when the gays who are doing the legwork are brought down by the gays who have their freedom as a result of those they're bringing down. Say what you want about Mormons, but we have yet to see Mormons imposing sacrament meetings in gay nightclubs, so the least those two guys could have done is extend some courtesy.

As mentioned at the beginning of this chapter, these ideals are transferable to every person and to every religion, and it's imperative that we all truly walk our chosen path with respect to others as they walk their path. My disclaimer, however, is that these ideals are about religion in the affirmative manner of which religion is meant to be approached, and not in the manner of which "radicals" carry out their alleged holy wars and hate-crimes against humanity.

Muslim radicals *(note the term "radicals")* believe that in order to enter heaven they must do at least 51% good over bad. I respect people's right to believe what they will, but people need to bring some logic into the equation, especially where radical religious convictions are concerned. First off, how does one go about measuring the good they've done? If one murders somebody, how do they measure the residual impact of that undertaking? How does one measure the heartbreak or the tears cried over that one lost life, or measure how many people will cry those tears? If one single life is attached to so much more than just a heartbeat, what of one thousand lives?

One simply cannot measure the good or the bad one does, and this is our best incentive for doing as much good as possible. The cowardly bullies who continue to murder, rape, torture and pillage in the name of their religion, and who continue to hold such extreme blatant contempt for life and for our Creator, are not in any way powerful, especially when you compare their numbers to all of the peaceful religions as a whole.

By peaceful religions remaining segregated from each other and doing nothing about the murderous *hate-clubs* that are the radicals, we not only extend to the radicals more power but we also grant them our approval. Where in this realization, among the massacres, rapes, tortures and bombings, is the religious man *living for God?* By allowing these radicals to continue in their endeavor, where is our love for our fellow man? I am not talking about raging war against the radicals, I am talking about all *affirmative* religions coming together to bring an end to tolerating the worldwide bullying that has seeped its way into every single country worldwide and is finding its way into our living rooms, our classrooms, our communities, our churches, our dreams and our lives. Regardless of our religious denominations, we all have the same basic understandings. Just because one man is against blood transfusions and another doesn't drink coffee and another man won't use machines on Saturday doesn't mean they can't all come together to ensure that they may continue to exercise their faith in peace and security.

As for exercising our faith in peace and security, perhaps my all-time greatest disappointment in religious practice is not in the actions of religious followers but rather in the practices of church leaders – priests, bishops, pastors, reverends and so forth. It is no secret that the job of a terrorist is to instill fear and terror in others, and to create unrest in the hearts and souls of man. This is done in order to bully and control humanity, and it is the hallmark of the lowest order of the human species. When the leaders of our churches stand before congregations and preach the end of days and fire and brimstone and a bullying

God and all that other evil stuff we've been hearing for countless generations, it is clear to me that many, and most, of these preaching men and women are the true terrorists of our land.

The profanity uttered each time we're told that God hates sinners while in the same breath we're reminded that we're never without sin, is sacrilege in the purest. When one goes to worship in earnest and seek a glimmer of solace within the confines of one's church, how exactly is one to come away feeling confident about raising their children when it's been made clear that our days are numbered? How many people over the generations lived in fear of the end of days and never lived their fullest life because they were *waiting for the end?* In short, if your church leader is scaring you, he's not working for God. Conversely, if you're a church leader and you're resorting to scare tactics to convince your congregation of the wrath and fear of God, perhaps you need to re-examine your approach, because people are waking up and you're about one sermon away from losing your flock.

I am also appalled by how convenient it is that the rules of religion only seem to change for some people but not for others. Who decided that women must remain silent, not teach and have no authority over men *(1 Tim 2:11-12)*, and who decided that now it's alright? Why is it wrong to use a car come Friday to bring one's family to a place of worship, but it's alright to be on an airplane during that same time in the name of financial gain? In my view, if you're *walking the walk*, then the Sabbath is the Sabbath; it is not negotiable! There are no rain checks or substitutes. This *pick and choose your rules* process is the biggest sham in religion and perhaps the biggest reason humanity is walking away from religion. As a footnote, I will mention that religious organizations who constantly tell children that they're little sinners are doing a great disservice to children and to God. Children are perfect in God's eyes and should be reminded of such. Children, if encouraged to dwell in God, should be encouraged to dwell in God *affirmatively*, not in fear. Any person who teaches children that they are anything less than perfect in God's eyes are simply bullying and terrorizing children, and they have no business being around children.

Ultimately, if people cannot come together affirmatively in order to protect each other and their rights, and the Truths which dwell within each religion which truly can bring us closer to God, what's the point in being religious? One thing is certain; if we don't begin to *walk the walk* today, we'll never experience the glorious residual awaiting us in the realm of an affirmative tomorrow...if we're lucky enough to see tomorrow.

Ten Commandments, Ten Gifts...

Assuming the *universal collective conscious* is an inherently affirmative organism capable uniquely of creation *(keeping in mind that everything including destruction is a form of creation)*, it stands to reason that any guideline delivered from God would have to be affirmative as well; all do's but no don'ts, for the do's imply the don'ts.

So, does this mean the Ten Commandments are applicable? In my estimation, the answer is a resounding *yes!* My disclaimer, however, is to heed the advice and then move on to affirmatively living for God and loving our fellow man.

Anybody who has ever learned anything knows that an important part of getting anything right is knowing what *not* to do. Conversely, anybody who has achieved any-thing knows that the success of their achievement has more to do with what they *did* do and little to do with what they *didn't* do. If we spend time focusing on what we shouldn't do, how can we give all of our attention to what we should do? If we focus on what we're not allowed to do, we then focus on what's missing and what we don't experience as a result of not doing what we're not allowed to do; stealing, cheating, coveting, etc. Furthermore, because what we think about usually comes to fruition, focusing on what "thou shalt not do" is guaranteed to constantly bring up the temptation. When we focus on the affirmative; on what we can do, we focus on the wonder that comes with rewards for a job well done, with being faithfully loyal in our relationships, and the energy that surrounds us when we're talking good about some-one rather than gossiping, to name only a few perks of affirmatively *walking the walk*.

So, how is it that if God is affirmative, and Moses was so advanced, that God told Moses what humans *must not* do *(Commandments)* instead of what humans *must* do? I'm not the world's foremost expert on the subject; I'm just a dude with a few opinions, but it makes sense to me that if the Commandments accounts are true, Moses asked the question and he either received the answer in a way God knew Moses would understand, or he received it in a way that God said it and then delivered it in a manner which the people would understand. I do wonder, however, that if Moses was truly working affirmatively with God, then what's with the forty-year desert excursion? I mean, after a year or two, most of us would have said, *"I'm outta here!"* or *"Maybe we should turn left at the cactus this time."* But forty years!? Yes I know there are many reasons for the forty years in the desert, and since everything I know about it could fit through the eye of a needle and still leave room for the camel, I'll move on...

Assuming the story about *The Commandments* is correct, we must remember that when people were first advised on the Ten Commandments *(apparently there were more, but let's stick with the ten for the sake of discussion)*, the world was a very different place. Language and education were not what they are today. The understanding of *everything* was not what it is today. There was little life guidance and there was little reference with which to create more guidance, and trial and error were what taught people, and at great cost. Today, we're smarter and more educated than ever (allegedly), and for most of us, trial and error are not responsible for our misery as much as we ourselves are. But how do we break hundreds, thousands and even millions of years of human nature? The answer is, we don't. We accept what's in our nature and couple that with our smarts and experience, as well as thinking, feeling and living affirmatively. And, we stop subscribing to the rules and judgments of ourselves and each other about what every human should or should not be allowed to do or be or wear or eat or whatever.

As I mentioned earlier, I don't claim to be the world's foremost expert on the subject of religion or spirituality or even being human, but one thing I do know is that you don't part a sea, or even a glass of water for that matter, if you're not living affirmatively. My theory is that Moses spoke in words that his people could understand at the time. Why, if Moses was so affirmative, would he resort to telling people what they cannot do instead of what they can or should do? It may have been more about damage control than anything else. Perhaps he thought he needed to stop his people from walking their destructive path before he could send them in the right direction. It may simply have been a question of damage control, and as such, the less than affirmative manner in which the Commandments were relayed was about setting boundaries for survival and to offer guidance for a good life, and a life truly worth living.

In this discovery lies the ideal that the Commandments were not introduced to please God but rather for us to live our ultimate lives; to ultimately please *us*. Many believe that if we fail to obey the Commandments, we'll go to hell, but failing to obey the Commandments affects our lives in the here and now, because the Commandments are guidelines for living our best lives while here on Earth. Yes, forsaking the Commandments may lead to hell after we die, but it clearly leads us to hell in the now, right here on Earth. Forsaking the Commandments and failing to reach our ultimate potential of becoming the kind of person we'd become, and living the miraculous life we'd live as a result of obeying the Commandments, is forsaking the ultimate experience we're actually here to live, and it ultimately forsakes our Divine purpose.

In actuality, the Commandments are not conditions designed to keep us from having a good time. They're actually the *life-manual* we're all seeking. On one hand, many people will be relieved to know that God will forgive their lying, stealing, cheating ways, so they'll continue to lie, steal and cheat because, after all, if God is unconditionally forgiving, why not do what we feel like doing, right? But the Commandments aren't about keeping us in line. They're about guidance, and they lead to a joyous reality that only those on a specific level of consciousness can ever experience. It's a level of consciousness that we arrive at only as a result of compliance of the Commandments. It is a level of consciousness to which no other substance or experience could ever bring us. And thus, the Ten Commandments could better be referred to as the Ten Gifts.

Nothing delivers us from the opposite of love better than abiding by the Commandments, but for those who think that a sinless life is a boring life; think again. The adventures and risks that come with the challenge of abiding by the Commandments are every bit as challenging, breathtaking and life-altering as any sport, drug or weekend excursion you'll ever experience. Like true religion, the Commandments are not an ideal, they are a process. Some moments are easy, others are challenging, and again, it's all about intention. For those who want to achieve it, it is possible. Without delving deeply into my personal experiences, I can personally attest to this. During the times when I've completely lived by the Commandments, the challenges were great. I lost friends, jobs and family, and a few times, I thought I'd lost my mind, but when you're *walking the walk*, other relationships grow, new ones are born, strong family ties become indestructible, new opportunities arise, and you understand that when you thought you'd lost your mind, you were merely waking up from the collective illusion we refer to as common *reality*.

As for Moses, it's very possible that he did say what *should* be done, and someone along the line with the best of intentions *(or not; who really knows?)* attempted to simplify things by saying, *"in other words, you can't..."* and again the gist of the affirmative message was lost in translation. For those struggling to respect the Commandments while living affirmatively and consciously, the key is to remember the ultimate ingredient: Love!

According to Christianity, Christ simplified the Commandments by advising humanity to *live for God and love our fellow man*. What's great about this simple idea is that only one of these two Commandments needs to be carried out, for if you do one, the other is implied. If you live for God, it implies you're loving your fellow man. If you're loving your fellow man, you're living for God. One simple guideline covers all your boundaries; every rule and every Commandment. Living for God and loving your fellow man, together or separately, implies no cheating, no lying, no judgment, no coveting, no stealing, no killing, and it implies allowing others to be who they are and live their lives as they choose. It is impossible to live for God and not love your fellow man, and it is equally impossible to love your fellow man and not live for God. True Love is to speak, feel, live, think and act affirmatively, every single moment of every single day, and the deed is done.

* * *

Questioning the Facts…

At the risk of sounding like I'm merely promoting organized religion, I want to yet again refer to the Bible, to examine its relevancy to our times and to humanity, and ask some challenging questions and view other perspectives. So, in an unbiased manner, let's get logical:

Previously I mentioned how important it is to the advancement of all humanity that people of all religious faiths affirmatively *walk the walk* of their faith. In actuality, however, of those who walk in the faith of their religion, very few actually possess a deep rooted understanding of what it is they're following, and fewer still have the courage to ask important logical questions. Here I'll refer to Christianity as an example, but this line of logical questioning applies to *all* religions. Also, whereas the previous chapters might have led readers to assume that I am promoting Christianity, this chapter may likely alter that assumption to the contrary. However, again, I'm not out to sell or deny anything; I'm here to encourage people to think.

The first logical question we need to ask is: *Is religion in any way logical?* Based alone on what good can come of religion – peace, harmony, love and the deepening of consciousness – religion seems like a very logical idea. It is however, the illogical manipulation of religion at the cost of the basic expression of life including blood-shed, violence, rape, torture, torment, murder and oppression in the name of something which is founded on absolute hearsay that should be questioned. As for examples of the questions we should be asking, here are just some:

Was/is Jesus God? The factor which differentiates most Christian religions from non-Christian religions is the worship of Christ stemming from the belief that Christ was/is God. It may seem certain that Jesus was/is God, especially in light of scriptures like *"Nobody enters the kingdom except through me"*, but where most Christians understand this scripture to mean we can only enter heaven through the *worship* of Christ, others understand it to mean that we can only enter heaven through observing the *teachings* of Christ and doing, being, believing and acting like Christ. Most Christians believe that Jesus is the middle-man; the one who delivers our prayers and fights for our redemption, so in effect, the glory goes to Jesus;

not to God. Unbiased, logical study of the Bible however, clarifies that Jesus, if in fact he did/does exist, was/is no more God than you or me, and here are the logics:

Jesus experienced anger, for example, at the market in the temple. Anger is something an all-knowing, all-compassionate, all-understanding, all-foreseeing God with no expectations would *not* experience. In fact, according to Christian belief, God *expects* us to sin, so why would he get angry at us for doing as he expects us to do? We're slow, we're weak, we're sinners, we know it and God knows it, so why would he get angry over it? The inanity that is the concept of God's wrath against His children is like imagining Jane Goodall beating a baby chimpanzee because it hasn't understood the hand-sign for the word *renaissance*.

Next, how could Jesus be "sinless" when he broke laws like working on the Sabbath for example? Even if his motive was to enlighten, he broke laws and created disharmony and unrest which only breeds more of the same. This negative form of teaching would not be the way of a Divine Creator. God wouldn't have to resort to breaking laws and having angry tantrums and creating unrest to make people realize the errors of their ways. God's a smart dude, and he knows a way to do everything affirmatively *(disclaimer: God might not be a dude)*. Just because we can't think of non-confrontational ways to teach humanity doesn't mean God couldn't think of a way. To imply that God would resort to discouraging, threatening, intimidating, bullying or employing other scare tactics is an insult to God's intelligence. God is unlimited. God would figure out a way to get through to us in a loving and affirmative manner. Humans who think God is anything other than Loving are simply narcissistic to think that God would negatively compromise himself on our behalf. Any time Love is compromised, it ceases to be Love. Love is God's way.

Next, Jesus possessed compromised faith. When upon the cross he asked, *"Father, why hath Thou forsaken me?"* If Jesus was God, why did he ask God why He had forsaken him? Even Job didn't think that God had forsaken him during his crisis, and what Job experienced was as painful to him as the crucifixion was to Jesus. As for the crucifixion, many believe that Jesus didn't have to die, nor should he have, but what can I say; people were jerks back then and still are today. Whether Jesus was God or just preaching the Word of God, if he actually existed, he was clearly a decent dude, but jerks being what they are found fault with something they refused to understand, and so they killed him.

Incidentally, we haven't changed much over time. If you don't think people would be cruel to Jesus today, just look at the cruel treatment we extend to people who do much good in our world today. Take for example Oprah Winfrey, Ellen Degeneres, Dr. Phil; all people who have contributed far more to humanity than they've taken, and who've contributed more to the world during each single passing year than most of us will ever give in our lifetime. In the midst of this knowledge, Oprah is nonetheless criticized for spending her own money to repaint a school that *she* built so that it was *just right*, and criticized for building a school in a country other than her own. Yet the fact remains, few of us, including most millionaires, have yet to build a school of *any* color, *anywhere* in the world.

To emphasize this unfair treatment, while Oprah continues to do good in the world, a negative non-creative ignoramus who makes her living by defaming others writes an unauthorized heretical biography about Oprah, and then a flock of dull ignorami actually goes out and buys it! On an affirmative note, controversy surrounding said autobiography provided billions of dollars of free publicity worldwide for Oprah, which results in more demand for Oprah, more power to Oprah, and consequently more *good* coming from Oprah!

I'm not comparing Oprah, Ellen and Phil to Jesus, and I know they're not perfect, we all know it. Heck, *they* know it! They're not supposed to be perfect. None of us are supposed to be perfect. I'm just saying that they are prime examples of regular humans who, in spite of being imperfect, are doing great things to affirmatively change the world, yet the best that many of us can do is find fault with them. If that's how we're treating our own at the height of their greatest potential, I'm not sure that we deserve a *savior*, and I don't want to know how we'd treat someone who claims to be savvier than the rest of us, and brings to our attention our downfalls in order to bring us into the light.

Perhaps the strongest testament opposing the ideal that Christ was/is God is the Commandment, *"Thou shalt have no other God before Me"*. This Commandment clearly commands us to worship God, *and God alone*. No exceptions! How is this Commandment not clear to anybody? This commandment is further underscored by the scripture; *No man can serve two masters (Matthew 6:24)*. Yes, Jesus may have brought people back to life, but so did the prophet Elijah. Furthermore, as for the many miracles throughout the Bible, if *miraculous* deeds are what make a man God, wouldn't Noah and Moses fit the bill? And for that matter, what about the millions of doctors worldwide who bring people back to life every day?

It has been suggested by scientists, historians and theologians alike that Jesus might have been a prophet, and although I am inclined to believe that Jesus, if in fact he did exist, definitely held a Divine position unique only to The Christ, I think that to imply Jesus was God and to worship him not only defeats his definitive purpose as defined by The Christ, but it ultimately *denies* who and what he really was, and as such, the worship of Christ as implied by the process of Christianity is as blasphemous to Christ as it is to God. Yes, I've heard the reasoning that Jesus and God are one in the same manner that one man can be both a father and a son, but I always follow a very simple rule; *when in doubt, go without!* Although I follow the teachings of Jesus, it is God I worship, and God only!

Assuming Jesus existed, I don't think it was his intention to be worshipped any more than being worshipped was the intention of Buddha or Krishna or any other *inherently affirmative conscious* individual. I think folks were as gullible back then as they are today, and it was just as easy to take something out of context and believe rumors back then as it is today, especially if people truly wanted to believe something. Today, thanks to television and the Internet, most of us have seen just about everything there is to see, yet we're somehow still impressed with the most menial of events, like a newscast depicting the face of Jesus in a cappuccino, or a snowstorm in December in Canada *(that's when you know it's a truly slow news day)*. Back then, however, people had seen very little and were probably as bored beyond belief as many are today, so even the most menial events could have sparked people's imagination, especially events surrounding a man with even the remotest sense of logic foreign to their archaic ideals.

I am willing to accept that Jesus actually did walk on water and raise the dead, but it also makes sense to me that a man who was so determined to teach logic would not have resorted to the illogical employment of illogical examples. Perhaps he did walk on water, or perhaps he walked on a sandbar. Maybe he did raise the dead, or maybe he knew the difference between death and a fainting spell. Jesus was a logical man; we need only be logical to understand him and what he *really* did.

Most Christians' attachment to believing that Jesus did all these things is stronger than their willingness to consider the possibility that he did not do them, even at the cost of remaining ignorant and stagnant. Furthermore, our beliefs exist because we *want* to believe and we *choose* to believe; not because they're factual. I'm all for respecting knowledge from thousands of years ago, but most of what was written at that time was written by men whose ideals and perspectives were anything but logical. Ultimately, regardless of whether we worship Jesus or follow his teachings, to study and live by the teachings of Christ does not have to imply Christianity, but to ignore the teachings deprives us, because even as illogical as their delivery may seem, the lessons are in essence of logic, of faith, of Love and of Truth.

On another brief note, the story of Job is meant to inspire faith, but I don't believe it happened that way, if it even happened at all. If it did happen, I can see a clear indication of how Job brought it on himself through the law of attraction. He constantly feared that his children sinned, and he feared God's wrath, and so he brought upon himself what he feared. I don't appreciate the implied negative intentions why God did what he did to Job. I don't believe God would test a good man to prove anything to the devil. I mean, would you test your child to prove anything to an evil person, say a predator or murderer? God doesn't owe the devil anything, and I don't believe God would, or even could associate with the devil. God is affirmative and associates with such.

And now to shift gears slightly. In light of the rapidly increasing populace of Muslims, I felt it appropriate to dedicate a few pages to Islam. Not in order to promote or deny Islam, but to clarify facts and challenge ideals. Before I proceed, I wish to mention that the ratio to which I support Islam is in direct proportion to that in which I support *all* religions. Something I do not support, however, is injustice. The ignorance behind the untruths preached about Islam is the same ignorance which fuels the radicals who carry out terrorist acts, and I feel this issue should be addressed.

The first order of business is to clarify that *true* Muslims are a peaceful people who recognize terrorism as a crime not just against Muslims, but against all of humanity. According to the Qur'an, God commands believers to promote peace and security in the world, and according to Islam, the act of inciting terror is forbidden. Anybody who has even lightly explored Islam recognizes that any association between Islam and terrorism is the result of independent radicals having nothing to do with the principles as outlined by Islam. Islam makes it very clear about where it stands on terrorism.

Anybody who makes even the smallest effort to learn about Muslims will learn some basic principles. Learning about Muslims doesn't mean you support Muslims, and it doesn't make you Muslim. You don't need to subscribe to a religion to familiarize yourself with a religion. As the best weapon against your enemy is to know your enemy, anyone you think might be your enemy should be studied. It is in study that one discovers any truth to hearsay. All education is helpful even if you aren't an expert. I know how to perform CPR and diagnose a concussion, but I'm not a doctor. I know how to pray, but I am not a pope. Before casting judgment, get the facts from the source. You don't need to be an expert or an *associate* to find the facts.

There's no denying that Islam is a powerful religion. There is, after all, strength in numbers. It's not entirely clear why so many people are becoming Muslim, Perhaps we're lemmings falling for a trend and Islam's got a great sales-pitch, or maybe we're logical people and it appears to be a logical process. At any rate, Muslim's seem to know what to say because people seem to be listening. However, inasmuch as I'm inclined to agree with many Islamic ideals, I honestly haven't seen any evidence that Islam is different from other religions, especially where the detriments of non-affirmative ideals come into play. Take for example the following excerpt from the Qur'an: *If all humans and all the angels banded together in order to produce a Qur'an like this, they could never produce anything like it, no matter how much assistance they lent one another.*

I can appreciate such conviction in one's faith, however, any motive to produce a Qur'an would not be to produce a Qur'an *like this*. The motive would be to *go beyond* its limitations as defined by the Qur'an's non-affirmative ideals. The motive would be to improve upon the excellence of the Qur'an (note the term *excellence* rather than *perfection*). The ideal that the Qur'an cannot be made better implies *no possibility of change*. Again, anything that does not subscribe to the law of *perpetual transmutation* is not a process and cannot exist. Any affirmative process must subscribe to the law of *perpetual transmutation* in order to be in harmony with all that is. The statement also implies failure to dwell within the realm of possibility. To dwell in God, one must dwell in affirmative possibility.

Implying that the Qur'an cannot be improved upon is as detrimental to the advancement of humanity as it is to Islam itself, if only for the following example. According to the Qur'an, a man is instructed to beat his wife. It has been explained to me by a reputable source that, although this act is prescribed in the Qur'an, women should only be beaten *lightly*. My rebuttal is, in the same manner of which it's impossible to only *lightly kill* someone, it's also impossible to *lightly terrorize* someone; either you're going up or down, you cannot be doing both at the same time. You cannot instill discord and at the same time instill peace. Even a *light tap* that *leaves no mark* is not affirmative. Abuse goes beyond the physical, and so do consequential *marks* and *scars* (and newsflash: women are not idiots; they can be spoken to...Welcome to the 21st century!).

I honestly do not believe that any man, Muslim or otherwise, would beat his wife in the presence of God. I strongly feel that we should never participate in any act in which we'd not proudly participate before many spectators and willingly have pictured on the front page of every newspaper worldwide and be willingly held accountable by our peers. I can accept the ideal that men are stronger than women (per the Qur'an). Logically speaking, most men in general *are* physically stronger than most women, and I'm okay with the reasoning that perhaps men are made stronger to protect women. However, the very idea that men might be stronger than women only emphasizes that men should never lay a hand on woman, as this simply implies bullying; the way of a coward.

The convenient translations of the Qur'an's archaic ideals are no different than the manner in which most religions approach the Bible. This is yet another example of a *pick and choose your rules* process. In my view, if you're truly a follower, then you follow. You either do what the book says, or, you don't. No supporting *some* beliefs, no changing laws, no translating things in order to make a religion look prettier than it actually is. If, however, the changes are carried out to affirmatively enlighten religion, then this process should not be limited to *some* ideals but made to accommodate consideration to *all* ideals. Absurdly, we'd rather be erroneously right about *everything* than take a brief hit to our ego and discover we might be wrong about *some* things, and finally get it *all* right. This is an unfortunate process subscribed to by all religions. It's unfortunate because there is Truth in every religion, and there is always room for new and additional knowledge and wisdom, and especially corrections.

As with the Bible, I have come to recognize that interlaced within Qur'an's many negative, limiting and oppressive content indwells all the affirmative answers we could ever seek about living a truly harmonious, prosperous life; personally and globally. To affirmatively learn and grow from the data therein, however, one must go entirely beyond the negative, limiting, oppressive content, absorbing all affirmative passages, and doing away with concepts which promote guilt, hatred, violence, and all that which limits the life-expression of others, for it is beyond those negatives and limitations where the true gold within the Qur'an, and The Bible, resides.

Debating what's true or false in our religious volumes is not easy for those who choose to walk in their faith, but God is not a trickster or tormenter, so, if your religious volumes are confusing you, do away with them for now; their gifts will be revealed to you in other divine ways.

Something we must recognize about the content of all great religious books is that, if none of these books existed, whatever good indwells them would still be made available to humanity. This is because all the goodness within the Qur'an and the Bible already exists in the consciousness of humanity. It's something which accompanies each of us to this existence; along with *free will* and the knowledge to know the difference between right and wrong, and between good and evil. The good that resides in those books actually existed before any book was ever written, and before all the ignorant, unenlightened, biased, power-hungry, narcissistic, controlling, scared ego-maniacs manipulated Truths and tarnished *The Word* with the concepts of limitation, fear and oppression. As long as there is humanity, however, the inherent, blessed, truly divine goodness that is *The Affirmative Word* will continue to live and grow and go forth to be recognized by those who seek it.

As for radical extremists, every religion is plagued with self-serving individuals and organizations which carry out ungodly actions and claim that their way is the manner in which the religion is meant to be wielded. Muslims, Catholics, Mormons, Jews, Religious Scientists, Methodists; every religion is affected by this infirmity, and it is only made worse when religions preach against each other instead of preaching love. Again, everybody should have the right to believe what they believe, but to imply that they *own* God is arrogant beyond reason, and the lack of intelligence behind such ideals goes beyond the realm of absurd. God belongs to all of us and we all belong to God!

With all religions in general, there is just too much hearsay to really *walk the walk* without messing up somewhere along the line. In order to bring order to our lives and our planet, we cannot encourage life by limiting life, and we cannot imagine God getting us through seemingly impossible conditions if we always imagine God as limited. We especially will not have our prayers answered by God if it isn't to God we're praying. Whatever our religion, we must see God as omnipotent and consider everything as possible, because, everything *is* possible.

Nothing breaks evil cycles better than love, and nothing fuels affirmative cycles more than love. We must respond *to* love and respond *with* love and respond *as* love. When a response to negativity is necessary, we must respond with the intention to surmount evil with love, not with more or greater evil. When faced with adversity, we must think not only on what Jesus would do, but also of what our *ideal self* would do. Admittedly, Jesus, whether mythological or real, is an ideal role model for all of us, but in actuality, you're not here to be Jesus; you're here to be you. You do this best by being logical, and by questioning anybody or anything which threatens you and the expression that is your life, and which threatens to hold back the best you have to bring to the world. Most importantly, always question whatever keeps you from Truth.

So, which is the one true religion? In a manner of speaking, the one true religion is a peaceful process which approaches all angles and aspects of life and spirituality in an *inherently affirmative* manner, from an *inherently affirmative* perspective. It is the religion which is derived from, and instills, commitment, discipline, absolute honesty and omnipotent faith. It is the religion which seeks to encourage, motivate, enthuse, and inspire, without resorting to scare tactics and guilt-trips. It is the one religion which sets the example of integrity with integrity, and sets the example of compassion with compassion. It is the religion which encourages and celebrates individual authenticity and our common golden thread. It is the religion which is always evolving, changing and improving to meet the needs of the ever-growing, ever-evolving, ever-discovering society that is humanity. It is the religion which Loves beyond reason, without prejudice, without arrogance, without judgment, without oppression, without condition. Simply put, the one true religion simply *"Is"*.

If we should draw anything from religion, it's that we are all equal in God's eyes. In the same manner of which a doctor is more useful to the sick, so is it that our love, compassion, acceptance, tolerance and our affirmative approach to humanity, religion and God, will better heal the world than ever will a narcissistic, self-righteous judgment of who others are, how they live their lives, or how they choose to view and embrace God. Therefore, for the Love of humanity, and for the Love of God: Let the healing begin...

CHAPTER X

=EVIL=

Evil isn't!

You'll notice this chapter is brief. It is this way because I wanted this book to have as much affirmative information as possible, and as such, for two main reasons, I didn't want to dwell on the topic of evil to any great length. For one, evil is a topic that is other than affirmative, and two, I didn't want to give more attention than necessary to something that doesn't actually exist.

In short, evil is merely the practice of going against the process of life; a simple exploitation of energy and action. I'm not usually one to put much stock in the meaning of anagrams, for example, I don't think that GOD is a DOG, or that ELVIS LIVES or that a MOTHER IN LAW is a WOMAN HITLER, but whenever I describe evil, I like to remind people that LIVE spelled backwards is EVIL, and LIVED spelled backwards is DEVIL, which *coincidentally* underscores the theory.

As for the devil, it's a fictitious character we blame for our failure to assume responsibility for our actions. *The devil made me do it* is just another phrase for *I didn't have the willpower* or *I'm addicted* or *I'm a bully* or *I couldn't keep it in my pants!* The idea that the devil is responsible for our actions is a sellout used by cowards since the beginning of time, and it's still used by bullies and petty thugs who have barely enough spine to walk upright. It's also a concept fed to children by parents, teachers and alleged role models who are the epitome of idiocy, ignorance and mediocrity at it's finest. When we subscribe to the idea of a devil – to the idea that the devil inherently controls us – we only weaken ourselves by not taking responsibility for our actions, and we relinquish our power. The worst part is, we relinquish our power to nobody!

Evil is a concept of fear. Fear is everything that opposes love. Love is a *Divine state of being* in action. Love and evil are born of thoughts. Thoughts lead to ideas which lead to decisions which lead to actions which lead to consequences which lead to circumstances which lead to states of mind. Thoughts, whether of love or evil, are creations of a state of mind. Every thought comes from either love or fear. Thoughts of love include joy, bliss, peace, faith, trust, patience, compassion, etc. Thoughts of fear include anger, anxiety, judgment, sadness, hate, guilt, etc.

Regardless of whether or not the devil exists *(hey, I could be wrong!)*, the fact remains that we generally attract what we dwell and act upon, and, regardless of what temptations the devil may or may not place before us, our actions are ultimately *our own* decision.

I decided long ago that it's better to ignore the concept of the devil altogether, and here's why: If the devil exists, why would I waste any time dwelling on him when my energy comes from, and belongs to, God? It's like taking money from my best friend and giving it to my worst enemy. Simply put, if I dwell in God and in Love and all that is good and right and affirmative, I'll attract the same energy. And, anything negative that comes along, I will be able to handle because of the omnipotent energy to which I am connected.

All this said, I recognize that there is evil in our world, but all evil is only ever sustained through *human action*. Like temptation, evil can never dwell in a human unless a human chooses to surrender, submit and subscribe to it. If you want nothing to do with evil, avoid those who do (or associate) with evil. It may be a lonely road, but not for long, for there are others like you. In the process, work hard, well, smart, and protect what's yours, and always stand for and protect those who cannot stand for and protect themselves. Most importantly, be sure that all thoughts, feelings and actions are rooted in firm faith, as much in yourself as in that force from whence you came and which promises to love, nourish and protect you always, regardless of what the evildoers and naysayers would otherwise have you believe.

Ultimately, aside from what we willingly put ourselves through, we don't go through certain things because the devil is testing us, but rather, because God is strengthening us. God is all there is: God and us. And it's up to us to keep our commitments, to take responsibility for ourselves and our actions, and to hold ourselves accountable when we don't follow through. So, let's take responsibility for ourselves, drop the charade, suck it up, and get on with living. Your real life is waiting to be lived!

CHAPTER XI

=Truth=

This chapter is whole and complete...

(The preceding chapter is whole and complete)

CHAPTER XII

=PsychicsMediumsTelepathsOthers=

And tomorrow's winning lottery numbers are...

It wouldn't be right to write about in-depth subjects such as God, religion and universal, scientific and moral laws without touching on the subject of paranormal and psychic activity, and of course, extraterrestrial life. These, along with angels, spirits, guides and everything else that's allegedly *out there* all exist, and they're all connected. To deny their existence out of lack of physical evidence or rational understanding is as erroneous as doubting the sun's existence because of nightfall. Also, to deny their possible goodness because of the negative manner in which they've been wielded and presented over time does not deny their inherent goodness or divinity.

When it comes to rituals of manifestation, contrary to religious belief, voodoo, witchcraft and other forms of magic and *spell-brewing* in themselves are not inherently evil. They're merely methods of communication and *creative manifestation*, just like prayer. In fact, they are prayer. Even satanic rituals are forms of creation and manifest-tation, but it is the *intention* behind the ritual that deems it as either evil or good.

Just like thought, meditation, fasting, and prayer, these creative methods are no different than any other form of sending thoughtful intentions out to the universe or to God in order to achieve a desired outcome. When changes are created in our world, whether through witchcraft or through mere thought, shifts must take place within the law of cause and effect. Whether one casts a spell to bring love or harm to somebody, or they merely think, visualize or pray for love or harm, the law is the law, and the lessons that we are meant to learn in life will be bestowed upon us whether we've manifested good or bad. You don't get something from nothing; only nothing comes from nothing. Whatever you manifest, there is a cost somewhere. Whether it is through blood, sweat, and tears, or through prayer, meditation and mental anguish; you reap what you sow! If you pray with and for evil, you'll get back evil. If you pray with and for love and light, you'll get back love and light.

This is how it works: Whenever we shift energy to manifest anything, universal law shifts that energy on our behalf. Whenever we send out vibrations of thoughts and feelings, those vibes come back to us, and we must deal with what we've created. Whenever we send out negative vibes, the universe restores our lives with *same* energy. Whether we perform traditional healing prayers or evil rites, whatever we give, we get. Whatever we manifest, there is a cost, and, pay now or pay later, make no mistake, we pay.

Practices such as voodoo, witchcraft, divination, mystic healing, to name some, get a bad rap because for eons these practices have been viewed for the evil they create, yet these rituals are merely forms of manipulating energy; like prayer in order to manifest something. Their employment for affirmative and peaceful practices doesn't stand out because those who wield such sacred practices for good wield them with utter respect and reverence, without vanity. Rarely, if ever, are these affirmative practices made public. There's no denying that there are many frauds out there. There is no shortage of insecure people wanting to be seen by others as *gifted* or *special*, and therefore claim themselves as psychics and healers, but they really are no different than those who buy things they can't afford, to please people they don't love, in an effort to cover up their own feelings of inadequacy. The difference is, however, that when a *would-be psychic* or *healer* does their thing, they're messing with people's lives and energies and with Divine Purpose, and almost always, they exacerbate rather than improve any ailment.

The fakes are every bit as responsible for making a mockery of mystic healing as they are for creating additional negative stigma and ideals of evil associated with mysticism. What these fakes have in common with people who subscribe to consumerism as a cover-up for their feelings of inadequacy is that they want to assume a title that must be worked for and cannot be purchased at any price. They want the same glory as an Olympic gold-medallist, or a prize-winning anthropologist, or a mother of well-behaved children who actually spends time with her kids, but they're not willing to work for it. It's comparable to buying trendy underwear and expecting it to turn your body into the athletic body pictured on the box.

Abilities of divination and healing are sacred gifts. They hold great power, require great responsibility, and involve immense discipline. They need to be protected, respected, and wielded responsibly, and they need to be nourished with discipline of the self; mentally, physically, and spiritually. Those who wield such powers don't take them lightly, and they definitely don't boast about them. In ancient times, not only would anybody not fake being an intuitive because it was disrespectful, but rarely did anybody want the responsibilities associated with such power. In current times it might not always be obvious who holds such powers, but where there's any hint of indiscipline in their lives, it's very clear who does not. Incidentally, the *real* reason that a *real* psychic would never mess with the lottery is because they see more than do most people, including the real costs of manipulating monetary energy, and they know the meaning of *real* riches. That's the real reason we've never heard of a psychic winning the lottery.

Other reasons why these practices are seen as evil is because the people who wanted power in the past manipulated others to believe that the powers that psychics held was evil. North American Native Indians, for example, were known for their powers. So powerful were the Natives in fact that they could, and still do, control even the weather, and as a result, they were made out as demons or missionaries of the devil. Yet what they did was not miraculous and required no spells. All they did was acknowledge rain and gave gratitude for rain. They simply thought, spoke, felt and believed rain, and so the rain came. Natives did and still do use their "mystic" abilities to manifest change in their lives with everything including health and healing, but they do it with a profound understanding of a price which must be paid for shifting universal energy in such a manner. It's an understanding which involves a True sense of commitment, discipline, sacrifice and accountability that those only pretending to be powerful cannot possibly fathom.

Natives should have been, and should be, revered for what they knew and know, but instead, humans, out of ego and greed, and a drive for power and control, chose another road. In the process, they preached that if someone was powerful enough to control the weather, what else could they do, and what force drove that power? This somewhat clarifies why minimal effort has been carried out over the decades to preserve the First Nations and their heritage, but alas, this subject reaches into political boundaries which are not what this chapter is about, so back to the topic at hand...

Without a doubt there is a dark power at work among humanity. A dark power, but not a strong power, and it has control over us not because it is strong but rather because we have allowed ourselves to become weak. This *dark side* of things is fed by ignorance. Our ignorance is fed by our laziness and our convictions about what others incorrectly preach. To overcome this dark side, we need to be silent, be logical, and seek out the real Truths, but we're living like a student taking an exam and cheating by looking over the shoulder of another student who all the while is also cheating off another cheater's work, and so the cycle persists, and nobody is really searching or applying discipline, commitment and *Conscious Affirmative Living*, and the dark side is gaining strength and power over our entire existence.

In keeping with my affirmative intentions for this book, I will not dwell deeply into the *dark side* of things, suffice it to say that the *dark side* exists, and it is in the awakening of humanity and the expansion of our consciousness that this *dark side* will be dissolved. It is also in the dwelling *upon* and *within* all that is affirmative and good and pure that we will remain untouched by said dark side, as any attempt by the dark side to assail light renders dark affirmative.

We're continually reminded of the power that one single candle has to expel darkness, but we must be mindful of just how fragile that single light is; that is must be protected and nourished. It should also be noted that positive thoughts and energy, contrary to what many *new age* books state, are not enough without action, discipline, commitment, faith and accountability. In fact, positive thoughts and energies are not inherently more powerful than negative energies, and as such, we must work harder to create and maintain positive energy in our lives. As sure as it takes just one negative person to disrupt an entire party, even a million candles will get blown out by one gust of wind. A perfect illustration of negative's power over positive's is in how much time it took to build New York's World Trade Centre, and how little time, little effort, and very little intelligence it took to bring it down and instill fear throughout the entire planet.

As for miracles and the hearsay of their actual nonexistence due to proof of how they *logically* happen, what I have come to understand about miracles is, just because it's logical doesn't mean it's not a miracle. Everything is connected, so it stands to reason that if God uses *some* things around us to get things done, he uses *everything* around us. I'm not denying that there are logical explanations behind miracles, I'm just saying that somewhere interlaced between the logic of time, space and reason, God is behind that logic. Sure, one might be able to explain how the taxi which was about to drive forth with the driver oblivious to my presence because he was reading something, suddenly stalled at the exact same moment that I tripped and fell in front of it. I can accept that coincidences are very possible. Anything is! However, these "coincidences" seem to be happening more often these days; to me and to many others around me, which makes me think that either they are happening more frequently, or we are simply becoming more aware of them with the expansion of our consciousness. For the record, I do not subscribe to the concept of coincidence. There really is a reason for everything. The real reason for every little thing however, is not always as profound as we like to think. Sometimes missing a bus means not having to deal with miserable people who'll ruin our day, but at other times it's just a reminder that we need to leave the house earlier.

When it comes to extraterrestrial life, it always overwhelms me that anybody could think that we are the only ones in the entire universe *(it takes a being with an ego the size of a human's to think such a thing)*. Even logically speaking, without hard physical evidence to prove the theory of extraterrestrial life, it seems illogical to think that, in all of the entirety of all of creation, *we're the only ones?*

From what most of us know, the alleged appearance of aliens always seems to happen in what we consider to be less than credible places and to less than credible people. One possible reason for this is that aliens simply don't mix with humans *(and it's very possible they do),* but regardless, aliens are probably not idiots. Maybe aliens appear to people who nobody will believe because they *know* nobody will believe them. And, maybe they can only land their vessels where there's less radio waves interference; for example, places where people have fewer electronics, like in the countryside. Another possible reason for the non-credible witnesses is possibly because the alleged witnesses are drunk or stoned or they're simply lying. Either way, just because we don't have proof doesn't mean we're the only ones around. When you consider the omnipotent entirety of all creation and existence, universally speaking, it seems illogical to consider the notion that it's just "us".

The biggest question I faced with acknowledging aliens was, what's their purpose? There are religions which believe that God is an alien, or that an alien gave birth to God. I am personally sold on the ideal that God created everything, including all the aliens, but then, I've always held God in pretty high regard, and not everybody shares this perspective. That said, when it came to my big ideas, I had to find a big answer to my big question, and of course, when I got tired of thinking about it, I moved on to the task of clipping my fingernails, and it was then that it came to me: Aliens are no different than us!

Aliens are on their search, misunderstanding God in the same manner of which we misunderstand aliens, researching us in order to better understand themselves in the same manner of which we research other species to understand ourselves. It's also completely possible that they actually do understand God but are more advanced and therefore can handle Truths in ways which we're just barely beginning to understand. Truths like why we're here, what comes next, what it takes to truly live for God, and, how exactly *do* they get the caramel into the Caramilk bar?

As previously mentioned, possessing great knowledge does not imply that life will be easier. It means you discover more of what you need to learn. If this is so, then aliens, possessing immeasurably more knowledge than humans, have their work cut out for them, including getting along with other aliens on different missions. Some things are so obvious that they never occur to us, like the fact that we're consciously seeing alien life all around us, every single day! For example, every single species of animal is actually an alien; we've just not been taught that it is such. Every cat, dog, cow, mosquito, bacterium, and yeah, every human, is an alien! We don't recognize them as aliens because they share our same planet, but in the same manner of which we are currently unable to decipher the origins of humans, so do we ignore the fact that all other species originated from some other place as well. We're not impressed by these aliens here on Earth because we see them all the time, but I can assure you that if we were to discover a giraffe on Jupiter, we'd be out of our minds in awe (then we'd go get it, bring it back, kill it, eat it, and pat each other on the back for our *human* feat).

Of course evolution is largely responsible for creating what most species have become over several thousands of millennia, but it's clear that all species did not originate on Earth, and as such, they are all aliens. We also overlook that aliens, whether living on Earth or elsewhere, are not necessarily our same size (much less our same form), so, if we ever do expect to make contact with beings beyond this planet, we must look as much inward as we do outward, and be prepared for something that looks nothing like anything we've ever seen or imagined.

What seems to have been overlooked by even the most seasoned of scientists is that the sum of all the galaxies of which we have come to recognize in *outer space* pales implausibly in comparison to the sum of all galaxies in existence, including those galaxies which exist within the omnipotent realm of *inner space*. While most space-related investigative endeavors have been and are emphasized on researching *outer space*, humanity nonetheless actually has far more to learn from *inner space* research, for therein lies discoveries which could far greater serve humanity at present. The easily, affordably retrievable data from research into *inner space* existence and quantum study, and *aliens*, far more represents humanity's current needs than does that of *outer space*.

The reason that spiritual sages have always said to *look within* is because when looking within, there's more to see, and that's where all the answers reside. I'm not suggesting that we should do away with *outer space* research; there's far too much to learn there as well, but even as a basic lesson from *inner space* research that anybody can understand, one need observe any basic strain of bacteria to recognize our common qualities and afflictions. On one hand, we must learn to work together – and equally – as do most all forms of bacteria, but we must learn to stop feasting upon the host that is this planet which nourishes and sustains us, as does Cancer. This one small lesson is a far greater tutorial for humanity than anything we've ever learned from *outer space* research. As we move deeper within the realms of *inner space*, beyond that which we have come to recognize as *the physical*, it is there that we will make the greatest discoveries about *outer space* and the *hyperphysical* which dwells therein and beyond.

As with humans, all aliens have their purpose and their missions. As for humanity's current state, I have come to recognize that we are not nearly as advanced as we'd like to believe, and that we're actually in fact an ancient and relatively barbaric society, which explains why we do the things we do. Things like lying and being dishonest in any way, shape or form, or constantly dwelling in fear, or being at war, or abusing our own family and friends, and the very fact that we feed on other living animals.

As for animals, I do not believe that animals were made to serve humanity as food, and that there is something inherently wrong about mass-producing living creatures for human consumption. I believe that we're not supposed to ever kill anything, and that animals, if in fact they are supposed to serve us, are supposed to serve us in a manner which helps the ecology, and offers companionship, and helps us get certain jobs done, to name just some tasks. Humans are, however, in the midst of transformational evolution and revolution, and we'll eventually get there. Meanwhile, if we're going to continue to eat animal flesh, we should, at the very least, recognize and care for the animals throughout their lifespan, and take their lives with love, dignity and gratitude.

So, we are what we are, and it's okay, because we actually are progressing – some of us faster than others – but we must nonetheless move on and grow. Otherwise, another species will use us the way we use animals, even if that species is an unidentifiable form of bacteria that kills us off because we were too arrogant to think there was a danger which was far smaller than we could see with a microscope, and far more cooperative with each other than we humans were ever willing to consider being with each other.

As for aliens, I do believe that people see flying saucers and other *space* craft, but I also believe that we're actually *surrounded* on a day to day basis by extraterrestrial life forms, and for various reasons. For example, in the same way a spiritual entity may be with us to carry out God's work, or because they cannot accept that it's time to move into the light, extraterrestrial beings have various motives for being with us as well. Some may be researching our progress in order to figure out our apparent ancient ways of doing certain things, while others are playing the role of guides, ensuring our universal purpose and leading us to a certain place or time, perhaps protecting us or ensuring we meet a destiny which guarantees our growth. There may even be the odd alien who thinks we'd go well with a Pepsi and fries, but I sincerely believe that aliens are a bit more civilized than that, or at the very least, if they were going to eat us, they'd prefer a Coke. All kidding and colas aside, I believe they are here and that they simply vibrate at a vastly rapid frequency. Sometimes we see their traveling device, and sometimes we see something else and only think it's their device. Either way, when we're ready to acknowledge them completely, they will let us know. We can, however, speed up the process by thinking past our limited thoughts

Limited thought doesn't only apply to mediocre minds. In fact, no one's impervious. This is just one of the many downfalls *(or perks, depending on your perspective)* of being imperfect. At the time of writing this, renowned scientist Stephen Hawking was reported to have suggested that it might not be good for aliens to mix with humans. He compared the concept of aliens discovering Earth to Columbus' discovering the Americas, and the resulting detriments it meant to Native Americans. I so admire Hawking's brilliance. In fact, he's one of the few people who can provoke from within me a true sense of envy. That said, I don't agree with his statement, because for one, to compare alien-consciousness to that of Christopher Columbus *(who couldn't find North with a compass)* is like comparing the consciousness of Steven Hawking to that of a typical monkey. And two, this kind of conclusion is what one arrives at when one considers the *immediate obvious.* Even mediocre minds have considered that aliens might be bad for us, so where is the brilliance behind this thought? Yes, Columbus thought within the realm of affirmative possibility – at least where his passion for sailing was concerned – but he landed in America only by accident, and his capturing of humans for sale into slavery only underscores his narrow level of consciousness. I believe that aliens have been aware of us for some time, and that in the same manner of which we understand the importance of honeybees to our existence, aliens understand how important humans are to the delicate balance of the universe, and how important it is to not upset that balance.

If aliens don't exist, then it means that we're all we have, and we should start taking care of each other. If aliens do exist, it's pretty clear that before we can get along with them, we need to learn to get along with each other. Although I do believe *they're out there*, as well as *in here*, I feel that governments are going about it the wrong way, because the real technology required to make contact is nestled between our ears and requires no computer assistance, regardless of how advanced our current technology may seem to us. I also have a strong feeling we've got to learn to get along with our own kind in our own world before we can discover them and their world. Here I'll resort to the term *"Occam's Razor"; all things being equal, the simplest explanation tends to be the right one (attributed to 14th century theologian William of Ockham)*: If we see the way we treat each other, treat our planet, treat animals, treat ourselves, it stands to reason that if aliens exist, they also see what we're doing, and I don't know about you, but if I became aware of a seemingly psychotic group of barbaric one-dimensional thinking, approval-addicted, glorified Neanderthals who rape their land and their people and have such immense contempt for life, I don't think I'd be too keen on making myself known, or inviting them to dinner, lest I be the main course!

Now, going back to psychics. You might now be wondering if you need a psychic, and my answer is; if you're dwelling in faith, you don't need a psychic. If you've got problems, it's highly probable that your problems are the result of your own compromised thoughts, feelings and actions coupled with a lack of commitment, honesty, discipline and faith. If you find yourself offended by this statement, it's a strong indication that it's likely applicable. If this is the case, then there's nothing a true psychic will tell you that you'll actually want to hear; about you or about what you have to do to change things. If, on the other hand, you've reached a point of complete consciousness in thought, feeling and action, and you're exercising commitment, honesty, discipline and faith, then you're able to tap into the realm of *affirmative consciousness* known as *psychic power*, and it will guide you through to the next step with what you need to know now in order to change things. This is because *you are* psychic. Nobody is born without this gift. Yes, some people are more advanced with their abilities than others, and some are meant to apply their abilities in a vocational capacity, but the fact remains that all people are psychic. This omnipotent realm of consciousness is open to all of us, at all times. One must simply choose to enter into it.

True vocational or professional psychics, clairvoyants, mediums, sages, or whatever term you use, are not in the business of fortune-telling. Their gift is about offering guidance and wisdom. It's not up to them what's to come into your life; it is up to you, as is the decision of whether or not to dwell in commitment, honesty, discipline and faith, and to take the actions required to turn your imagined fortune into actuality. In short, there's always work to do in order to achieve wealth, health, abundance, glory, ideal relationships and peace of mind, and nobody needs a psychic to tell us this, because it's no secret. There is always a price to pay, and there's always work to do!

So, why am I an authority on the subject? Well, it's like this: That realm of *affirmative consciousness* is from where I extract the *energetic Truths* of which I write at the introduction of this book, and throughout these pages, and which I arrived at by *subscribing to* integrity while *applying* integrity. It is a place to where I have reached time and again, and from where I have fallen time and again. Like anything, however, there's always something to learn, and it's an ongoing balancing act. Admittedly, it's a place that requires the kind of integrity which is often challenging to maintain moment-to-moment, but this Divine endeavor is well worth the human stumbles and setbacks, and I have seen, and I recognize, that it remains a worthwhile journey, now and forever...

CHAPTER XIII

=Relationships=

A journey of *self*...

The topic of relationships is vast beyond measure, and as such, rather than attempting to cover all aspects of relationships, this chapter serves more as an introduction to healing, attracting and maintaining healthy relationships than as a *one size fits all* solution to every relationship issue. I say *introduction* because the only way to truly understand the complexity of relationships is through personal, practical experience. Some of these ideals are practical, some are unorthodox, but all are logical. As such, I'd like to begin by first sharing some very basic, logical facts about relationships. These are truths that, once recognized, have the potential to bring any and all relationships into clearer perspective, and heal us – each and all of us.

Perhaps the most basic yet most overlooked truth about relationships is that the most important relationship we'll ever have is the relationship we have with our *self*. The relationship we have with our self is the basis upon which all our relationships are built. It is the blueprint for all our relationships and how we *relate* to anything and anyone.

Whereas our best relationships are indicative of the healthier aspects of our blueprint, our worst relationships are indicative of where our blueprint is compromised. For any relationship to be healed, or be created, one must first recognize that insofar as a relationship – like life – is a process, it is also a structure. As such, the structure of a relationship, like a chain or a machine, is only as strong as its weakest component. Usually the weakest component of any relationship can be linked to its foundation; generally where the relationship begins, and the motives behind the relationship.

Lack of attention to the foundation of any new relationship clearly explains why many relationships, romantic or otherwise, don't work out. On an intimate level, people are often attracted to somebody not so much for whom the other person is, but for what they represent; financial standing, physical appearance, even fashion orientation. This can be detrimental to the basic structure of the relationship, as well as the mental and physical wellbeing of all involved, especially if one's attraction to another has to do with negative attachments to old patterns. Regardless of one's motives, moving around relationships is the greatest task humans will ever encounter, because we are in a relationship with every person who lives and breathes. How we relate to anybody, whether we share their city or we share their bed, tells us about our own relationship with our *self*.

When it comes to difficult relationships, it's not always the outcome, but how we respond to and feel about the outcome that tells the story about those involved. What people must recognize is that *all relationships* are salvageable. Relationships in turmoil, however, can only be salvaged if all parties involved are willing to do their part.

Yes, it might be advisable to stay away from certain people; sometimes living in harmony means having our own space, but, living apart in animosity, and living apart in harmony, carry completely different significances.

Throughout this book, the idea of the law of attraction comes up time and again. It wasn't planned this way, however, in all my research on all aspects of life, I have yet to discover any aspect of the human experience where the law of attraction doesn't play a role, for better or for worse. In the same manner of which we attract experiences, so is it that we attract relationships. In the same manner that where we are now is the largely the result of past thoughts, feelings, words and actions, so is it that our relationships are largely the result of the same. This is why it is important to recognize and master our own thoughts and feelings surrounding other individuals, and why forgiveness must be at the forefront of stressed and compromised relationships. Extending forgiveness is the best way to avoid attracting more of the same kind of negative people and relationships into our lives, but, because nobody is perfect and we all hurt somebody at some point along the way, it's also the best way to attract forgiveness, understanding and compassion when we fall out of line in spite of our intention to love others.

Like electricity, universal law is unbiased when sending back to us what we send out. What we give to each other, we give to the universe, and it always comes back, and when it does, it's guaranteed to be multiplied. This is great knowledge for those who have attachments to ideals of revenge or taking justice into their own hands, for nothing brings justice to the unjust better than universal law. Sure, it can be argued that some people spend their lives bringing misery to others, and then they die without seeing justice, but the fact remains: *It doesn't end here!* Life extends well beyond our physical experience, and what we don't accomplish here on Earth becomes homework. So don't worry about those who are not nice to you; they'll get there's eventually no matter what. Meanwhile, you just continue to be nice, and be forgiving, and spread your kindness wherever you go!

As a side note, most of us have heard it said that no one can make you feel bad without your permission. This, however, is pure giraffe-poop! We are human and we are all connected. Although we may be able to choose not to dwell on the misery someone dealt us, we'd be disconnected if we were entirely unaffected. In other words, when someone makes you feel bad, there's nothing wrong with you and it's not necessarily your fault that they may have succeeded in sharing their misery. The true fault lies with the one who served up their misery. That fault, however, can only be shared by you if you *choose* to dwell on it. Attitudes are energy in motion, and energy is contagious. The more conscious a person you are, the more likely you are to be affected by this energy. Conversely, the more conscious a person you become, the more adept you will be at not dwelling on it. In this ideal lies the realization that you are as susceptible to the effects of a bad attitude as you are susceptible to a common cold virus within your environment. So, although it is highly unlikely that you will never be completely unaffected by someone's bad attitude, you have the power to defuse it and not dwell on it, and to move on.

As for healing, attracting and maintaining relationships, we must recognize and accept that we cannot create healthy relationships while in a state of disharmony, hate, anger, jealousy, animosity, fear and war. As everything begins with a thought, so do our relationships, and each time we approach a new relationship, or look to heal or rekindle an old one, we must look at the thoughts which surround those first steps towards our endeavor. By considering the thoughts which are the creative force behind our relationships, we again must consider the process of how our thoughts lead to ideas, which in turn lead to decisions, which then lead to actions, which lead to consequences, which lead to circumstances, which lead to the state of mind that ultimately creates the thoughts which drive our continuous cycle of creation. As previously mentioned, everything is created from thought, and every thought comes from one of two places: *Love or fear.*

So, what is love? Well, I'm definitely not the first to attempt to answer that question, and I most definitely won't be the last, but in my search, this is what I have come to understand:

Love is a Divine state of consciousness in action.

Contrary to popular belief, love is not an emotion. Emotion is the messenger; not the message. Emotion broadcasts our state of mind to our awareness. Perhaps the best way to describe emotion is to imagine a peaceful crowd of people sitting quietly, patiently waiting for a ball game to start. Suddenly, the game begins, the star batter from the home team hits a home run and the crowd goes wild. The mass reaction is a *disturbance* which indicates the crowd's state of mind. A disturbance in itself is not good or bad; it's merely a message. In this case, the disturbance indicates an affirmative state of mind. When we understand love as a *Divine state of mind in action*, we are then better equipped to comprehend that love is not attachment – emotionally or otherwise – but quite the opposite. When we apply this concept of love to ourselves first and foremost, we are then suitably equipped to love others accordingly.

Perhaps the most important message I can share regarding improving our personal and planetary relationships is to suggest that the answer to healthy relationships is the same answer to everything else: *Education*. Any time we recognize ignorance as the barrier which keeps us from our goal, the first thing we're confronted with is the fact that we don't know what we don't know. If we don't know what we don't know, then how do we *learn* what we don't know? Often the awareness of what we must endure in order to overcome our ignorance is our single motive for remaining ignorant. We can learn through communication, meaningful reading and the conversing of ideas, but the burden of overcoming our ignorance would be greatly reduced if we were to first overcome our arrogance. By arrogance, I mean living with the perspective that we already know everything, or that we're always right, or that we've never – or don't have the capacity to – hurt others.

A staggering problem with our arrogance isn't our lack of communication, but rather, our *mis*communication, both taken and given. Considering how archaically ancient humanity is at present, the technology surrounding our communication capabilities is overwhelmingly advanced, yet, like the cobblers children who walk about shoeless, our current communication process is no match for our capability, and as such, with so many forms of communication at our disposal, we're not communicating, and our communication skills are not at a standstill, but rather, sliding back at an alarming rate.

A large fraction – perhaps the largest fraction – of what goes on between married couples has much to do with miscommunication, but also to do with overlooking our basic nature. If we don't understand our nature, how can we understand what and why we're communicating to each other? And, how can we discover our inherent nature or communicate or innate needs when we're all glued to our telephones, computers and televisions? I want to get onto the subject of basic human nature where it applies to relationships, but before I do, I want to make a few basic and easy to understand points about communication.

Indisputably, the fundamental distinguishing attribute of communication is honesty. Without honesty, there's miscommunication. Where there's miscommunication, there's disharmony. When it comes to getting the answers to what plagues our relationships, the process is clear: To get the right answers, we must ask the right questions. To know the right questions, we must get to the root of the problem. We get to the root of the problem by *being honest*.

To repair and improve relationships with others, we must first repair and improve our relationship with our *self*. This starts by being *honest* with our *self* – without making excuses, without hiding a single truth about our authenticity, and especially without ever placing the need for approval – from anybody – at the forefront of what or who we are, or what or who we or anybody else erroneously thinks we should be. This equates to perfect self acceptance. This is the only way to be harmonious in any relationship. This is the only way to be authentically accepted and authentically loved by others who authentically accept and love their *self*. There is no other way to attain true authentic harmony in any relationship, and there is no quick fix. The *healing* is truly in *doing* and in *being*.

Acceptance of the self means that honesty dwells at the forefront of every relationship one has, including – and most importantly – the relationship with the *self*. Where there is honesty with the authentic *self*, there is true freedom to *be*. Anyone who denies, or attempts to deny, or attempts to get you to deny your authentic *self*, is absolutely denying their authentic *self* – no exceptions. In fact, that's the first sign that somebody is denying their own authentic self; they try to get others to deny themselves – through judgment, through oppression, through hypocrisy, through guilt, through manipulation and so forth.

In a love relationship, two people don't need to be perfectly aware of their authentic self; often the realization and acceptance of the self comes to life *because* of intimate love relationships. However, in order for a relationship to grow and prosper, and for all parties involved to feel free to *be* who they truly are *in essence*, all parties must be willing to learn who and what they are, accept it, communicate it, and encourage the other to do the same, without conditions or shame, and with total respect for the individual journey of the other party while walking together.

Any untruths, drama or secrets willingly dwelt within by either party – individually or as a unit – will destroy any sense of liberty for either. This is because untruths, drama and secrets are killers, and as certain as these negative factors make one person sick, so is it that they make all parties of a relationship sick, because these negative factors are what ultimately make, and keep, any relationship sick. That's their job! Untruths, drama and secrets are meant for entertainment purposes; they belong on a stage and on TV and on the big screen, but have no place in our relationships. Individuals attached to untruths, drama and secrets are utterly entertained by such practices and their resulting consequences, and these individuals are in the deplorable, non-paying, oversaturated business of making people, relationships, and our entire planet, sick. These are the people who don't accept their own authentic *self.*

Beyond self acceptance, our relationships are frequently affected by issues outside of our relationships, but there is great power in understanding the difference between our life *circumstances* and our life *experiences.* The process of performing exercises that will assist in the healing of all your relationships can either be a tormenting task, or it can be an intimate journey in your own heart and mind. Our experiences and the way we feel in our day to day life don't have to be dictated by what goes on in our day. Where someone might allow their entire day to be ruined by a challenging situation, another person will choose to let it go, thereby remaining open to all the good things the day has in store for them.

In the same manner that some consider a dental visit to be terrifying, others see it as a moment to lie back and relax. This all comes down to *perspective.* When you make the decision to change your perspective of any situation on the basis that your whole life experience depends on it – *and that your best life lies just beyond that situation* – the entire process can mean the difference between a mere *tough moment* and a perpetually miserable existence. It truly helps things when you can differentiate a life circumstance from a life experience, because you don't let the circumstance dictate other aspects of your life or taint all the good experiences. Sure, you may owe back-taxes, or be getting a divorce, or be slated for chemotherapy tomorrow morning, but that doesn't stop you from being in the glorious *here and now*, unless you allow it to. Even if you've got a long day ahead of you tomorrow, you can still drop to your knees and eat a Popsicle with your kid while you play with Lego or dolls together. In fact, doing just that kind of thing tonight may be just what you need to get you through your day tomorrow.

Beyond outside challenges, when it comes to healing relationships, communication is the first step, so be honest and be accountable. If you suspect or want to know something regarding your relationships, ask the necessary questions. If you're afraid of what the answer might be, ask anyway and deal with the truth rather than lingering in the illusion of harmonic bliss that is your ignorance. If you weren't honest about something, ask yourself why you weren't honest. For those who believe in the power of prayer; pray, but don't just leave it up to God; pray and take action.

Since nobody is perfect, many of us are at some point the culprit or the *bad guy* in the relationship. When this happens, it's important to forgive ourselves and our past mistakes. In the same manner that we need to forgive those who cannot love (some people are simply too hurt to love), we must forgive ourselves for not allowing ourselves to love, or for not allowing love into our lives. If you discover that you are too hurt to love, get help, otherwise find a way to deal with your issues, because your lack of love is hurting people, and it's hurting you. Acknowledge where your relationships are, the good ones and the bad ones. Acknowledge the actions and attitudes you carried out in order to create those relationships. Look at what you can and will commit to doing to create better relationships. Decide what changes to make, and make a commitment to those changes, and get professional help if necessary. For those who don't like the sound of that last suggestion: *Put your pride away.*

Relationships and finances have so much in common that they're actually far more connected than we usually imagine. For example, everything we do that affects the wellbeing of our finances will also affect the wellbeing of our relationships. For this reason, it's important to break bad habits. Eliminate addictions like smoking, drinking, gambling and unnecessary spending. Addictions and bad habits are the first sign that your relationship with your *self* is in crisis, and when you're in crisis with your *self*, you're in crisis with the world.

State your intention and intend your statement *(say what you mean, mean what you say)*. Each time you tell your spouse or child or anyone else how much you love them, do your actions reflect your words? Are your boundaries firmly set? Have you made and do you make your boundaries clear to others; not only through words but through actions? Nothing makes your boundaries clearer to others than the practice of showing that *your own word means business* when it comes to your own boundaries. Also, when you say *I love you*, are you just expressing your attachment, or are there actions surrounding those words?

Moving on to other aspects of our relationship with the *self*, it has been my observation that there is no better evidence of how a person feels about themselves than by how they treat their body, and as such, there is no better evidence of how someone treats their body than by the general overall appearance of their body. A person who abuses or neglects their body will ultimately abuse or neglect their relationships on some level. I'm not suggesting that people with perfectly sculpted bodies don't have relationship issues; a sculpted body can reveal an obsessively insecure individual who feels worthless inside, and in the same manner which nothing is ever good enough with what they see in the mirror, the same usually applies to the way they feel about everyone around them. Nonetheless, insofar as it's inaccurate to judge a person's level of goodness by their physical appearance, I've personally yet to meet any individual who treated their body in any manner which is not in harmony with the way they feel about themselves. If they love and approve of themselves, they feed and care for their body temple, and it shows.

Changing the way we feel about our body and our *self* doesn't happen overnight, and we shouldn't expect it to. Any change for the better is actually a dramatic change, and to move along at a pace that is overconfident can be as traumatizing to the body as it is to the mind. The key to change is to start making changes we can handle and take on commitments we can fulfill. Whether bettering our *self* means dieting or better parenting or being more patient with others, it's also ideal to spend time with individuals who have the same mentality, or better yet, who live healthier lifestyles than ours. What better way to pick up healthy new habits?

A healthy relationship with the self implies a healthy relationship with the mind, and what we feed our mind is just as important as what we feed our body. Affirmative books which encourage, challenge and/or comfort you during your changes are ideal. And, unless it's filled with truly affirmative information about your goals, *forget about magazines!* If you absolutely must read magazines, be strongly selective about what you believe, especially where advertisements are concerned. Most advertisements are designed to remind you that you are inadequate without their product or service, and, preying on our alleged inadequacies is how those advertisers survive.

Whether looking for friends, colleagues or a new love-interest, settling for less than what's truly important to you in other people is the same as settling for less in any other area of your life. Remember: *When you settle for less, you'll get less than what you settled for.* When it comes to actively looking for an ideal mate, set your goal and expect – and accept – only your intended outcome, or better! When it comes to seeking out an intimate relationship, it's entirely okay to be on the lookout. It's absolutely natural to want to be with someone, and it's in our nature to be on *the hunt* and to want to mate. Anyone who tells you otherwise is denying their basic human nature and is trying to deny you yours. The key to harmonious *hunting*, however, comes down to honest communication. Everyone's into different things, and guaranteed, whatever you are into – as vanilla or as flavorfully warped as it may be – there's someone else out there who's into the same things as you are and is looking to be *hunted.* You just have to send out the honest message, and stop hiding your *self.*

My strongest suggestion in the realm of intimate love relationships – beyond honest communication – is to not begin a relationship unless you are in love. Yes it's normal to date and see if things can develop, but pursuing a relationship because it *seems ideal,* or because you're lonely, or because *they're* in love with you, or because someone's made you feel guilty or obligated, or *(UGH!)* because you're biological clock is ticking, will ultimately lead to disaster, or at the very least, lead to an unhappy, unfulfilled existence. A true love relationship is rarely ever easy, but it's worth all the work. Any relationship lacking in true love just becomes a job, and rarely ever a happy job.

Interestingly enough, the thing we desire of intimate relationships is to make a connection with another person, but as much as we've retained our natural instinctual desire for intimacy, we still can't seem to bring uninhibited honesty into the equation. At a time where honesty should be king, we're all *consciously* being dishonest and leading ourselves and others on. It would be one thing if the game was part of our nature, but the games we play in relationships are largely based on fear rather than on real needs according to our basic human nature. Again, we're dishonest with others in relationships because we're dishonest with ourselves, but it's not necessarily always intentional, or even conscious. Intentional or otherwise, however, lack of honesty with our *self* ultimately leads to unfulfilling intimate relationships, if for no other reason than for the relationship's lack of true intimacy.

CHAPTER XIV

=Marriage=

A truly defining relationship...

Some may find it perplexing that I opted to separate the chapter on marriage from the chapter on relationships, however, in light of how complex both subjects have become despite their intricate simplicities, I truly felt they each merited their own undivided attention. This even with the realization that marriage is not only a relationship, but in all actuality, an *ultimate defining* relationship.

Regardless if you choose to label marriage as a *union* or *institution*, marriage is quite fundamentally, before anything else, a relationship. Now, I'm not talking about marriage in the legal and allegedly ethical mumbo-jumbo standards under which the essentially beautiful truth of marriage has been crushed, crippled and raped, yet remains miraculously still barely alive and breathing. I'm talking about the relationship aspect of it. The "truth" at the very essence of the union. That vital *life source* that is meant to unite souls who love each other in a divine and miraculous way.

Although it's also a lot more than a mere relationship, marriage is clearly beyond anything as measureable as an institution. As with any profound relationship, marriage is ultimately about love and commitment, and it's as ridiculous to assume that anyone has the right to tell us whom we can or cannot marry as it is ridiculous to tell us whom we can or cannot love. Love is Love. We cannot choose being in love anymore than we can choose to escape it. We can only choose to *experience* it, or *deny* it. When love happens, nobody except for those involved should have the right to prevent any form of celebration in its honor.

In regards to same-gender marriage, we've all heard questions like, *"Where does it stop?"* and, *"If a man can marry a man, what's to stop him from marrying a goat/dog/guitar/giraffe?"* The answer is simply that it stops with the human race. Marriage is about consenting adults who willingly choose to profess and pledge their love to each other and commit to a union, either before God, witnesses and friends and family, or alone on a beach somewhere, or at any other place they feel is right to celebrate their union. They should be as free to choose the how, the when and the where, just as they should be free to choose the whom.

As for those with religious viewpoints about what marriage is, it's probably a good time to point out that marriage and the concept of *coupling* existed long before religion was even a notion. The concept even exists among the animal kingdom. Furthermore, natural things like falling in love and sexual orientation are not something we choose, whereas religion *is* something we choose, along with everything many religions imply; judgment, hatred, oppression, limitation, etc. Religion aside, just because some folks might use what is right to do what isn't right, is that a reason to not allow what *is* right?

Many *straight* people get married for financial or political reasons, or out of guilt or fear or denial, and they do this while professing *love* and *God* as the foundation of their union, and this has been for centuries the accepted norm; accepted by those who claim that same-gender marriages somehow corrupt the institution of marriage. In light of this ongoing insult to the institution of marriage, to God, and to all of humanity, it is clear that the face of marriage is changing, but if religion insists on preserving the sanctity of marriage which includes traditional aspects of love and commitment, then why not open the doors to those who are marrying for just those exact reasons; love and commitment? So a dude wants to marry a dude and a dame wants to marry a dame; what's the big deal? If they are going to hell, what does it have to do with you? I've never cared about what my neighbors do with each other in their own bedroom; it's none of anybody else's business but their own. If what they are doing to and with each other is wrong, God will deal with them. If we have time to judge anybody under any circumstances, then it's clear that we're not loving hard enough!

To limit marriage to the idea of a mere institution is to limit what marriage is about; love, respect, commitment, to name only a few factors. When marriage is viewed as an institution, it becomes the rules, limitations and ideals that are the institution; something reminiscent of a prison. These limiting ideals about marriage are just as supported by those who oppose or are *offended* by the notion of marriage (as if the notion of marriage being offensive isn't absurd enough), and therefore the inaccurate ideals which have become reasons for *not* getting married are just as damaging to humanity as the fanatical ideas surrounding the radical reasons why we *should* be married. At the rate we're going, everybody's going to get fed up with marriage altogether, and a once beautiful concept celebrating a union of souls will be nothing more than an all-vanishing memory.

The ideal of marriage as per how we perceive it in most countries limits the concept to the union of two souls, but this concept is not shared by nations which permit multiple spouses. For many religions, the ideal of having more than one wife is blasphemous, and to those who look beyond religious convictions, its puzzling how such a marriage could work – *How can a man love more than one woman?* I've personally never considered marrying more than one person, but not because I feel it's wrong; it's just never occurred to me. I do believe, however, that a woman or a man can intimately love more than one partner. I actually believe we're designed to do so; it's called unconditional love. If a father can love all his children individually yet equally, or love his parents as such, why would the concept of *multiplied loving* be limited to remain outside of marriage, especially since it's very clear that humans are not inherently a monogamous species?

What's foreign to some is normal to others, and *our* marriage ideals might seem silly or psychotic to *theirs*. While some cultures feel that all the good guys are taken, other cultures figure, *"Why fight over a really great man when you can just share him?"* Perhaps the latter concept is a natural process which ensures that every woman who wants to be married to a good, hardworking man and have kids can do so in spite of the fact that there are more women than men on the planet, and of those men, some aren't into marriage, and some aren't into women, and this provides a way for everybody to get what they want.

Like with all things, marriage is about perspective and education, but we must keep in mind that how we see things and what we're taught are not necessarily Truths. How we see things – *our perspective* – is typically by choice, and these choices are based on our comfort zone, and our comfort zone is habitually dictated – or molded – by those who've taught us what we know, and by society; an assembly of unconscious lemmings being held back by their own refusal to relinquish obsolete thought, and by their own acceptance to live by, and thereby support, the disastrous oppressive untruths which impede the progression and freedoms of all humanity. Silly lemmings!

As a whole society, we're still struggling with the ideal of maintaining *traditional marriage*; something between a man and a woman. These limitations are usually set by religious addicts, and by political activists trying to please those addicts, and by closeted homosexuals doing their darndest to hide their true authentic self *(all three of which are typically the same person)*. My question is, since most of us aren't religious addicts, why are we all subscribing to these limitations?

It's interesting that the same people who our society gives the right to the freedoms of their religious beliefs and limitations are the same people who are robbing everyone else of their right to be free, even in their own bedrooms. If we're to maintain all past traditional values, where do we draw the line? Do we return to putting women back in the home, making it so that they're not equal to the husband but rather his property? Should we revoke women's right to vote or teach while we're at it? If so, should we go as far as forcing all people to practice the same religion, place blacks at the back of the bus, and revive Hitler's cause? How far do we go? What are the boundaries, who's right, who's wrong and who's in charge? Fortunately, we usually do evolve, and there's a reason we don't go back. It's called progress. Our progress with most things is painfully slow, but we're progressing nonetheless. Changing our perspective about what we *assume* is right or wrong along with communicating honestly are all pivotal factors in accelerating affirmative change among humanity.

If we truly desire to preserve the sanctity of marriage, perhaps we should start by making it illegal to get a divorce. Perhaps we should hold people accountable under strict laws and severe penalties for breaking the sacred vows they took to honor each other, and the promises they made in writing, before God. It seems to me that keeping a promise to God, in writing, on official government documents, in the presence of friends, family and legal witnesses would be important to God, whereas offensive to God would be preventing others who have the capacity to keep promises to God from making those promises.

Much of the idea that a man can only marry a woman stems from the idea that men and women were made to procreate. Although our bodies are in fact designed to come together and multiply, the fact remains that it's the destiny of many people to procreate, and it's also the destiny of many people to do otherwise, even if the parts are there. Most of us are born with arms and legs and have an ability to dance, but we're not all inspired to dance, and many of us who are inspired are much better suited to other forms of movement, whether it be swimming, running, sewing, or sitting on our blessed fannies and painting pictures or writing poetry. I realize that it is written in countless places that marriage is between a man and a woman, but whatever has been written anywhere was written out of *perspective*; much of it limited. It's time to broaden our perspective.

Should society impose upon all its citizens to aspire to become Olympic swimmers because other humans are gold medallists? Of course not; because it would be ridiculous to place everyone in one same category. It is as ridiculous a notion to do such a thing as it would be ridiculous to terminate the life of any woman who is unable or unwilling to bear a child. We all have our missions in life based on what God has handed us, and when the sacred call to intimately love someone graces our lives, nobody has the right to stop us from answering that call or deny us that gift. This is a human right!

God knows what he's doing, and when we completely surrender our trust to God's *divine purpose*, we understand that there is a master plan, and we best participate in that plan when we approach everything with Love, including the things we don't understand. We best serve divine purpose when we love others and allow others to freely express their love to those willing to receive it. It's truly unfortunate that marriage is not as popular as it once was, and that so many are offended by the sacred divinity of marriage – although I do feel that most people are less offended by the idea of marriage than they are by the idea of commitment. Still, people should have the right to marry, or not marry, according to what they feel works in their lives. Once society – all religions and government especially – stops spending precious time, energy and money enforcing laws which prohibit nuptials among those inspired to unite themselves before God, we can get on to other more important things like uniting couples with the millions of orphaned, sick, dying, homeless children worldwide so that every kid knows what it's like to have a family.

It pains me to think of how many same-sex couples there are in the world that would make excellent parents and could provide loving homes for orphaned or homeless children, yet society isn't opening its eyes to discover an excellent solution to a horrific reality. Millions of children worldwide are orphaned and/or homeless; fatally succumbing to the daily tragedies of ill health, abuse, neglect and unimaginable forms of exploitation, on all continents including North America. On one hand, it can be argued that children might not feel completely comfortable being raised by parents of the same gender, but, being raised by even mediocre adoptive same-sex parents who provide only the basic essentials is considerably more favorable than spending an entire childhood without bedtime stories, hugs, encouraging words, boundaries, discipline, food, water, medical attention and education (note: adoptive parents are rarely ever *mediocre parents*). Denying same-sex couples the basic human rights to which they are wholeheartedly entitled is denying humanity its rights, and preventing adoptive parenting is just the tip of the colossal iceberg that is the evil which society nourishes at the price of precious life. While much of what holds human progress back has to do with religious reasoning, no scripture clarifies the validity of gay marriage better than *John 8:17; The testimony of two men is valid.*

Marriage between gays is not only important for the good that it can accomplish for others, but also for the advancement and progress of gays themselves. Once society gets to the point where homosexuality is no longer an issue, children who grow up to discover their sexuality to be out of *the norm* won't have to hide it, won't commit suicide over it, won't spend a lifetime pretending to be something they're not, and especially won't have to turn to the gay community for guidance. Admittedly, the gay community provides immense support and guidance for gay teens and young adults, and is largely responsible for building up the self-esteem of otherwise distraught and destroyed gay youth; something that is completely the responsibility of the parents. This support, guidance and understanding of something as personal and intimate as one's sexuality, however, should be accessible at home, among family; not among strangers, and definitely not among communities which emphasize sexual promiscuity, as this merely creates more confusion to a developing, impressionable, fertile adolescent mind. In short, parents who discover their children to be gay should not concern themselves with attempting to *straighten* their children out, but rather, direct them to respect themselves and seek to be good people and make good choices.

Gay, straight, bi or otherwise, when it comes to searching for the ideal mate, we often get so wrapped up in the current dating fads that we either overlook, or have no energy for, the normal things we should be doing. As such, I've included some helpful ideas here. If you are single, these ideas may be of some assistance. If you know of someone who could use some advice, please pass it on.

Some major relationship tools I am about to suggest have been overlooked by most singles because they're seemingly inconsequential, but in actuality, they work! What's great about what follows is that much of this advice can be applied to every relationship we have, including our relationships with our siblings, our children, our parents, our in-laws, our neighbors, and especially and most importantly, our *self*...

Ignore everybody

Forget what anybody says about who you're attracted to. Your attraction is your business, and anybody who ridicules who you're attracted to is not your friend. Go for who you want in life, especially when it comes to Love. (This is applicable to non-dependant-based relationships; if it's an addiction, it's not healthy. If you're into kids; please get counseling.)

Make it fun from the start

Get involved in activities you love, especially on a first date. Nobody's more attractive than when they're experiencing joy and expressing passion for what interests them most. If you want to get to know somebody, forget going for a coffee and find out what they love to do and set it up. This works well for new friends, too, and at the very least, if the dude or dame is a dud, you've had a good time.

Go virtual

Online dating works beautifully, but only where complete honesty comes into play. I know of several people who have met through Internet sites and singles ads, and along with being honest and being themselves, they also credit their success to participating in an activity rather than just going for coffee or a meal. Honesty is so important here because people are online for many different reasons, and your honesty will play a huge role in whom you contact online and whom you allow to contact you, thereby drastically improving your chances of finding what you desire.

Make a wish list

This suggestion comes up in just about every relationship book, video, talk, seminar, conference and bathroom wall – um...er...depending on where you pee these days – and although it's such a powerful tool, I am always surprised at singles who don't do it.

Most times people don't do it because they don't know what they truly want and/or cannot commit to an ideal mate, even if it is just in their mind. My rebuttal is always; if you cannot commit in your mind, how will you commit when they show up?

This process is simple:

Write a list of all the qualities you seek in a partner, including both the important and the unimportant qualities you'd like in a mate, then check the items that are most important to you, and never ever compromise on those core essentials. What's interesting about this process is that, everybody I've known who has done this and then met someone reported that, not only were the core essentials there, but in all cases, most or all of the unimportant qualities were there as well.

An important element worth mentioning about the wish list process is the old axiom; *watch what you wish for, you just might get it*. If you want a sensitive man, then don't get miffed when he cries at a movie or doesn't like playing contact sports; sensitivity, like most qualities, is *spherical*, and again, the way someone is with one aspect of their lives tends to be the way they are with most other aspects as well.

Become the person you want to attract

Become the person your ideal mate would want. Let's face it; the man with the hardcore gym-body, active life and bank account that proves he's smart and hardworking probably won't be interested in a brain-dead couch potato with a shopping addiction. If your ideal mate is financially responsible, you may want to get your finances in order, because like-minds attract like-minds. This is not about being rich, it's about having control over your finances rather than the contrary. If you want someone who likes to cook, acquire some top-of-the-line cookware for your kitchen. If you want someone who gardens; start gardening! Often people have their life together but are not confident about their appearance and thus have a hard time imagining that someone else will be interested in their face or body or scars, but not everybody likes the same things. Some guys like skinny girls, others really like the softness of more corpulent women. As for scars, some people love imperfections. Being the person your ideal partner desires includes accepting who you are; scars, bones, fat and whatever else. Many people hope to meet the person who will encourage them to change their ways, but it's in changing our ways that we will draw to us the person we desire.

Compromise but don't sell out

Don't sell out, but also understand what compromise really means. Compromise is a complex issue in relationships, so when looking for the ideal person, although you might like blondes, meeting a bald person is not really a sell-out. Where life quality is concerned, substance-abuse is a sell-out. To simplify, remember; there's a difference between making intelligent concessions *(compromise)* and selling out!

Recognize what already exists

Recognize that the qualities you seek in a partner already exist in your life, in others around you. Imagine for example that you want a smart, funny partner who cooks. Now, look at the people in your life and name one who's the smartest, then name one who's the funniest, then name one who cooks well. When you realize these quailties are in your life, it's easy to imagine what the qualities feel like. On the other hand, if you meet someone who lacks one of these qualities, you can acknowledge that your life is not lacking in that area. I use this example to make the point that no *one person* can or should be everything in our life. This realization makes it easier to deal with someone who isn't everything you'd hoped for. For the record, if you do dwell on the qualities in the people around you, the same qualities are pretty sure to appear in that partner you seek.

Get to know the person

This one gets major neglect. Take all the time you need to get to know someone. A worthy person will give you the time you need. Anyone who rushes you, especially after you've requested time and stated your boundaries, doesn't deserve a moment more of your time. No exceptions! When it comes to sex, the *three-date* rule works like a charm to weed out boundary-crashers. Having a minimum of three dates before sexual intimacy is introduced not only ensures ample time to get to know someone than would one or two brief visits, but it's also a great way to build up healthy anticipation and desire which only fuels sexual energy for those who discover they want to *get it on* after three dates.

Get priorities straight

Priorities go well beyond deciding where to meet dates or what you're going to wear. With relationships, like anything else, your health and wellbeing come first. Without health, you have nothing. Where many people are understandably not willing to give strangers their bank card or house key, somehow, they go into complete stupid-mode when it comes to sexual relations, and sex-now/question-later is the game – without protection, without common sense. I can think of many reasons why people should not participate in casual sex, especially prior to having at least three dates, but I can't think of one reason not to protect oneself if they do participate. When it comes to casual sex, you'll never regret keeping it safe.

Know the secret to keeping your partner happy

Although there's much to be said for not making your partner miserable, it's not your responsibility to keep anybody happy. The quest for happiness is a personal journey. Make yourself happy in your relationship and you'll have done your part. Magazines and books peddle the alleged secrets to making your partner happy, but the truth is, there are no secrets. Just use your brain, your heart, your gut instincts, your intuition, and for the love of all that is good; be honest! Otherwise, dudes, keep the toilet seat down, and ladies, stop asking him what he's thinking about every five seconds – That's it!

Discuss and observe their values

If you don't ask them about their values on the first date, you'll be in for trouble. Also, do their actions speak their values? Most importantly, do *their* values match *yours?*

Observe compatibility

Is the person right for your life? Is this relationship conducive to your goals, and are your goals conducive to a harmonious relationship? Is it enough to have an agnostic partner who respects your religion, or is it vital that they walk in your faith? If you're looking to be a traveling career woman, is it fair to settle down with a man who wants to be married to a homemaker? If he's not interested in children and you dream of it, is this good enough for you, or will you resent him and yourself later? Which is more important? Only honest and open communication will clarify these issues. Compatibility goes well beyond the bedroom and favorite television shows, and even beyond shared values, so look deeper than the obvious.

Don't keep score

Many relationships end over *him* or *her* allegedly not doing their part. Yes, it takes both partners to create the one hundred percent of what a relationship *is*, but what people don't seem to get is, it's not about you giving fifty percent and your partner giving fifty percent; the one hundred percent that is a relationship is created by both partners giving one hundred percent of themselves at all times. It takes two whole hearts to make a relationship work. That way when the occasion arises – and it will – when one partner is unable to give their all, the relationship can be held together by the wholeness of the other partner. And forget about remembering who did more when the other was down. Spend that energy instead on gratitude for *what is*. This is perfectly balanced relationship contribution and distribution.

Know what you're forgiving

Every relationship will go through troubled periods, and when it does, it's not enough to forgive; you must know *what* you're forgiving. For many, the difference between a *mistake* and a *betrayal* is unclear, but understanding the difference will clarify if and why you can forgive and regain the trust of your partner. Forgiveness doesn't imply rekindled trust or immediate healing, and anybody who tells you different needs to further examine the process of forgiveness. I have a friend whose boyfriend accidentally broke her foot by letting a door close too soon as she entered a building. The man felt just terrible about it, and of course she forgave him, but regardless of her forgiveness, the pain was still there and the foot took the time it needed in order to heal. This is a concept we must apply to emotional healing. When it comes to forgiving mistakes, it's sometimes challenging to trust that the person won't make the same mistake again, but our mistrust isn't necessarily in *the person* as much as it is in the person's *competence*. When it comes to betrayal, that's a whole other thing. In the instance of a *mistake*, something is done *unintentionally*, but where *betrayal* is involved, *intention* is the essence of the act. A man might *accidentally* lose his wife's keys or *accidentally* break her favorite vase, but when it comes to infidelity, a man doesn't *accidentally* ogle another woman, *accidentally* kiss her, *accidentally* remove his clothing, *accidentally* penetrate her, and *accidentally* carry on an affair. Weakness and clumsiness are not the same. Certainly, both a mistake and a betrayal can be forgiven, but understanding the difference between the two exposes what it is you're forgiving, and to what extent your trust in that person has been compromised. It may also indicate whether the road to healing will be a long one, and if it will ever end.

Learn how to apologize

We're all angels. We're all jerks. No exceptions! This is why we all need to understand how to apologize for our unfortunate misjudgements and regrettable treatments of others. Understanding what an apology signifies can mean the difference between utter peace of mind and pure hell.

An apology doesn't mean making excuses for your actions or defending your alleged reasons – valid as those reasons may be. After your apology, there may come a time when the other party will want or need to understand the reasons for, and motives behind, your actions, but imposing those reasons or excuses along with, or instead of, an apology may seem as if you're attempting to defend or justify your actions. Although you may be able to explain your actions by providing perfectly valid reasons, nothing can or will ever justify the hurt that you may have caused. Also, insofar as *you* may have come to understand and accept the "what and why" of your actions, *they* may not be ready to accept these things.

The golden rule in making an apology is to take ownership of what you did; not to *justify* what you did. So, when you're ready to apologize, don't explain anything unless an explanation has been requested. Simply tell them that you were wrong (because you likely were wrong), and that you realize how badly you may have hurt them, and tell them that they did not deserve what happened. You can also offer to do whatever it takes to help make it up to them, but your apology should not be about making yourself feel better; it should be about making *them* feel better. Furthermore, your apology has a far greater chance of being accepted if it's not laced with excuses, reasons, or attempts of justification.

The Second Chance

Whether a person made a mistake, or whether they intentionally betrayed you, the concept of a second chance is meant to offer someone the opportunity to make right the error of their ways. When we first meet any new person, we don't actually "trust" them, because true trust is earned over time. What we do is extend to them *trust on faith*, like a loan. This is our investment in the relationship. They in turn either make good on the loan by showing you over time that they are who they alluded to being, or, they bankrupt themselves. Either way, in time they'll show you who they really are. When someone messes up, if you feel they're worth the effort, it's okay to give them a second chance, but they must understand that the chance does not mean another *trust* loan. In fact, it must be made clear that you *don't* trust them, and that not only do they need to repay or repair the mess they've made (without exception), but that instead of giving your trust, this time, they must earn it. In this manner, they've got their work cut out for them, and if they are not willing to do it, then they're not worth the second chance.

Understand fidelity and monogamy

Fidelity is not monogamy; they're two separate concepts. Fidelity means being faithful to the deal you make with the partner. Monogamy means having one partner. In business, monogamy means having one client whereas fidelity means being faithful to all clients. For some couples the deal is monogamy; one partner, whereas for others, the deal is approval of sexual activity with others but with limitations of certain actions, times or locations. Then there are couples without sexual restrictions but who limit what they share with others emotionally. Because relationships constantly change, you need to be clear about what's important to you at the beginning of an intimate relationship, and continually throughout as time goes by.

You decide

Don't let others manipulate your decisions about your relationship. Your relationship is *your* relationship. If you need to talk about it, make sure you're clear about what you need: Do you need to just vent, or are you looking for divorce counsel? A true confidante will listen to you, and they can usually decipher whether you are venting or if you are in crises, but you need to be clear from the get-go about what you need. Don't waste people's valuable time if you're upset about the toilet seat being up (or down); just adjust the seat as required and get over it. On the other hand, if you're telling a friend that your partner is abusive, don't get angry when you're advised to end the relationship. Also, if you're burdening somebody with your relationship problems, at the very least, have the decency to be completely honest with them. It's surprisingly helpful when they have all the facts, including what *you* did to make the problem what it has become. When reaching out for advice, remember that it is advice you are seeking, not a decision made on your behalf.

Get the facts

Never make decisions about somebody based on rumors. I've seen time and again where a good person is dishonored because of the jealousy of others. If you're interested in somebody, get the dirt on them *from them*. In some cases, there may be truth to rumors, but there are often reasons behind what people do in their lives, and a good man or a good woman might just need a good partner to become all they can be. Otherwise, when all else fails in the face of an uncertain character, be confident, trust your gut, and pray about it. As for rumors and gossip, just remember, those who gossip *to* you will gossip *about* you; and they will – every single chance they get to do so.

Anger

The problem with anger in relationships is not anger itself but rather the way we respond to anger; both our own anger and the anger of others. Our response to anger is not usually a response to anger itself but rather a response to how we feel about the cause of our anger. When a person is angered because their partner has not taken out the garbage, and they completely lose their temper, I can assure you that what angers the person has nothing to do with garbage. As for anger issues with new relationships, if you're dating a guy and he explodes, or dating a girl and she's mean, be honest and express your concerns, or do yourself a huge favor and make that date the last date with them. Misdirected anger doesn't always show its ugly little head in the beginning stages of relationships, and thus, it's just one more reason to take time to get to know somebody, and another reason to apply the three-date rule.

Dress Up

For those chronically single folks, here's some really good advice: *Stop looking like a slob!* Destiny may be at the corner store the next time you drop by to pick up some milk, so look decent, or at the very least, fix your hair! First impressions truly do last. A perfect example of this is when a friend I've known for some time recently complimented me on how well I dress, yet this person has only ever seen me dressed up on one occasion; the very first time we met. Even though I see this friend regularly and I am almost always wearing jeans and a t-shirt, her image of me is one of refinement because I was wearing a suit the first time we met. Also, first dates should always be treated as golden opportunities, because many of them turn out to be exactly that.

Abusive relationships

If you're being abused in a relationship, get out and get help! If he beat you once, he'll beat you again. You will not change him, and you are not a hero for putting up with him. Spousal abuse is not only about abusive men, it's also about abusive women, and nobody is required to be abused. This applies to verbal abuse as well. Staying in an abusive relationship is indicative of extreme low self-esteem – an issue that requires immediate attention. So, if you're being abused, get out now, and get help!

Instinctual Communication

Newsflash: People lie! That said, most of us know when we're being lied to, and people know when we're lying to them, so just be honest from the get-go. By being honest you never have to remember anything you lied about, so you don't have to remember what you've said to cover up a lie. One reason it's hard to keep up with lies is because dishonesty weakens the body and the brain *(imagine what it does to the soul)* whereas honesty strengthens us. Just observe the physical or mental state of anybody you know who's a habitual liar. Second, in the same manner that animals communicate beyond words, so do we, so whether lies are apparent through a look in our eyes or through a stench we release in the air, the communication is clear. Most of us are attuned to lies, but we'd rather deny facts in order to maintain people's approval, however, if we truly have someone's approval, they'd never lie to us. Yes, relationships are complex, but out of honest communication, they can be healed and improved upon. When we heal and improve our relationship with our *self*, then all other relationships cannot help but fall into order. For some, this means overlooked relationships will grow, and for others, it means people moving out of their lives. Regardless of what changes take place, when you're harmonious, the changes will take place harmoniously.

Be confident

Is there any wonder why so many nerdy geeks are getting the hot girls as much in movies as in real life these days? It's mostly because nerdy geeks usually have avid interests and they let it be known, and they don't pretend to be something they're not. *Geek-ness* is like a truth serum; you don't usually know you're a geek, so it doesn't occur to you to try to be something you're not. Since it's no secret that nothing shows a person's true colors more than when they're completely engaged in what interests them most, it explains why geeks are emerging more alluring than the surplus of over-plucked, over-waxed, insecure posers who have nothing going on in their lives other than trying desperately to stand out from the crowd, yet in the process, ironically resembling their fake poser counterparts.

Confidence isn't about believing you're *all that*. It's about not believing you're less than that, whatever *that* may imply. Whenever we tell ourselves that we're not good enough for someone, we're saying that we're not good enough for ourselves. We're complex people living in a complex world, all trying to please everybody, all craving approval on some level, almost always trying to be something we're not in order to conceal the horror of what we think we are. For some it's more obvious than for others, but we're almost all affected by this affliction.

When it comes to our confidence where it applies to dating and finding an ideal mate, our perspective, like with everything, *is* everything. Our insecurities are one hundred percent unfounded. If you think you're not good enough, you're wrong! If you're not what most people would go for, it has nothing to do with you. Sure maybe you'd like to have a better body, or longer hair, or curly hair, or simply *have* hair, but the person who will love you will love you no matter what your hair situation, your size or your age. What people like and dislike about you has very little to do with you. People's ideals about what's hot or not has to do with their education, upbringing and all they're exposed to *(thank you media)* about what an ideal mate should be.

Insecurities are illogical and unrealistic, and are born of fear. Where one man thinks he'll be alone because he's got a scarred leg, another man is happily married in spite of the fact that he has no legs. When it comes to appearance, shape, size, color, age, anomaly, there's always someone who's hot for what you've got, and there's every reason to flaunt your stuff, if for no other reason than to attract the one who's interested. One cannot account for the likes and dislikes of another, one can only celebrate everything one has, or doesn't have, and celebrate it with confidence!

Don't fake it

Faking an interest, whether it's an interest in something or someone, is like faking an orgasm; it's a waste of valuable time, it's a waste of valuable energy, it's dishonest, and regardless of what anybody thinks; nobody's fooled. As for faking orgasms, here's a little tidbit of info for those of you who do, have done, or plan to fake an orgasm: MEN KNOW! They always know. The thing is, just like with many things, they don't care. When you fake it, they can stop working at it, roll over, and go to sleep. When a man doesn't have to work at something, he'll play stupid, as long as he can get himself off. Don't believe me? How is it that most men can't seem to work a stove or clean something properly, yet they are the ultimate barbeque king, and their tools are often cleaner than their teeth? Playing dumb gets people out of a lot of responsibilities, and this applies as much to women as it does to men. Somehow, she can't seem to program the VCR or PVR *(or whatever they're calling those recording devices these days)*, yet she can drive a car down the highway with a coffee, a cigarette, a telephone and an eye liner pencil; all in one hand!

Both sexes are exceptionally creative when it comes to skirting responsibilities, and playing the incompetence card works beautifully. Honesty in our world applies to our kitchen table as much as it does to our beds, so always keep it honest. And for women who are frustrated with men who can't find their special *spot,* don't spend your relationship waiting for him to find it; tell him where it is, tell him how to work it, and make him work it. Then get him to pass the vacuum and wash your car, with the understanding that if he does a good job, you'll let him please you again!

Play with destiny and choice

One of the biggest discoveries I've made about life is where *destiny* and *choice* come into play. I realize that this chapter seems somewhat of an obscure location to place such an important discovery, but nowhere is this discovery more obvious than with relationships.

There are two main reasons why people don't commit to relationships. For one; they're afraid that someone better will show up and that they shouldn't control fate. Two; they know they're leading themselves on because they're not being honest about what they want, and so they don't make a choice.

The discovery about choice and destiny is that not only do choice and destiny both exist, but they *coexist* on a multidimensional level. In this discovery I have come to understand that choice and destiny cannot exist one without the other. In our current consciousness, it's somewhat difficult to imagine how such a theory could be possible, but when we open our minds *spherically* to this concept, it not only becomes clear that choice and destiny are not in conflict with each other, but that they're completely *reliant upon* each other. Our confusion on the topic stems from the one dimensional perspective which dictates that only one or the other can exist. This inaccurate theory is a result of our habitual one-dimensional thinking. Multi-dimensional thinking is how one discovers that which resides on multidimensional levels.

With relationships, if you stick to your guns and await your ideal mate, never compromising your worth, then your choice and your destiny will converge. Equally, if you are with somebody and want to commit but are scared that your choice will mess up your destiny; keep in mind, some things are *written* and life will find a way to harmoniously marry your choice to that which is written. The best advice here is the same advice which applies to all matters of the heart: *Be true to you!*

No matter who we are, whether straight, bi, gay, transgender or otherwise, marriage is about being together and enduring what life throws at you; it shouldn't be about enduring what you throw at each other. Kindness goes a long way in the short time we're here on Earth, especially in the lives of the married. I often wonder what divorce statistics would look like if kindness were at the forefront of all marriages. I wonder it there'd even be any divorce statistics. Yes, some people get married for dumb reasons, and some people change but don't always change together or at the same pace. Sometimes people fall out of love over the years, sometimes it happens overnight, whereas others discover true love many years into their marriage. Some people become more superficial and others become deeper. There's so much about love that is completely out of our control, but one thing is certain; what *is* in our control is how we approach the ones we love. What we do and what we say to, about, around, and in the absence of the people we love, tells us, and them, how we feel about them. These factors are also an ever-present indication about our relationship with our *self*; this being perhaps the one most important thing in our entire world.

CHAPTER XV

=OurChildrenWhoArtOnEarth=

To teach children honor, simply honor the children...

Mahatma Gandhi said *"The greatness of a nation and its moral progress can be judged by the way its animals are treated"*. If there is any truth to his statement, I shudder to think how a nation is viewed when judged by how it treats its children. Above that, what of *a world* which is judged accordingly? I believe that if there is one single thing we could do outside of ourselves that would have the greatest impact on humanity and on what we give to God, it would be to change the way we educate and love our children.

Now more than ever before, our children are being born unto an awakening, but beyond this, more than ever before, they're also being born *awakened*, with limitless, omnipotent capabilities, in body and in mind. However, never before have children been born into the world unto parents who knew more or had as much access to resources, knowledge and education as is available at this time. The dilemma is, however, that our children have new and different needs, yet most parents are not doing their job, and they're not *stepping up* to meet the needs of the way their children are being born. Parents are not pushing or disciplining themselves into progressing towards all that they can be, and as such, they're not applying these vital actions to *parenting*, and the results of their oversight and plain laziness are proving to be devastating to the entire planet.

The problems with our children have little, if anything, to do with the children themselves and everything to do with how they are raised, how they are conditioned, how they are nourished, what is and isn't instilled in them, and what they experience, see and hear in their chaotic and undisciplined world. In their half-baked attempts to mold their children, most parents overlook the fact that children actually have the capacity to mold themselves, and parents need only mold their children's *environment* in order to provide an enriching, fulfilling life experience rather than merely a mundane existence. Parents best provide a vitally fertile environment for their children by conscientiously awakening and molding themselves; both as people and as parents.

An awakening of the self is a choice; it is not something that just happens. And it does not matter how you were raised or what you were taught. If you know the difference between right and wrong, then you also know the difference between basking in one's ignorance and progressing towards affirmative consciousness. We are also just about beyond the age if *information gathering* and into the dawn of *information sharing;* information which is easily accessible, so there's never been an easier time to get what we need to go beyond our demons in the name of becoming finer humans and superior parents. No matter what you've been through, there's somebody out there who's been through the same and can help you deal with your old wounds, or there's information out there that's been made available to help you grow as a human and as a parent. There really is no excuse today for being a negligent parent, and there's no excuse for laying our problems on our children or not providing their basic needs.

Many books on religion and spirituality; new and ancient alike, consistently make mention of a *great awakening* which is taking place in our world, and as much as I'm inclined to agree with the basic concept of a collective awakening, I also recognize that this collective awakening is reliant upon the personal choices of each person who makes up humanity. In the same manner of which we must choose whether to go back to sleep or to wake up in the morning to go about our duties and follow our dreams and stand up for what's right and just, so must we choose to wake up on a conscious level, especially where it applies to raising our children.

The era of a *collective conscious awakening* is in fact upon us, however, like love, *conscious evolution* is not imposed upon us. We are free to take part in it, or to do otherwise. *Conscious evolution* is ours for the taking, but the stepping stones are love, commitment, discipline, faith and humility. In the same manner that our current generation's children are being born unto a great awakening, so is it that their parents were born with the great special gifts required to provide the necessary guidance and wisdom for the next generation to evolve into their full potential. These great special gifts must be *consciously* and *decisively* awoken by each individual; they don't just appear and get to work on their own. Much like an individual doesn't just one day become a doctor; they must study and apply their actions and themselves over years, so is it that each individual must study and apply their actions and themselves to that which is *conscious awakening* in order to *consciously awaken*.

Ultimately, our children are born perfect; all knowing, all loving, all creative and affirmative. These factors, however, must be nourished in order for them to grow and become the character traits which will become the child, and ultimately become the path they will follow. These factors are nourished when parents decide to do the absolute best they can to set prime examples of what it means to be good, honest and integrous people. When parents seek to do the right thing and to better themselves under the watchful eye of their children, children will follow suit.

As parents, we can only work with what we have. This means working with the level of intelligence and comprehension abilities which we have been handed. Admittedly, some parents are smarter than others, but this should not keep us from reaching beyond our apparent limitations. I have come to understand that, in our world, despicable people have the run of most things, but I have also come to recognize that the despicable are not the ignorant doing ignorant things; ignorant things, after all, are what ignorant people do. The despicable are actually the intelligent who do as the ignorant do, and most of us make up the populace of despicable people, because most of us are actually *highly intelligent* people doing *highly ignorant* things. Those of us who *consciously* continue to do as the ignorant do in spite of the fact that we know better are *choosing* to be despicable, and we further the works of the despicable in our world. In this lies the realization of why our children are becoming what they're becoming, where they're headed, and the distressing legacy we're leaving for them.

On our planet there is currently an increasingly common ailment referred to as Attention Deficit Disorder (ADD), and nowhere in the world is there a higher level of ADD both in volume and per capita than in North America. Regardless of what the public is fed about ADD, ADD is merely a disorder brought on by the absence of discipline, education and firmly set boundaries. Where an authentic deficiency in the ability to give attention is truly present, said deficiency would not be selective, and it would affect all things requiring attention such as video games, television, movies and so forth. It would not just apply to things requiring discipline and responsibility. The lack of education, discipline and firmly set boundaries are not remedied with a pill, they are remedied with exactly these factors; education, discipline and firmly set boundaries; all factors which must be affirmatively taught and instilled.

Interestingly enough, ADD is virtually non-existent in India, China and Japan, to name only a few countries. More interesting is what these aforementioned three nations have in common. Of course, to the list of countries throughout the world which are generally unaffected by ADD, we could add many (most actually) countries, but for the sake of discussion, let's focus on just two of the aforementioned nations and one common thread they share, which is, *discipline.*

Whether or not you admire or approve of China or Japan, the fact remains that they are among the most disciplined nations on the planet. They are disciplined about business and work ethics, about their education, their diet and their families, and most importantly, they're disciplined where their children and their children's education are concerned. It is this discipline which, over countless centuries, has helped them retain their sense of tradition; that same sense of tradition which teaches family members to respect one another every morning when they awaken, and is the same factor which brings families to-gether to sup at the same table at the end of each day. Yes, I am perfectly aware that China and Japan, as well as all nations, have been and are doing their fair share of holding back humanity, but where it comes to disciplining children compared to North America, China and Japan have the general idea.

The term *sense of tradition* means a lot of different things to a lot of different people, and its ideals are often as detrimental to our progress as they are instrumental, so it really is about balancing our progress — what works, what oppresses, what kills. When it comes to the affirmative aspects of tradition, bringing up children in a stable environment with loving parents who actually *live* together and who lovingly discipline their children is definitely a great way to encourage a planet to progress together. Mommy and Daddy *(or Dad & Dad or Mom & Mom)*, after all, are the world to kids, and if the parents can't get along and live together and forgive each other and keep their commitments, how can anybody else do it, and why *should* anybody do it? Even if Mommy and Daddy are present, attentive and disciplined, however, what's the point of instilling a sense of tradition if a child is guilted into pretending to be something other than she is, or aspires to be, whether it be a doctor, lawyer, dancer or a great wife to another woman and an excellent mother?

When tradition stems from ego-based attachments, fear-based beliefs or misunderstood information passed on by mediocre thinkers, it will, at all costs, continue to hold humanity at bay. Conversely, when tradition stems from truly tested, tried, true and wisely logical and affirmative foundations, it can only catapult humanity forward, one brilliantly loved and disciplined child at a time. China and

Japan get this; at least with discipline and education. Yes, these countries have much work to do in the arena of breaking free from many of their own self-imposed traditional ideals which plague them, such as women's place in the world, their archaic form of government, and of course their view of sexual orientation, but then again, so do most countries.

I mention in the beginning of this chapter that if there was one single thing we could do that would have the greatest impact on humanity and on what we give back to God, it would be to change the way we educate and love our children. I say this because, nothing tells us more about ourselves than how our children feel about us, and nothing tells God more about us than what we've instilled in our children. Once again, this comes back to our relationship with ourselves.

For most of us, the lives we've created for ourselves are largely based on our parents' aspirations for us and what they prepared us, or didn't prepare us, for. If a parent abused, tormented and instilled fear and loathing in their child, those are the basic building blocks with which that child builds his/her life. Because most children during the same generation are raised in the same common manner, generations of children use those same building blocks to build their society, and that, before anything else – before genetics and before material and monetary inheritances, is the legacy each parent delivers to their children. This legacy is not left to our children after we pass on, but rather, this legacy starts at home, when a child is born, and it is with them for all time. Sure, an abused and neglected child may rise to the top, above the crowd on many levels, but, rich or poor, sick or healthy, regardless of what he may acquire in life, the essence of what his parents instilled in him is as much his legacy as it is his ongoing reality and his ultimate destiny.

When it comes to discipline, humanity is severely out of balance, and this imbalance, although having much to do with compromised traditional values and archaic thinking, mostly comes down to ignorance. What's interesting about the word *ignorance* is that it implies to "ignore". To ignore something generally requires intention; in this case, actively *choosing* to ignore, and this action usually involves a motive. The motive behind maintaining one's ignorance usually has to do with guilt, fear and the need for approval, and sometimes it's just plain laziness. Either way, dwelling in ignorance is a choice. Although we don't know what we don't know, there's no excuse to remain ignorant. If we realized that all of humanity and its purpose in the universe are further at stake with each day we wallow in our ignorance, we'd think a little more, we'd judge much less, and we'd practice love like it was our very last breath.

The reason I bring up ignorance is because if we'd just think about it, we'd find within ourselves what discipline *truly* means. As I mention a few chapters previous to this, we're physically beating our children based on what we understand an ancient book appears to be suggesting about disciplining our children. The book says to guide our children with a firm hand, but it is not meant that we are to guide them by striking them, but rather, by providing firm boundaries and guidance with a *loving* hand. This ideal is supported by the scripture; *Fathers, provoke not your children to anger, lest they be discouraged (Colossians 4:21).* Is there anything that could better provoke and discourage a child than being struck in any manner by his/her parent?

Placing such immense emphasis on raising our children is important to humanity because as much as it is for the legacy and destiny of our children, it is also a gift we give to ourselves in the present. It is our gift to ourselves because in order to love our children to the absolute best of our ability, we must absolutely love ourselves in the same manner. When this self-love occurs throughout a generation, all of humanity changes drastically, for the better.

Since parents who abuse, neglect and torment their children are usually themselves victims of abuse, neglect and torment, the mere idea of moving forth to encourage, discipline and love their children unconditionally would mean acknowledging the encouragement, discipline and unconditional love they require *of* themselves and *for* themselves, before they can give it to their children. If every parent knew how damaging their own low self-esteem, self-loathing, self-hatred, and especially lack of discipline was impacting their children for the rest of their lives, and if they knew that *that* is the legacy, reality and destiny they are *willingly* imposing upon their children, they might realize that it's time to give more to their children. In the process, they'd have to discover how to love themselves.

All religious traditions advocate that life is meant to be abundantly prosperous and harmonious. In our society, for those of us who recognize the potential for universal peace and harmony, we've become accustomed to visualizing peace and harmony in the future but rarely, if ever, do we take a moment to recognize the peace and harmony that does, or could, surround us in the now. In this process, our children don't experience peace and harmony, and thus, their compromised *life programming* is set to guide them for the rest of their lives. This applies to all of humanity.

What is perhaps most damaging to a child's sense of peace, harmony and general overall wellbeing is when it comes to the physical abuse which is corporal punishment. As adults, most of us are rarely faced with the actual fist-fights, wrestling matches and physical bullying that we went through as children, but what we did get through as children was a result of the fact that most schoolyard violence took place with people of our own general size and strength. The *physical* feeling, however, that comes with a giant hand hitting, slapping or pushing a little body is bad enough, but the *psychological* feeling of helplessness, hopelessness, vulnerability, embarrassment, insecurity, shame (the list goes on) which a child experiences each time they are physically reprimanded is life-altering; every single time it happens. When it comes to the prosperity, abundance, peace and harmony that our life is meant to be, how exactly is a child supposed to feel at peace when someone twice or three times or more their size strikes them in any manner, especially when the abuse is coming from the people who are supposed to protect them from just such abuse, and from whom they're supposed to love, trust, honor and learn from, and are generally the same people who have made it clear that they wish to be loved by their child?

Whether in the home, at school, or anywhere else, there is a harmonious way to teach. If we'd recognize how learning *harmoniously* and learning *affirmatively* results in *learning more*, we'd actually get somewhere with these brilliant minds of ours. Our children would learn more if we took time to offer direction instead of wrath. In the process of teaching a child to ride a bike, it's ideal to not simply give the child a bike and just tell them not to fall off; you'd give them directions on what to do, how to steer and of course how to stop. This concept seems simple enough on paper, but millions of households worldwide scold their children for spilling their milk, when in fact, spilling milk is part of the learning process. Although we don't want to encourage more spilled milk, scolding and especially physically reprimanding a child over spilled milk only works to reinforce the child's acknowledgment of spilling more milk which in turn ensures he'll repeat the process. This process not only ensures that the child will do as he's been trained to do *(spill the milk)*, but it also ensures a healthy dose of attention each time the milk is spilled, which is exactly what children thrive on; *attention!*

Regardless of one's religious views, there is no glory in abandoning, beating, tormenting, abusing, or neglecting our children, and the world is not better as a result of this practice. I don't believe for one moment that if God came and stood next to any parent, that they would ever be proud to strike their child in the presence of God. When it comes to reprimanding our children, one law we tend to overlook, or of which we are simply unaware, is the law that says *like breeds like*. Humans breed humans, birds breed birds, bees breed bees and so forth. This concept applies equally to what we teach our children. Violence breeds violence, compassion breeds compassion, love breeds love, like-energy breeds like-energy. This is a basic law to which childrearing is not in any way impervious. It is a law which applies to all and to everything.

When it comes to raising children, a key component to acknowledge is that it is the parents' job to love their children; it is not the children's job to love the parents. Many would argue this point, but it is our job to teach our children everything from holding a glass of milk to the concept of love, and they will learn this through what they see and hear from their parents more than from any other source. Yes, children need to learn to *honor thy mother and thy father*, but children learn to honor by being honored. They learn by example.

It is evident to anybody who stops to pay attention that the human race has squandered, and continues to squander its gifts, and nowhere is this more evident than with what we've done and are doing to our children. It is our responsibility to raise children and prepare them for life, and as a society overall, we're failing miserably at this task. We are failing because, in the process of providing all our children's *wants*, we're overlooking their basic *needs*. Children seek attention, discipline, boundaries and approval, and one way or another, they will find a way to get it. Providing children with the kind of boundaries, discipline and approval which will propel them towards a harmoniously prosperous life requires affirmative action on our part.

Too much of the action parents currently take is negative, whether it's actions such as using damaging coarse language, not keeping their word, physical abuse and so forth. Constant use of seemingly inconsequential reinforcements used in verbal directives such as, *no, don't, can't, won't,* are excessively confusing to the mind, but nothing is more verbally damaging to the self-esteem of a child than when their first name is used as a reprimand. As much as verbal abuse is damaging to a child, I realize it's a difficult task to be mindful of every single word we utter, however, the difficulty of the task is no reason to keep us from doing our task.

When it comes to corporal punishment, in my mind, there is something *(everything, actually)* so wrong about it, but for those who insist upon it, it's important to keep in mind that the process is meant as a tool for *direction* and not as a venting platform for parents' rage. The ramifications of corporal punishment are feelings of insecurity and other self-esteem issues including embarrassment, shame and permanent physical and mental damage, and suicidal tendencies, to name just some. I believe that corporal punishment is inherently wrong, period. That said, in the highly unlikely event that I am incorrect in my estimation, I will say that, if you're unsure whether you're effectively administering corporal punishment, here's a hint: *If you're angry; you're not!*

Where this practice, well-meaning as it allegedly may be, is meant as a corrective measure, it is nonetheless traditionally carried out as a result of impatience, frustration, self-loathing and anger, each of which breeds more of the same. Any calm, intelligent, well-meaning parent can get through to their child without getting physical with them. If you're a parent who tends to lose it each time your child steps out of line, try a hug and a whispering tone. You just might be pleasantly surprised at the results.

The concept of striking a child as a form of affirmative directive is comparable to hitting a malfunctioning car and expecting it to run properly. In both cases, where compromised function is concerned, the answer is to research the root of the problem and correct it *affirmatively*, whether the cause of the problem is a dead battery in a car or spilled milk at the breakfast table. In the case of the child, however, more often than not, the child is actually acting out exactly as he has been directed to act, or they're trying you tell you something. Either way, in all my research, prayer, meditation and thinking, I have yet to find any indication that corporal punishment is an affirmative form of discipline and guidance, or is anything other than an act of a primitive ignoramus.

Don't agree? Consider for a moment if you were physically struck each time you made a mistake. How encouraged would you feel to want to continue? How would you feel about your every next step? What's more, how would you feel about the person administering it to you? What we tend to forget as adults is that we make mistakes throughout our day, and children are no different, so why should they be struck because of their mistakes when most adults wouldn't be able to handle the abuse every time we made a mistake? As adults we often take legal action if someone even nudges us, yet we expect our children to put up with it. Something is seriously wrong with this process!

When it comes to the general overall health of our children, the main problem with most children, again, is that they have no discipline. This is not because they can't learn to be disciplined, but rather, because their parents aren't disciplined and therefore can't and don't instill discipline, and thus, the cycle continues. Many of us have come to associate the word discipline with beatings and other forms of corporal punishment, and for many of us, the word discipline means *discomfort*. Either way, it's a scary word for most of us, but in reality, the word has nothing to do with abuse of any kind, and everything to do with self-respect and commitment. The discipline we must instill in our children must first be instilled within ourselves. The value of discipline we instill in our children will be in direct proportion to our own commitment to properly raising our children. Furthermore, in regards to diet and nutrition, this area has nothing to do with children; they're not the ones who do the grocery shopping, so why are they to blame? Currently, our children are not only dehydrated and malnourished by processed foods, they're also being poisoned by these foods, as well as by elements such as toiletries, cleaning products, fluoride, pesticides, and other poisonous additives, toxins and contaminants. Along with being poisoned, although they're being fed, their little bodies are actually starving. The malnourishment factor alone is responsible for ailing and killing our children more than any plague or epidemic the planet has ever known.

Ultimately, it's important that all parents ask themselves the following questions: Who's raising your kids; you or video games? You or their teacher? You or their nanny? You or their coach? You or the television? You or the Internet? You or social media? These are the very first questions we should all be asking ourselves. And, in regards to technological past-times; if your child each day is getting more than a half hour of video games or Internet, or more than one hour of television, then your child is in trouble!

As previously mentioned, a scientific fact about the subconscious mind is that the subconscious cannot decipher between fantasy and reality. If a child spends hours shooting at people in a video game, then subconsciously, he believes he has shot those people. If he watches someone kill another person on a television show, his subconscious mind believes this to be real. Sure, he might not grow up to shoot anybody, but he will be desensitized to these actions when they are placed before him. This alone is one of the detriments to the illogical censoring process carried out by most media regulatory organizations. TV programs are consistently censored so that viewers are not able to see nudity or hear coarse language, yet throughout an entire broadcast day, viewers are inundated with images of people beating and murdering and raping other people, and not surprisingly, we've become exceptionally desensitized to what would normally *freak us out*. Most of us are so out of touch with ourselves that we don't realize how agonizingly disruptive images of violence are to our physical nervous system. This mass desensitization, however, is purely on a conscious level. The subconscious mind, on the other hand, is every bit as affected by those images and is shaping our kids' minds, and their world, and their wellbeing, or lack thereof.

Whoever it was who decided that something as normal and natural as a human breast was more dangerous to see than watching somebody take the life of another human being, definitely needs to re-evaluate their priorities, as does anyone who supports such a perverse notion. I personally support the general censoring of gratuitous nudity in television programming, especially since everybody entertains different television viewing habits and since we (apparently) can't always control what little eyes are watching. I also support censoring coarse language during prime-time hours, however, any movie which has coarse language is probably more damaging visually than auditorily, and again, if there's violence, bullying, rape or murder, then coarse language is not the biggest problem. Nudity, however, is nothing to be ashamed or scared of, and it definitely shouldn't be the first thing we censor when it comes to television. We're born naked, we leave here naked, and most of the importance things we do; making love, showering, using the bathroom, are done in the nude, so nudity is just plain normal. All that said, that which minds see and hear is that upon which minds feed, and this is especially applicable to little *developing* minds, so we really should be minding what our children watch and hear on a day to day, moment to moment basis.

When it comes to academics, there are many lessons we could learn from other countries; especially China, about how to educate our children. The amount of time a child spends in school in China outweighs that of the United States at a painfully embarrassing rate (243 days in China, 180 in the U.S.), or at least we'd be embarrassed if we were educated enough to know that we should be embarrassed.

Beyond days spent at school in China, the actual time spent is utilized efficiently so as to get the most education out of – or put more education into – every hour of schooling. There's a lot to be said for improving academic systems to accommodate more effective learning, but even the most effective education process can yield only so much in just so many days per year. If you want to get something *from* school, you've got to spend ample time *at* school. There is no evidence confirming that the Chinese are *smarter* than Americans; all evidence indicates that the Chinese are simply more *disciplined* than Americans, and, although the decision to be disciplined alone is an indication that the Chinese might just be smarter, discipline is *taught* and *instilled*, and it is something that even animals can be taught, so we as humans have zero excuse for not choosing to be disciplined.

I recognize that China is known for often taking academics too far, with a severely imbalanced learning-to-playing ratio making for a joyless childhood experience for many. Playing, after all, is not just about pleasure; it's a necessity beyond ABC's & 123's, important for the development of motor and social skills, and learning in itself, among other things. I'm not implying that America should employ the same extreme academic practices as does China, but applying just *some* of China's systems would greatly add to the *sum* of what our children are getting from North America's current systems.

Resorting to changing things like physical education classes *daily* rather than just *weekly*, for all children, in all schools, would yield immense affirmative change. Exercise stimulates the body and the brain, and it relaxes and settles otherwise rambunctious and restless students; something teachers struggle with greatly in light of the ADD/ADHD issue. Beyond physical education, to get more from school, children simply need to spend more time at school. Children also need to be taught to respect their teachers, respect each other, and respect themselves. This requires that parents play a role in the process, because respect is taught, before anywhere else, at home.

This brings me to another point; if parents don't respect and support their children's teachers, why should the children? With classes growing bigger by mass and volume, and lack of education funding, teachers need parents to support them; to remind children that the teacher is the boss, that teachers have a job to do and are to be respected, no exceptions! There was a time when teachers could control a class because, back then, pupils were taught at home to respect the teacher. Today, a teacher is on her/his own; facing abuse, knives, guns, behavior-modifying drugs and energy drinks and telecommunication devices; as much wielded by parents as by students. Incidentally, if you've got kids in school, just assume your child's teacher is overwhelmed, and offer her/him one day per month of your assistance, whether grading papers or organizing things or helping with a class project. If every parent did this, then every teacher, ever day, would have a helper.

I admit there is no shortage of teachers who deserve to be strung up by their toes for how they discourage and disempower the young hearts and minds of pupils which they're blessed with the honor of teaching. I have nieces and nephews who tell me of what goes on in school, and although I'm inclined to not believe everything a disgruntled child tells me about their teacher, of the factual accounts, I do realize why many kids are appalled and outraged. I look very forward to being a dad someday, but the thing that concerns me the most about being a parent is the people who will be teaching my children.

I have a particularly brilliant young niece who is a celebrated scholar in her school board region; a science & math aficionado with whom I've been able to discuss profound concepts since she was in grade school. Her biggest challenge is her teacher's negativity and lack of passion for what she does, and the horrible things she says to her students, and her constant yelling. My niece is consciously hungry for knowledge, but most kids aren't, and having so few days to learn is one thing for such a brilliant young mind with so much potential, but additionally having a teacher who hates teaching, hates kids, and hates herself, can only encourage children to do and be the same. Such conduct is unacceptable behavior coming from teachers, and they make all teachers look bad. If there's any doubt about a teacher's conduct, then ensuring they have a helper each day, especially a helper who happens to be a pupil's parent, will confirm or defuse any speculation. It's also a great way to hold pupils accountable to learning and to their own actions.

Perhaps the worst thing with our education process is in how we don't encourage young minds to consider, discover and dwell in possibility, regardless of the alleged answers, and don't reward them when they do. My niece is often met with inexact data in textbooks and in the classroom, and when she brings this to her teachers' attention, she's reprimanded and told that the information is correct, which is unfortunate, because these kinds of discoveries made by students in China would actually be rewarded. We, however, choose to continue teaching the inaccurate information because it's easier than admitting that a student is smarter than a textbook or a disgruntled teacher.

As a child, I wasn't nearly as unrelentingly devoted to learning as is my niece, but I recall being at school and being required to answer this riddle: *A scientist announced that he invented an acid which can eat through anything. Explain why this would be impossible.* As a student, I saw no reason why this could not be possible and I responded with, *"It is possible!"* I was then told that I was incorrect. The *alleged* correct response was that it would be impossible for the scientist to create such an acid because if the acid could eat through anything, then it could eat through a vial and therefore could not be contained and consequently could not exist. Regardless of the riddle's *alleged* correct response, even as a child, I dwelt in the affirmative realm of possibility. I knew that just because the scientist couldn't *contain* the acid, it didn't mean he couldn't have *developed* the acid *(many things are non-containable, yet they exist)*. I figured that the acid would become completely corrosive upon the addition of a final specific elemental ingredient, at which point it would simply eat its way through whatever was *containing* it, then eat its way through the table, then through the floor, then through the ground below, continually eating through whatever it touched until it exhausted its compositional resources. Beyond this, in my mind, it was very feasible that a scientist who could develop an acid that could eat through anything, could have also developed a method to *seize* the acid, even if others couldn't comprehend that method. My teacher rejected my ideals, citing his brilliant rebuttal: *The riddle's answer couldn't possibly be wrong because it was in print.* Incidentally, he's also the same teacher who insisted that the name Sean can only be pronounced "seen", even in light of the fact that there was a Sean – *pronounced "Shawn"* – in the very next class.

To this day, this same riddle, along with the same *alleged* correct response, is taught in schools. This limited form of educating humanity, where creative thought is cut off at the knees, is just one of our downfalls. Lack of attention to this mammoth downfall is one problem, but it's nothing compared to our willingness to continue to give little or no attention to the educational process which not only ensures that we instill the absolute minimum into the minds of our children, but it also ensures the minimum of what we can expect of them, and what they can expect of themselves.

Teaching young minds, whether at home or at school, to look beyond the apparent and beyond the *alleged* apparent, and encouraging creativity in all they do, and letting them know they're part of a cause far greater than they will ever imagine, whether it be God, their country, their neighborhood, or their family, is the first step towards affirmative change for all of humanity.

Changing our ways with our children would change us all, because in order to love our children in an inherently affirmative manner, it would mean re-evaluating everything we've come to know about ourselves – each of us individually; all of us as a whole. Before understanding how to approach our children in the same way, we'd have to first understand what love, discipline and integrity really mean, and we'd have to apply it to ourselves, and that's when change truly happens.

If we were all to drop what we are doing right now and committed to sincerely loving our *self* at all costs, we'd discover just how important it is to really listen to our instincts, intuition, thoughts and feelings, not to mention seek to find the answers to all the questions we could ever think of asking, and we'd teach this to our children. At that point we'd feel less secluded, less scared, and less lonely in the world. Only then could we and can we bring the best of ourselves to our children and set them up for a life truly worth living and a story worth sharing when they report back to the Divine Creator when it's all said and done.

If we honored our children, they would honor us. By honor, I most certainly don't mean *spoil* them, but rather, if we truly loved and adored them, and placed them on a pedestal as the gifts from God that they truly are, and if we acted like the gifts we're meant to be to them, then on one hand, ADD would be known for the absurd notion of which it truly is. On the other hand, the results of our actions would change our children's world, change *our* world, and change the world as it applies to the advancement of all of humanity, and to the entire universe, and to God. This single act would project us all into realms of consciousness which we currently cannot imagine. Realms of consciousness that this current realm of *unconsciousness* which we refer to as "reality" would pale, implausibly, in comparison.

CHAPTER XVI

=ProChoiceProLife=

Life begins at...

The agonizingly delicate issue of abortion has plagued humanity for literally centuries, and although the solution to the problem is astonishingly simple, the many facets of the solution are, for lack of better explanation, easier said than done. In order to tackle the issue that is abortion, we must first examine what makes abortion an issue in the first place, which is in all actuality the disregarded pre-existing issues which precede unwanted or compromised pregnancy. As much with abortion as with anything else, society has become accustomed to *fighting* for rights, whether they're that of the mother, or of the father, or of the unborn fetus, but in essence, abortion is not a *rights* issue at all; it's a *responsibility* issue. As with any issue concerning humanity, we must stop examining the result of abortion long enough to spend some time examining the *root cause* of the issue. That root cause is *all of us*.

Before I continue, I should mention that, as much as I am an advocate for *affirmative living*, I maintain that any decision a woman makes about her body is her God-given right, as I take into account that her actions are between her and her body, between her and her child, and between her and her God. Conversely, I'd also like to suggest that anyone who claims that a fetus is not a *person* until it is born is undeniably a first-rate ignoramus. I'd also like to remind anyone who believes that nonsense, that in many continents – including North America – a woman was not recognized as a *person* until recent decades, and in many countries, this is still the case. In my estimation, a human being that feeds and grows *is* a person, whether she's in my country, another country, an incubator or in the womb. The issue of whether or not a fetus is *legally* recognized as a person has no impact on the fact that the fetus *is alive*. Human life begins before birth regardless of its legal fixed address. If it absorbs nourishment and grows; it lives!

What I discovered during my search for answers to this issue is that one cannot be any more pro-choice without being pro-life than they can be pro-life without being pro-choice. Both are entirely one and the same and as vital to each other as breathing in and breathing out are vital to sustaining life. If you're pro-life, then you must be pro-everything life implies, which includes every person's God-given right to choose. If you're pro-choice, then you must be pro-everything choice implies, which includes allowing every living thing its *right to live* in order to exercise its *right to choose*. It quite simply cannot be one or the other.

Continual segregation of pro-life activism from pro-choice activism can only continue to breed the same endless cycle of banter which continues to nurture confusion and frustration on both sides. Both pro-life and pro-choice arguments are correct, however, arguments either way are not *action* towards a solution, but rather, *reaction* to the biased convictions of the other side. The solution to the abortion issue can only ever be discovered by the amalgamation of both sides; a joining together into one assembly of affirmative thinkers and doers with an agenda to discover an affirmative solution which effectively serves all lives involved, and which preserves the right to choose. A solution which already exists but which we have yet to discover as a result of the one-dimensional perspective which suggests that we must pick one side and abandon the other.

Incidentally, for those who are still on the fence about whether life begins at birth or at conception, here's my suggestion; life begins *before* conception! The egg is clearly a *living* organism; there's no question about that. Whether or not the egg has a consciousness may be uncertain, but there is no denying that the sperm is alive and possesses a consciousness, and here's the reasoning:

Intention requires *consciousness*, and when a sperm cell swims its way towards an egg with a clear objective of penetrating the egg, it does this with *intention*. Intention requires consciousness; consciousness implies life. If there is life *before* conception, how can anybody deny that there is life *at* conception? Ultimately, it's perfectly evident that a fetus is clearly a living human being at the time of conception and thus deserves to live its life and deserves to exercise its right to choose.

I mention that the solution is simple, but I in no way can honestly imply that it's a painless solution. When we let others walk their chosen path, we risk them walking down a path contrary to our preference, but the fact remains, it's *their* path, it's *their* life, it's *their* right to choose, and it's not our place to judge; it is our place, and our Commandment, to love. I'm not implying that we shouldn't do our absolute best to encourage life. As a matter of fact, I feel there should be laws in place to protect living fetuses. After all, a prime example of loving our fellow man is to protect and defend the survival of those who cannot protect and defend themselves. However, along with laws that would protect living fetuses, there should also be a soaring caliber of *care protocol* for women in such crises — a *care protocol* which supports and protects a woman as much as it supports and protects the fetus — for one human being is as important as the other. This cutting-edge, *spherical thinking* kind of care protocol is how we must deal with this issue. It is the *only* way to deal with it. Otherwise, no matter how we feel or what our religion might suggest, it's not our place to judge; it's only our place to love. *"Judge not lest ye be judged"* doesn't only apply to how you feel about your friend's new haircut; it applies to *everything* and *everybody*, as does the Commandment, *"Thou shalt not kill"*.

Commandments aside, the abortion issue isn't actually about terminating life, or having a child, or even about speaking for and defending the life of the fetus. It's about what led to the pregnancy or what created the compromised health of the fetus or the mother *(depending on the motive for considering termination)*. It's about responsibility, accountability, priority and self-respect, as much on a personal level as on a global level. It's also about ignorance and our arrogant ego-driven contempt for life. Rectifying this issue is about not dwelling in fear, and it's about living in the realm of *affirmative possibility*.

I don't believe there is one woman who ever lived in all of history who intended on getting pregnant just so she could go out and have an abortion, and thus, the women involved deserve better treatment than they receive. On the other hand, where unwanted pregnancy as a result of being irresponsible is concerned, if appropriate decisions were made prior to conception, many women facing the abortion issue as a result of unwanted pregnancy wouldn't be there *(note: "many" women facing the issue, not "all" women)*. At any rate, the issue of abortion wouldn't even exist if we dealt with the core root factors which we fail to acknowledge and which ultimately contribute to the issue.

When our *global society* that is humanity, and our *collective consciousness* advance to where we all truly *live consciously*, we'll raise our sons and daughters to respect themselves and each other, as well as respect their bodies. Our children in turn will make better decisions about whom they spend time with, whom they make love with, and the lengths they'll go to protect the temples they call their bodies. This process will also have a profound impact on other areas of their intimate lives, in everything from contracting sexually transmitted diseases to marrying the right person. Furthermore, with divine consciousness comes absolute understanding of the complexity and the miracle that is life, rendering the *contempt for life* that is the mere idea of abortion not only a thing of the past, but possibly even forgotten, unheard of, or at the very least, an absurd notion.

The term *live and let live* applies to everything and everyone. This applies to those who, thanks to the miracle of technology, are discovered to be imperfect – physically disfigured, emotionally challenged or otherwise *different*. If a life is strong enough to survive long enough to be born, it deserves its chance to live. It's not always clear how to raise children who are born into the world with extremely challenging physical and emotional needs, but just because we're not clear on how to go about raising and providing for these children doesn't mean there isn't a harmonious way to do so, or that they shouldn't be permitted to live, and it certainly doesn't mean they don't have a divine purpose bigger than our own. Regardless of whether we're for or against abortion, and regardless of how difficult it is to face facts, we have to be completely honest with ourselves at least long enough to consider the bigger picture.

When it comes to considering abortion for reasons other than health detriments to the mother or the fetus, again, we must consider the issues preceding contemplation of abortion. For example, consider the scenario of a child being conceived through rape. Of course there are many logical reasons a woman under such circumstances might consider terminating the pregnancy; the idea that the child could become a rapist, the idea of growing something inside her that belongs to the person who violated her, and then there's the looking into the face of the child and possibly seeing its father's face every day, not to mention the thought that a child might infringe upon personal life plans; all this to name just some reasons.

First off, there is no *rape gene*. Rape is merely a form of bullying, just like spousal abuse and pedophilia, so it's highly unlikely a child would grow up to be a rapist just because its father was one. Second, although the child is partly the aggressor's child, it's also partly the victim's child. At any rate, this kind of reasoning means nothing to a woman in such a crisis state, and the reasons to terminate overwhelmingly outnumber the reasons not to. This scenario, however, has nothing to do with the issue of abortion, but rather, has everything to do with the issue of rape and the lenient laws which we support and tolerate; laws which mean nothing to those who perform violent acts against women as a result of how they are raised and knowing what they can get away with in our society.

What exactly is wrong with society in this day and age that any woman should have to endure such an ordeal? What is wrong with us that we continue to tolerate such gross oversights where the law is concerned? What exactly is it going to take for us to finally take care of ourselves and each other? Once we – by we I mean *all of humanity* – create serious zero-tolerance laws which mean something, and we lovingly raise our children to respect others, and we all look out for each other's wellbeing, then issues like rape and the resulting unwanted pregnancy will be a thing of the past.

Where the notion of terminating pregnancy due to health issues is concerned, there is also a solution. We've heard of instances where a fetus is diagnosed with acute health issues; severe physical anomalies or mental impediments, and the question often comes down to whether or not to terminate the pregnancy. With our current level of consciousness, it's virtually unfeasible to consider just what possible reason God would have for permitting a human to live under such conditions. That said, just because our current level of consciousness won't allow us to imagine the possibility of any quality of life for a child born with such ailments, it doesn't mean the quality of life doesn't or can't exist.

When it comes to birth defects, physical or otherwise, or the health threats to the mother, again, the true issue has nothing to do with abortion but has largely to do with environmental issues as well as our own compromised states of consciousness which create the anomaly(s). Everything from the foods we eat, to the air we breathe, the cleaners we use, the chemicals in our cosmetics and toiletries, the thoughts that pass through our minds, the words we speak and the things we do – it all plays a part in what's happening with our children, whether they're in the womb or in their bed. Clearly, we're not currently at the point where we can identify all the reasons for fetal health issues, and until we get to that point, we can only deal with the issues as they arise, but there's nothing stopping us from bettering the way we deal with things in the interim.

As much as I support the right to *choose*, I can't help but acknowledge abortion as the defective service it truly is. On a scientific level, it can easily be argued that a woman's decision to opt for abortion is just one of nature's ways of controlling the world's population, however, when one considers the resulting unnatural death of the fetus, and the consequential psychological ramifications enforced upon the women who undergo the procedure, it becomes clearly evident that abortion is not a natural solution at all, but rather, an *easy way out* of a challenging predicament. In all my studies about the laws of nature, I have learned this basic truth: *Nature never takes the easy way out!* On the other hand, it is perfectly natural for humans to want to bring an end to pain and fear. When a desperate crisis arises, it's natural to consider desperate measures, and the difficult decisions we must make in our times of crises are only made more difficult when political confusion enters the picture.

When I was eighteen years old, I worked at a ski resort in St. Jovite, Quebec, called *Grey Rocks Inn*. During that time, I had served in the dining section where renowned pro-choice activist, *Dr. Henry Morgentaler*, ate his breakfast. Breakfast that day was a buffet style service, so I didn't actually serve as much as I picked up the used dinnerware and thus didn't really converse much with him. I recall wanting to say something – anything – to him about what he does *(for those unaware; he performs abortions)*, but the thing was, he was such a gentleman. He was so kind and so polite, that I couldn't say anything. To make matters more interesting, he was there with his son; a beautiful child of about six or eight years old. Although I said nothing, I wondered if Dr. Morgentaler realized the role he played in depriving potential mothers the same divine love which he enjoyed with his own son. Yes, on one hand, his child was probably planned, as opposed to the majority of the fetuses he terminates, but in the same rite, I wondered if he had ever said to a woman; *you can have this child if you put your mind to it, you are a woman; women are resilient, love is resilient, you can do this!* On one hand, I suppose that kind of talk isn't good for business, but on the other hand, I don't think it's *all* about business.

Dr. Morgentaler, like all practitioners who execute the same work, is merely providing a service, and contrary to popular belief, they're doing some good. If they don't perform the abortions under professional and legal conditions, most of these abortions will be carried out in some other manner. Many of us have heard the horrifying details of self-administered abortions and illegal, botched, semi-surgical procedures and the consequential injuries, mutilations and fatalities endured by the women involved. As desperate times call for desperate measures, the measures a woman will reach for in the midst of her pain, anguish, fear and sense of hopelessness, should not involve self-mutilation, and it should not threaten her own life. Nor should it unnecessarily prolong the already excruciating death of the fetus. If a women us absolutely going to terminate her pregnancy, it should be done in a manner which does not add to the agonizingly painful experience she's obviously already living. In contrast to the alleged affirmative side of these professionals and their clinics, I do wonder how many women would come to such a decision if abortion clinics didn't exist and if it were more of an ordeal to get an abortion.

In 2008, it was announced that Dr. Morgentaler was to receive the *Order of Canada,* which is the highest honor of merit administered by the Governor General on behalf of the Queen. This is an award which most Canadians understand is meant to, among other things, honor an individual for an overall extraordinary contribution to their country, and to recognize, on some level, a magnificent body of work. On one hand, the recognition of Dr. Morgentaler in this capacity is nothing short of a veritable travesty of immeasurable proportions to the majesty of the *Order of Canada*, yet, on the other hand, Dr. Morgentaler deserves ten times over this award for crashing through barriers by fighting for women's basic rights and ultimately saving so many lives by professionally attending to women at the crisis time of their lives.

In 1969, Morgentaler opened his first abortion clinic and performed thousands of procedures which were at the time illegal. Morgentaler, a trained physician, argued that access to abortion was a *basic human right* and the women should not have to risk death at the hands of untrained practitioners in order to terminate their pregnancies. That said, I do wonder how a man; *a trained physician* who takes an oath to *save lives* and then overwhelmingly compromises his oath by *killing* human lives, can be inducted into an organization of individuals who dwell in *excellence* and the *affirmative realm of possibility.*

Furthermore, in order to achieve what he did in 1969, it required that he break the law in a grossly substantial fashion in the name of what *he* thought to be right; not in the name of what necessarily was right. Where Dr. Morgentaler did fight for women's right to abort, at the same time, he denied the rights – and lives – of thousands of humans, which included thousands of future women, and that aspect makes up the largest part of his body of work; a body of work that makes one wonder if it truly merits an *honor of merit*.

Ultimately, Dr. Morgentaler's award, along with his reputation and his career, would not be the enduring controversy it is and has been had we all woken up and looked at abortion for what it is: An *easy way out* of a consequence resulting from personal and global irresponsibility, our lack of accountability, and our contempt for the miracle that is life.

When one thinks on the immensely sensitive subject that is the issue of abortion, one cannot help but consider the possible, as well as the probable, issues humanity faces as a result of all the millions of human lives which did not come to be as a result of abortion. Of those millions of aborted fetuses could possibly have emerged the doctors who might have saved lives, the researchers who might have found cures for current plagues, the peacemakers who might have spread peace, the politicians who might have saved the economy, the avatars who might have discovered how to express truth in a manner which we could have all understood, or, even possibly, the messiah who might have brought peace to the lands. It also makes me wonder how many soul-mates and life-partners so many humans will never know because their prospective partners were simply not permitted to join humanity, and thus, a vast amount of us walk alone.

A popular rebuttal to this perspective is that, if no fetuses were aborted, along with doctors, researches and avatars, there would also have been murderers. However, the fact that there are currently more doctors than murderers, more researchers than murderers, and more avatars than murderers, and even more regular good people than murderers, clarifies that a lot more good than bad would have been born unto this world had they all been permitted to live. Even if there were murderers among those potential lives, perhaps the one murderer we could have learned the most from when it comes to forensic science was the one that got away. Either way, we'll never know. One thing is certain, however; if we were to couple the process of allowing these numerous lives to live, with the process of *Conscious Affirmative Living*, the world would be a completely different place, undeniably, for the better.

In researching this topic, I interviewed countless women who've had abortions. Of the entire group, none of them were completely at peace with having done it, and all of them expressed varying degrees of longstanding regret over it. In conversations with women who have walked this road, I learned that they unanimously agreed that many of their reasons for considering abortion at the time were merely fear-based excuses. All women interviewed recognized that, at the time, their fear, uncertainty, sense of shame, anguish, anger *(the list goes on)*, coupled with questions like what would happen if they had the child: What would they do, what would people say, who would help them, how would they care for the child, how would they finish school, who would adopt the child, would they be good to the child *(again, the list goes on)*? All this coupled with hormonal changes and confusing advice led them to ultimately make the decision according to what they felt they were faced with, and according to their emotional capacity at the time. In the end, they made their decision based upon the fact that it was the only thing over which they felt they had control. Ideals along the line of not wanting to bring a life into *this miserable world* were also excuses, but they later realized this excuse was not reason enough to make such a drastic decision. By the time they had come this realization, however, it was too late. The one constant heard from most of the interviewees was the lack of care and compassion, and general lack of services required to help ease them into making a different kind of decision.

Incidentally, if you're personally reading this in hopes of finding an answer to whether or not to terminate your pregnancy, you should know this: *The answer is within you.* Should you move forth with having your child, in the years to come, you will never regret *not* having aborted. In your search for direction, there will be no shortage of people to remind you of your *rights*, nor will there be a shortage of people to guilt you into giving your child life, and you know that additional confusion and guilt are the last things you need. That said, just because your current perspective may deny you to imagine joy does not mean the perspective of your child will deny him joy. In the same manner that you've laughed in the past, I promise you; you will laugh again. In this same manner, there is every reason in the world to believe that this child you carry will also laugh much in his lifetime, and cause many others to laugh as well. Wouldn't it be wonderful to know that, no matter who raises that child, you are the reason he'll experience that laughter?

Warnings about emotional burdens which follow abortion are not hearsay; they are fact. Abortion is not like suicide where we have no proof of what lies beyond. There are countless thousands of women who have been down that road and will tell you that abortion comes with deep and painful regrets. For the woman who reads this and is unsure of which path to take, just in case no one has yet told you: *You are a woman; women are resilient, and love is reliant. Allowing for and embracing life...you can handle this!*

No matter what the opinion, there is no denying that the reason abortion is such a big issue is because we're all intelligent. And, because we're intelligent, we all know that abortion isn't about merely terminating a pregnancy, it's about terminating a life; an innocent, defenseless and utterly precious life. Whatever our stance on the topic, whether pro-life or pro-choice, none of us can deny this fact. At least, none of us who *think*.

CHAPTER XVII

=Health=

Healthy people *think* healthy...

Okay, let's get right to the goods: There are five stages of health in which the human body can exist. The first stage is the *optimum health* state. When the body is in the optimum health state, there are no aches, pains, growths, acne, rashes or other disease-related symptoms. The *optimum* state of health is that under which all humans are intended to live.

The second state of health is the *crisis* state. Many people mistake the crisis state for the *optimum health* state because they feel that, if they're not taking any prescription medications or suffering any chronically debilitating diseases, then they must be in *optimum* health. Unfortunately, the *crisis* state is a very treacherous state, because it's where most individuals commonly overlook the signs and symptoms of what's really going on inside the body, and those dangerous words, *Maybe it'll go away...,* are vainly and foolishly uttered. Symptoms during this state are anything that brings an individual out of the *optimum health* state. All symptoms – from acne, rashes and dandruff, to fatigue, aches and pains – are all part of the *crisis* health stage. Like an infant or a teenager, any time the body is in crisis on the inside, it will ultimately announce its inner *state of being* on the outside; usually in a manner that's not becoming, and it won't be shy about it. And, like an infant or a teenager, ignoring the outer message is never a good idea.

The third state of health is the *sick* state. The sick state is where symptoms become unbearable and when individuals typically find the courage to visit their doctor(s) after they didn't have the courage to listen to their intuition and change their eating, living and *thinking* habits and addictions. This is when one or two prescription medications are prescribed to replace or accompany generic painkillers and other over the counter symptom remedies. Individuals under such medical supervision commonly consider themselves *optimally* healthy because their symptoms have been relieved and controlled by a foreign toxic substance, but, make no mistake; once a body is at the mercy of, and controlled by, prescription drugs, the body's natural healing process has been acutely compromised, and the individual is well past the *optimum health* state and far beyond a mere state of *crisis*. They are officially *sick*. Typically accompanied by the most perilous of attitudes – *denial* – the *sick* state is usually the most short-lived, routinely and rapidly giving way to the next regrettable state of health.

The fourth state of health is the *dying* state. Classically accompanied by the most perilous of interdependent diseases – denial & addiction – the *dying* state is usually the most lengthy and arduous state for individuals living outside of the *optimum health* state. When I speak about the *dying* state to individuals to whom it applies, the most common response is denial – this even while sitting in the midst of their vast collection of prescription and over the counter medications, medicines and remedies that would kill – literally; not figuratively – the mightiest horse. The unyielding denial of *sick* individuals stems not only from their leisurely progression from the *crisis* state into the *dying* state – a process which most individuals don't perceive with the passing of time and only find impossible to perceive due to the effects of prescription medication on the mind – but their denial also stems from addiction.

The two things to which individuals in the *dying* state are most addicted – beyond their medications and the attention their ailment ensures them – are their actual illness and the idea that they're somehow getting better and working their way towards being healthy. In all my personal and professional experiences, I've never witnessed any person in the *dying* state ever improve their state without first coming to terms with their denial and addiction, and without employing a substantial attitude change on their part. Everyone else in the *dying* state just dies. If you're reading this and you're taking more than two prescription medications, please take note: You're not sick; you're in the *dying* state. No exceptions!

The fifth state of health is the *transition* state. One can transition either negatively or affirmatively between states of health, and they can even go back and forth. When an individual is in the *optimal health* state, there's still room for improvement, because nobody ever has perfect health (which is why the term *optimal,* and not *perfect,* is used). Whether it's to maintain and improve optimal health, or to transition from the *dying* state to the *sick* state, or from the *sick* state to the *crisis* state, or from the *crisis* state to the *optimum health* state, the same ideas always apply: Affirmative shifts in thought, perspectives, actions, nourishment and alternative forms of personal care are vital.

Regardless of which of the first four health states you may find yourself, it must be understood that we are *always* in the state of constant transition. The transition state is generally on a decline for most individuals because most individuals are not *conscious* about their health, their diet and their own responsibility to constantly maintain and *self heal* themselves. They also associate *aging* with *illness,* however, there is absolutely no correlation between the two. In fact, there are countless well-aged, well-preserved fit, non *prescription-drug-reliant* seniors who can outrun, out-swim, out-dance, out-wrestle and generally out-live most of today's typical teenagers. Age simply has nothing to do with health. Sure, we maybe don't have the same vitality at fifty as we did at fifteen, but that's not a result of the body weakening; that's the body relinquishing the overkill of energy and interest required to fight against our enemies, to revolt against our parents, and especially to procreate. The *adolescent* and *young adult* phases of our lives are filled with energies required to do a specific job. As we age, we don't need to do those jobs anymore, which is also why we don't have to deal with the ravages of acne and all the other horrors that come with being a teen. Incidentally, if you are experiencing acne after the young adult phase of your life, it is a sign that your health is in the crisis stage.

Ultimately, as we live, we cannot choose whether or not to age, but we can – and do – choose whether or not to be healthy. It is the conscious individual who recognizes the sacred divinity of their body, and who recognizes their own responsibility to maintain that body. It is also the conscious individual who takes the less frequent path of health and healing, which is commitment, discipline, and self-respect.

Like with many things – relationships, money and so forth – our perspective on health is quite backwards. Our mentality of *putting the cart before the horse* not only prevents us from attaining and maintaining optimum health, but it also ensures quite the opposite. In an ideal world, there would be no health issues, however, we're not (yet) in that ideal world, and as such, when health issues do arise, they must be dealt with. My *cart before the horse* statement is entirely supported by the manner of which we approach *healing* illness, or rather, the way we embrace, coddle and worship illness as opposed to *preventing* illness.

Instead of treating the *cause* of illness, we have adapted ourselves to treating the *illness,* or worse, the *symptoms* of illness. So accustomed are we to treating the symptoms in fact that the idea of treating the *root cause* is often foreign to us. It starts with us treating a headache or stomach ache or nausea or heartburn or joint discomfort or dizziness or numbness – all symptoms (signs) that something else is transpiring in the body – without giving any thought to what those symptoms are trying to tell us. In truth, there is no such thing as *just* a headache or *just* nausea or *just* the other aforementioned symptoms. These and all the other symptoms (signs) are messages from the body telling us that something else is going on. Yes, sometimes a headache means you need to slow down and take a break, just as heartburn can just indicate you ate too fast or ate the wrong thing. Nonetheless, these symptoms – when reoccurring – are generally a message that the body is not in harmony, and that it needs attention, now!

Treatment of *the cause* of an illness can only happen when we *discover* the cause, but in so many cases, we're neglecting our search altogether, and we're spending time, money and lives on treatments and cures for *symptoms* when, in actuality, the true cure for most any ailment is *prevention*. Our current process of dealing with disease, especially ailments such as cancer, not only diminishes our chances of finding the cause and thus ever finding a cure, but it also affirms the presence, and ensures continued growth, of the disease.

I will admit that I am very impressed with the advances modern medicine has made, and continues to make, and I am not knocking all the countless millions of miracles for which modern medicine is responsible, however, it would be inaccurate to state that medical science has not played a role in holding humanity back in its own rite. That said, it would also be incorrect to state that medical science hasn't tried to get humans to just take care of themselves. Doctors spend much time lecturing patients to exercise, cut salt, reduce sugar, quit smoking, drinking, drugs and so forth, and patients continue on their destructive path, knowing that they are killing themselves, and then they complain how insensitive doctors are becoming.

As for the pharmaceutical industry, I've got to say that many humans are really a bunch of ungrateful lemmings! The pharmaceutical industry has gone above and beyond to provide cures that even by today's advanced standards are nothing short of utter miracles. If humans would have had a simple bottle of Tylenol or Advil two hundred years ago, I think it would have blown their minds *(think of how many people died because they simply couldn't get a fever down, and today all we have to do is pop a pill!)*. Now here we are in the twenty-first century with everything and anything at our disposal, and we're griping about how selfish the pharmaceutical industry is and that they're not really looking for cures for our ailments.

Yes, *big pharma* wants to make money, but if the pharmaceutical industry is providing disease control instead of cures, it's not because they're greedy; it's because they're giving us what we've been asking for: *Keep us alive while we kill ourselves.* We know we're not supposed to eat, drink, smoke and do certain things, but we do it all, and it makes us sick, and then we complain when the residuals of our actions can't be remedied. We all know how to prevent illness, but we just don't want to do it. Pharmaceutical companies might seem greedy, but if they are, we're the ones who give them the power. If we'd all just eat right, take care of ourselves, and stop getting so stressed out about everything we think about, we'd all be healthy, and the pharmaceutical companies would go out of business, just like the telegram companies did not so long after the widespread usage of Email technology made telegrams obsolete. Maybe *big pharma* figures that if we're going to keep killing ourselves, they may as well learn from us, and make a few bucks along the way. In short, the responsibility of our personal health is *our own*, and as much as medical science is doing its part to heal the world, it is our responsibility to feed our bodies and minds properly, and exercise them regularly.

Beyond pharmaceutical endeavors, our health is not the fault of a national *healthcare system*. Yes, nations should take care of their people, but it's the responsibility of people to first take care of themselves. Governments should provide complete healthcare for children and seniors since, after all, they are the ones who are usually the most vulnerable, but here's where the limitations should come in: Everybody should get healthcare, but if a person smokes, heavy-drinks or uses drugs, they should be completely exempt. If people don't maintain their ideal weight within a certain *(generous)* ratio, they're also cut off; why should everybody pay for the results of detrimental eating habits of others? Yes, all sick people should be medically cared for, but if they don't take care of themselves, they should be billed for services. The deal with healthcare should be: *We'll take care of you if you take care of you!*

Clearly, healthcare isn't free; someone has to pay for it. It's at this time that I would like to correct anyone who thinks that healthcare in Canada is free *(thank you, Michael Moore)*. First off, not all medical services are covered in Canada; dentists, optometrists and many tests for example. What is covered – whether or not it's used – Canadians pay for through very high taxes. Although Canada has great doctors and nurses and caring orderlies, it's very common to have to wait many hours to be seen by a doctor. These reasons, coupled with the fact that healthcare keeps declining, should encourage us to eat better and take care of our health, especially since we all really do know better.

It's illogical how people will plant themselves in the dentist's chair, feeling sorry for themselves in the midst of having a root-canal treatment and thinking, *"If I'd have only known this would have happened, I would have brushed, flossed, rinsed, etc..."*, but the truth is, they've known all along that brushing and flossing are essential to oral health maintenance. This same pity-process applies to most health issues. We know exactly what to do, or what not to do, but we do very little, or nothing at all, to prevent health issues and to maintain our bodies. Then, when it all comes crashing down, we get on the horn to anyone who'll listen, which is pretty much everyone, because we love the drama and enjoy playing the hero/savior game as much as the *sick* enjoy being the victim, and so the cycle persists. Of course, lack of nutrition and exercise are not the only culprits when it comes to health, and many people do take good care of themselves, otherwise, why else would more serious afflictions affect us? For example, how does a perfectly healthy, well fed, well exercised, well educated child develop a terminal disease? How does an expectant mother who does everything "by the book" miscarry or develop a disfigured fetus? How does an athlete who is healthy, strong and focused, develop cancer?

In all your searching, you will never find a stronger advocate than me when it comes to the power of employing affirmations for health and healing. However, it would be inaccurate to suggest that all illness is attributed to just *attitude* or *thought,* or that it can be cured by just doing affirmations. There's a lot more going around each of us than just what goes on inside our heads and our hearts. Things like electricity, radio frequencies, microwaves, radiation and an abundance of energies we haven't yet discovered how to manipulate, and energies we haven't discovered period. When you consider the magnitude of these energies alone going through our bodies, it's easy to imagine how they can and do manipulate the body's cells and thus compromise our health. When you add those energies to a body that's led by a mind which continually emphasizes negative thoughts, then couple that with unhealthy diets and lifestyles, then fascinating conditions, negative as they may be, can't help but develop within the body.

Energy and thought aside, consider for a moment a typical healthy woman in her thirties residing in a major metropolitan city. Consider the cosmetics she uses each day – a combination of petroleums, oils, colors, dyes, chemicals, hydrates, chlorides and so forth. Consider her hair dye and perm treatment, laundry detergent, fabric softener, shower soap, shampoo, conditioner, perfume, lip liner, lipstick, lip gloss, eyeliner, eye shadow, concealer, foundation, powder, fingernail polish, polish remover, hair mousse, gel and spray. Now consider her toothpaste, mouthwash, antiperspirant, contact lens solution, feminine odor/itching cream, sanitary napkins, and hydrating body creams and lotions.

When pharmaceutical companies develop anything, they must ensure all ingredients which go into their various products are compatible with each other so the products are safe for consumers. The problem is that, although chemicals in a product from one manufacturer may be basically harmless to the body, those chemicals might not be compatible with the chemicals of another product from another manufacturer. Whereas most eyeliner chemicals are fully compatible with most lip liner chemicals, neither are necessarily compatible with the contents of other products, cosmetic or otherwise, and that's where the dangers come into play. On one hand, all may seem harmless since, for example, the eye-liner is on the face and the antiperspirant is under the arms, and the food byproducts are in the belly, but the mix takes place *inside* the body, under and within the skin, where everything is absorbed. To a scientific researcher, what can and does happen as a result of this mix is a very exciting phenomenon, however, to the person whose body in which this goes on, it is usually devastating.

Now consider the same woman stepping out into the smoggy air she breathes daily. Then consider the stagnant air she breathes inside her office, and the office chemicals; copy, fax and printer machine ink, computer radiation, carpet fiber chemicals, carpet freshener, cleaner chemicals, bathroom cleansers, air fresheners, radio waves; all taking into consideration that this office is up to code, yet noting that most offices are commonly not completely up to code.

Now, combine this woman's exposure to everything previously mentioned, multiply that by five years, and then try to imagine her *not* developing some kind of ailment. Keep in mind; in all that the woman is exposed to, I've not included compromised dietary rituals or habits such as smoking, drinking and use of recreational drugs. I've also left out personal factors like work-related stress, personal relationship stress, lack of sleep & rest, and chemical traces of product substances left by colleagues. Then there are artificial sweeteners, seasonings, basic antibiotics and other prescription and over the counter medications. Over the process of a few years, the chemical absorptions which the body endures all add up, and the body has no natural way of processing them. In some cases, the body either finds a place to *dump* the chemicals which lead to lumps of whatever cells by which they are joined. In other cases, worse or better happens, depending on if you are the scientist, or if you are the patient.

Where optimal health is concerned, history, science and technology have unanimously revealed that the cure for anything is in the research into, and in the prevention of, the cause. Continuing in the past and current manner of which we largely do, to cure disease by merely cutting away the results of an ailment, is about as logical as swallowing a box of bandages in order to stop internal bleeding. When it comes to medicine, forward thinking shouldn't be about creating the ultimate insulin, it should be about healing and preventing illness of the pancreas.

On a related topic; a process which is quickly becoming a fad at an alarming rate among women with a history of breast cancer in their family gene pool, is to undergo a double mastectomy, even after extensive testing proves their bodies to be absolutely healthy and cancer-free in the immediate. The idea is that if you remove the breast, you've removed the chances of the breast developing cancer. This fad is largely growing out of fear than anything else, and it is a practice that is as barbaric and destructive as it is appallingly archaic.

The whole point of preventative therapy of any kind is not only to avoid the ailment itself, but to avoid anything the ailment causes, including the need for treatment resulting in consequential scarring and psychological trauma. Although removing the breast may prevent cancer from settling in *the breast*, and for some *(note word: some)* provides an excellent excuse to get breast implants with the benefit of sympathy instead of judgment, everything a woman feels as a result of such a procedure is every bit as traumatizing and damaging. Yes, it does make a difference for a woman to undergo said procedure without having to deal with chemotherapy, radiation and the other medications that actual cancer treatments may require, but just because removal of the breast may suggest *no breast cancer*, there is no guarantee that cancer won't develop in other areas of the body, and, anybody who will develop cancer to the breast can develop it anywhere else in the body. Ultimately, any alleged preventative procedure which requires cutting away the very portion of the anatomy which it alludes to protect from disease, is not a measure of prevention; it's a measure of mutilation. This archaic ideal is equivalent to executing a traditional abortion in order to save a fetus.

One much overlooked fact about our genetic makeup is that, much of what we inherit from our families has more to do with ill *thinking* than with ill *bodies*. We inherit our family's ideas; their way of thinking, their pessimism, their negativity, their anger, their sadness, and usually their way of eating. Ensuring that we don't inherit Mom's breast cancer or Grandpa's diabetes has far more to do with changing the thought patterns we've inherited from Mom or Gramps. If you're not entirely sold on this idea, just pay attention to someone who is accident-prone *(all thumbs or clumsy)* and then take a good look at one or both of their parents, and you'll find a connection. Usually the clumsy person is that way because they grew up watching Mom or Dad or someone else in their life getting much attention from *goofing up*, and thus, they continually goofed up to get that attention, whether it was good attention or bad attention. Being accident-prone is not an inherited ailment; it's merely carelessness nurtured, and so it grows and flows through the generations – this usually based on the payoff that is the reaction to the *alleged* inadvertent mishaps. Our generation to generation thought-process is far more responsible for our inherited ailments than actual physical genes. In this discovery lies the ideal that, if we're to cut away anything as a *preventative* measure, we must cut away negative though patterns before anything else.

Beyond thought, the process of finding the cure for any ailment requires that we *observe* the ailment. Removing the breast is *not* removing the problem, because the problem isn't the breast; the problem is cancer. In truth, cancer isn't the problem either. Cancer cells are actually vital to our genetic makeup. Cancer *sickness* is actually about our body and our cells being out of balance. The problem with cancer is first and foremost nutrition. Our bodies are starving, dehydrated and chemically toxic, and cancer is a resilient cell that can endure such extreme conditions. All that said, a harmonious world is not a world of healthy young women medically mutilating their bodies because of a health scare. Harmony is not examining one's self, searching for "the lump" each time one steps out of the shower either (although I do recognize that in current times, at least with self-examination, one's chances of maintaining optimum health are greater than with unnecessary surgery). Nonetheless, genetic health issues are not only the result of physical dynamics but also the result of diet, environment, and especially mental conditioning; much of which are factors passed on through generations. Either way, any doctor will tell you that even when the genetic factors go from *possible* to *probable*, there is still no *guarantee* that cancer will absolutely develop.

Before this popular new fad of de-breasting women becomes a trend, we need to ask ourselves; if every single young woman with a family history of breast cancer should undergo a complete double mastectomy procedure, how will this affect entire generations of children to follow who will not be breastfed? How will this process affect the mentality of the women we know as our mothers, grandmothers, aunts, sisters and daughters? How will this process affect the world after just one generation?

For anybody not concerned with future generations on the basis that you aren't involved or won't be around long enough to be affected, keep in mind; *life doesn't end here!* You are involved whether or not you like to think you aren't, and on some level, in generations to come, it will involve you and *it will matter.* This is one example of *energetic Truths* that I cannot explain with words without compromising its *core value,* suffice it to say; do your part, get involved, because it matters today and it will matter in generations to come! This concept also applies to knowledge and education. Learn everything you can, because all education and knowledge accompanies you beyond this place, and it will always serve you, and it will serve God.

In the event that this archaic medical procedure becomes the norm, where do we draw the line? If eighty percent if all men are to develop prostate cancer in their lifetime, does this mean that all men should have their prostates removed well before this could happen? Does this also mean that anybody with AIDS, knowing the likelihood of them dying from the disease, should just call it a day and take their life now? This process bothers me because, in humanity's fight against cancer, we're so determined to win that we're letting cancer win before it even has the chance to develop. It wins because, whether a woman removes her breast because of cancer, or she does it because of the *fear* of cancer; cancer wins. Cancer *illness* is like a bully, and too many people bow down to bullies, to the point that people – adults and children alike – commit suicide over bullies. Ending one's life because of a bully is no different than compromising one's health over the *fear* of cancer. Our planetary society is young, and we're still all about fighting, and I can accept that this is where we are at present. In my view, however, if we're going to fight this thing, let's really take it on; let's not remove the battlefield and pretend we've won the war on this thing.

For a moment, I'd like to draw your attention back to the *affirmative living* process mentioned throughout this entire book. Whatever we think about, the universe (God) is responding to affirmatively. The answer is always *Yes*. If every person were to think, speak, feel and act *affirmatively* every moment of the day, then that is what the universe will offer back. If we remind every single woman, through television, though books, through magazines, through ribbons, through music, through whatever medium, that she needs to *"beware of cancer"*, she will live in fear and she will experience cancer. If a woman is to examine herself every time she gets out of the shower, she's on the search for cancer, and even for the healthiest woman; s*eek and ye shall find!*

Once again, I completely acknowledge that thought and attitude are not the only factors responsible for disease, however, the difference in thought and attitude for a person at risk might just very well be the difference that tips the scale in their favor. For anybody who is remotely concerned or obsessed with statistics, here's a great idea; eat only the best foods available, live every day and every moment as affirmatively as possible, and just think about *optimum health.* If your friends don't click with your new attitude, find new friends. Do this because your life just may very well depend on this change. Do it now! Again, thought and attitude alone are not solely responsible for illness, but when removed from the equation of all the things that are out of our control, affirmative thought and attitude serve as building blocks leading *away from* illness rather than leading *towards* illness.

On a grander scale of consciousness, it's not the methods of which we go about healing ourselves that should convince us of our ancient and obsolete thinking, but rather, it's the mere fact that we even get sick in the first place. We humans are at a point in our emotional and spiritual developmental stage where we should not only be able to heal the body with the mind, but also be able to *prevent* illness. As previously mentioned, one major reason we get sick is because we don't listen to our bodies when our bodies are trying to tell us that something's not right. We do this with relationships, with jobs, and even with money matters. We don't listen to that inner voice which speaks through our bodies. When it comes to our health, we especially don't listen. Most of us can feel when the body needs to rest or when we're stressing it beyond its capacity, but for those of us who choose to be conscious of our body-awareness sensitivity, we still neglect to heed the body's warnings.

A prime example of this in our current day is when, instead of understanding that our heartburn means the body is trying to tell us not to eat that chili-dog, we eat it anyway, along with a handful of cheap antacid. When the cheap antacid no longer works, we move on to the more expensive antacid. When that no longer works, we move on to the prescription acid-reflux medication, but at no time will we accept that the chili-dog must go. Obviously this is just one example, and I can already hear the arguments about how "even salad gives me reflux", but trust me; the salad gives you reflux because foods like the chili-dog damaged your system. Furthermore, when a drug no longer works for our ailment, it's not the drug that's the problem; it's usually an indication that our ailment has worsened.

Diabetes is among the absolute best examples of a completely controllable, reversible and emotionally fed illness. Yes, there are children who are born with diabetes or who develop it due to other factors, but when it comes to the vast majority of all diabetics, they not only bring it on, but they nurture and coddle their ailment like it's their new best friend. The first major detriment is in labeling oneself *as* the illness rather than claiming to merely *have* the illness. *Being diabetic* as opposed to *having diabetes* works to *encourage* the illness because not only are we dwelling upon the illness, but we're actually *being* the illness.

For most diabetics, their basic mentality is stuck in the past; either dwelling on what never came to be and what could have been. It's also a controller's disease (people who like to control), and it's the disease of those carrying deep grief and who possess attachments to that grief. Unresolved and blocked anger has perhaps the most to do with diabetes. I admit that I have never met a person who was *diabetic* who didn't have major unresolved deep-rooted anger issues. Regardless of what causes illness, it's very clear that in order to heal the body, we must first heal the mind. Conversely, if we worked on healing our emotions, then the ailments which develop within the body as a result of unresolved emotional strain would never develop in the first place.

Obviously another major reason we're so sick is because of what we put our bodies through, whether it's the wrong foods or the unnecessary stress we put ourselves through each day. Some of the many unnecessary stresses include working at jobs we don't care about and dealing with people we shouldn't be dealing with, but we've been programmed to let our guilt and our need for approval rule all of our decisions, and in doing so, guilt and approval addiction rules our lives. As a society, we have learned to live with the idea that *we gotta do what we gotta do*, whether it's dealing with a dead-end job or putting up with an abusive partner. In all actuality, however, we don't *gotta* do anything, but we do it to be good little boys and girls so that everyone will approve of us and we won't feel guilty, and that is the norm.

Jobs and relationships aside, it's the small day to day, moment to moment decisions we make, and the stresses we take on which really make up our lives. Stresses like our indecisiveness, our lack of commitment, and our inability to prioritize what's important in life. And then there's getting into debt, eating toxic foods, smoking, drinking, drugs, refined sugar, sweeteners, and arguing with stupid people about stupid things that make us want to quit our stupid job, leave our stupid partner, drink that stupid drink, light that stupid cigarette and get this stupid life over with! As a society it looks like we're pretty stupid, but in reality, we're actually all-brilliant beings just doing stupid things.

Our words are perhaps the single most powerful tool we possess when it comes to healing or wounding ourselves and our world. Think about the word *love*, and there's something distinctly special about its energy. Conversely, think about the word *hate*, and feel how the mere thought of it sounds in comparison to the word Love. Words, titles, names; they're all very powerful, especially when attached to anything that has to do with healing. Take for example organizations with names reminiscent of *Fat-Controllers*, *Hospital for Diseased Children*, and *Unidentified Addicts*. Compare these titles to names like *Slim-Club*, or *Kids-Healing Center*. As for addiction programs, addicts would have more success if the various programs didn't carry the ailments' name in their titles, constantly reminding addicts of the problem plaguing their lives.

Before I continue, I wish to make a point that most organizations geared towards healing are truly great organizations; they save and affirmatively change thousands of lives every day, and, let's face it, their names are about marketing, and they make it very clear about what they do. That said, I can appreciate the fact that the only way an alcoholic can heal himself is to first admit that he's got a problem, however, how can a person truly heal if he stands in front of a crowd every week for the rest of his life and says *"I'm an alcoholic!"*? Additionally, how can he be healed if he's constantly reminded that he will *never* be healed and that alcoholism is his lifetime illness? I believe that anything and everything is curable, and I also believe that alcoholism is not an illness but merely the result of the lack of self-control, self-respect and discipline. Addiction in any form is a decision. As with all forms of addiction, alcoholism is a *conscious choice*.

To underscore the ideal that addiction is not an actual *illness*, consider this: A woman with cancer does not necessarily consciously and willingly put cancer into her body, whereas an alcoholic does consciously and willingly put alcohol into their body. Furthermore, if you take a woman with cancer and place her on a desert island with the basic essentials – food, water, shelter – but you don't treat the cancer, she'll die. If an alcoholic, however, is placed on a desert island with the same basic essentials, they're most likely to survive. This is because cancer is an *illness* whereas addiction is a *state* arrived at through the unwillingness to rectify underlying factors. For example, if alcoholism is the result of depression, then depression is the illness; not alcoholism. Alcoholism is merely the bandage or calling card, or the cry for help. It is not the actual illness.

In an advanced, *conscious* civilization, alcoholism would not be a problem, because we'd know how to have an amazing time without chemically altering our minds, and we'd know how to get through difficulties without drowning our sorrows. The fact remains, however, that alcoholism is a problem and requires attention, but convincing people that they are anything else than healthy can only keep them ill. If a breast cancer survivor went back to the clinic every week for the rest of her life and declared to everybody that she has *(or is)* cancer, and she is committed to the ideal that she'll never be healed, what do you think her prognosis would be in the weeks, months and years which followed?

Twelve-step programs are very useful, but their basic concepts are in dire need of revamping, to say the least. I personally approve of acknowledging a problem, taking responsibility for oneself, making amends, and especially developing a relationship with God; whatever that means to each person. These are marvelous steps towards healing addiction, but the idea that an addict will always be an addict implies that addiction is beyond the person's control, and this is simply false.

The vast majority of people who attend twelve-step programs are slated to attend the program for the duration of their lives. Alcoholics, for example, are supposed to participate in the program to heal, but at best, they end up trading one addiction in for another addiction. Coffee and cigarettes are usually the first addictions, and of course there is the sympathetic attention that comes with sharing personal drama with the masses *(which brings us back to the past, leaving us feeling powerless in the now)*. I can appreciate that some people have had difficult times in life, but the truth is, almost all of us have had tough times, but we're not all resorting to addiction. Addiction is not a sign of sickness; it's a sign of weakness. One can only conquer weakness through discipline. In an ideal world, we'd know what to do, but we're not in that ideal world. Or, are we?

Dealing with addicts in our lives is simple. This is my proven method, and it works like a charm every single time. This applies to everybody, regardless of age or relationship. The rule of thumb here is simple: If an addict is in your life, then *you* are involved. If you're involved, then you enable it and therefore are part of the problem. My system is, *don't be part of the problem!* I have made the irrevocable decision that addicts have no place in my life (*addicts; not recovering addicts*). If and when I discover an addict in my life, I offer them help *once*, I then give them the ultimatum, and they get *only one chance!* I make it very clear to them that they either get it right the first time, or they are out of my life.

Anyone who knows me knows I mean business when it comes to who I *hang* with. In a world filled with so many people doing their best to better themselves and make the world a better place in spite of what life has handed them, and so many of them wanting to be my friend, why would I waste my time on someone who chooses a line or bottle over me? I have all the compassion in the world for addicts. I feel for their pain; I know it's real, but I have zero tolerance for the victim game, and I do not tolerate liars.

This process applies to your child as well, no matter how young. You may have absolutely nothing to do with your child's addiction, but if you don't do all that you can do *right now*, you are part of the problem. If he's thirteen and he's brought drugs into the house, have him arrested. Drugs are illegal; your child knows this and must understand the consequences of his own actions. How children escalate to the point of illegal dealings is not always clear, but most boundaries are established in the home. If you are responsible for your child's lack of boundaries, then don't have him arrested; get help *now* for both of you.

Contrary to what the traditional twelve-step programs have been suggesting since their humble beginnings; healing addiction *is* possible, but it is only possible once an addict taps into the motive behind the addiction. Furthermore, avoiding a casino doesn't mean you've got gambling licked; going to a casino and being *indifferent* to participating does. The same goes for smoking and drinking. Addiction is an *obsessive habit* which can only be broken, or cured, by overriding a person's current state of consciousness. Every person can do this.

When we apply this thinking to *dieting*, we clearly see why the majority of weight-loss programs don't work. *Weight-Watchers* is perhaps the most well-respected and renowned weight-loss organization in the world. One reason for their success is because they were one of the first to recognize that *diets don't work;* lifestyle changes do. They understood long ago that people didn't merely want to take off the weight; they wanted to keep it off, but nobody wants to diet forever. Consequently, *Weight-Watchers* researched what people could do on a day-to-day basis to keep the weight off and still be able to eat like a normal person. Concepts such as portion control and points systems overtook old ideals of abstinence and fat & caloric intake, and people learned to eat, live and feel like normal humans again. In the process, many broke the cycle of 'eating disorders' and were healed because they were educated on how to eat; not trained that they were sick and couldn't be healed.

Again, my only objection to most health-aimed organizations when it comes to health consciousness is their names. The reason I bring this up is, if a person is struggling with weight or alcoholism, having the word *weight* or *alcohol* as part of their thinking isn't conducive to attaining a goal of being *slim* or *sober.* This is why banks utilize terms like *money* and *savings* and *interest* rather than *pact*, *debt* and *buyer's remorse*. Consider what comes to mind when you compare the words in the name *International Fat & Chunky Group* with the words in the name *Slim & Trim Health Team*. With which organization would you rather be identified? Which one sounds more goal-oriented to you? Which one better describes your intentions? On the surface, words may seem minor, but words are powerful tools which work for or against us throughout our entire day. If fat is someone's biggest struggle, the word *fat* will ensure the struggle continues. This concept is applicable to whatever we're struggling with. Just think of what the word *collection* means to a person who is constantly in debt. Then think of what the word *collection* means to someone who has several beloved priceless classic cars.

Words are powerful, and they, along with thought, feeling and action, must play a role in healing the world. This is an all-encompassing, multidimensional, *spherical* concept that should be applied to all we say and do, right down to the advertisements and names of organizations aimed at healing. Moreover, the idea behind every healing organization should be geared towards *healing;* never suggesting that people will never be healed, or that their healing is beyond the *realm of possibility*, for it is only a matter of time before we all accept that the mind that heals is the mind that dwells at the very core of that *conscious affirmative* realm.

CHAPTER XVIII

=SexAndSexuality=

Sex isn't overrated; it's merely improperly exercised...

I strongly suspect that, at this point, a few readers will probably want to burn this book, especially after arriving at this chapter, but what can I say other than; *Ah, the joys of a no refund policy!* When I considered that some people might take offence to this chapter, I decided that their prudishness is not my problem; it's theirs. I figured that if people are going to be offended by ideals surrounding the most important and glorious form of human creativity, I probably lost them at page one. My intention with this chapter isn't to offend, but, in the event that people are offended, I make no apologies, because if there's any topic we should be openly and freely discussing, and having fun with in the process, it's definitely sex. So, let's get it on!

For most of us, while growing up, there was no shortage of people who were determined to make us feel ashamed about the idea of sex or thinking about sex or needing sex or wanting sex. Between parents not wanting to discuss sex, and parents miscommunicating the facts, whether due to their own shame, upbringing, religious convictions, or merely their attempts to protect us, they messed us all up real good. The ideals that came with their convictions had little, if anything, to do with the facts, and even less to do with love. Sure, their hearts may have been in the right place, but they weren't dealing with their hearts, they were dwelling in fear and ignorance, and as a result, for generations, humanity has been taught to despise, loath, fear and feel guilty about the one single solitary concept that we can say is indisputably the most natural and necessary thing about humanity. And that's just the damage inflicted upon us by our parents!

God knew what he was doing when he created us. He made us sensitive in just the right places in order to make sex feel so good that we'd want to do it again and again and...well, you get the idea. And to spice things up and to ensure an ancient ritual would always be fresh and alluring, he made us all just a bit kinky! That's right: ALL OF US! The truth is, we all want something more than merely inserting a key into a lock, even if it's just incorporating a mere *wiggly-jiggly* at just the right time. This process, with or without the *wiggly-jiggly,* is not an accident. It is part of God's divine purpose, and it's about time we take a chill-pill and stop making a mockery of one of the greatest gifts God ever gave us, and put an end once and for all to the guilt, fear, shame and lies imposed upon human sexuality.

I'm all for moralistic integrity, but there's a line between encouraging morals and *living in denial,* and that line is not in the least bit fine. The idea that someone has the right to tell anyone what they can and cannot do with other consenting adults in the privacy of their home is ludicrous beyond reproach. The kind of control over nature that we're suggesting by trying to control humanity's sexuality is not only impossibly dangerous to our existence, but it's quite simply impossible. Humanity has learned to associate the very notion of sex with fear, guilt, immorality, sin, wickedness, disobedience, misbehavior, depravity, corruption, dishonesty (have I turned you off yet?) and the list goes on. Is it any wonder why sex hurts so much the first time for so many? This inhumane thought process of sex being evil is the seed of which ideals of alleged punishments for transgressions are born. Ideals like unwanted pregnancy, venereal disease, death, hell, and anything we think is a punishment for having sex.

Humans are extremely talented at rejecting anything they can't understand, and no exception is made when it comes to the idea of homosexuality and bisexuality and tri-sexuality *(I don't know what that last one means, but I think it has to do with whipped cream and jumper-cables)*. The biggest barriers working against homosexuality are the ideals resulting from religion. Just as we habitually reject and find fault with anything we don't understand, so is it that we reject and judge homosexuality because we have been, and still are, unable to conceive of what possible use God could have for the concept that is homosexuality. For centuries, millions upon millions of people; both men and women, have been deprived of their God-given right to sexual self expression because society simply didn't understand the concept and thus chose to persecute homosexuality. It has been this way for thousands of years, and we still do this.

I am not an advocate for homosexuality; I am an advocate for Truth, and I have yet to witness any indisputable evidence to deny the process of homosexuality as normal and natural. Why is it that we can't take the word of a person who is homosexual; that it is normal to be homosexual, yet we can take the word of any woman that it is normal to yearn for a child to the extent she is willing to go through the inconceivable pain of childbirth? Yes, it's clear that childbirth is a natural process of life, but just because we don't *see* the natural process of life implied by homosexuality does not mean there isn't one.

In spite of what many people think, homosexuality is not a choice. It is no more a choice than heterosexuality. In the instance of bisexuality, one can perhaps choose which "lifestyle" they're going to pursue, but even then, many bisexuals opt for the *straight* life out of fear and shame. If homosexuality actually was a choice, I'm quite convinced that most gays would *choose* to be straight, if for no other reason than to become wonderful moms and dads instead of being merely wonderful aunts and uncles. The theory that homosexuality is not a choice is emphasized by the lengths most homosexuals will go to hide it. It's no secret that many artists (I'd venture to say *most* artists), whether actors or singers or otherwise, are gay or bisexual, and for many (many; not all) of them, their career choice is often largely based upon the approval they crave and/or are addicted to. If a person were so adamant on getting such mass approval, the last thing they'd do is choose to be gay or bisexual in a society where being gay or bisexual is so frowned upon.

Our sexuality is just one area where labels truly do affect us in the most negative of ways. Most people have had or will at some point, on some level, have a homosexual en-counter, whether it's a simple kiss, or the whole *lay me down and do me* experience. Some will like it, some won't, and some will feel shame about it, and they'll try to con-vince themselves and anybody else who finds out about their experience that, *I'm not gay!* First off, you don't have to be gay to have sex with the same gender; plain sex with a man or with a woman is just sex; plain and simple. You don't need to be straight in order to have sex with an opposing gender any more than you need to be gay to have a same-sex sexual encounter, but you also don't have to convince anybody, including yourself, of what you are or aren't because of your experience. Judging people by their orientation or experiences is simply immature.

Currently there are many groups, religious mostly, who do their best to try and change homosexuals and make them "straight", and there are even people who claim to have been changed as a result of such "training", but you can no more train a man to be straight than you can train a man to be gay. Brainwashing can definitely work to convince a man to live in denial, but it will not change a man's essence.

Some years ago, a man appeared on a popular television talk-show, claiming that he used to be gay and that with the help of God, he became straight. I admit that I cringed at the first few words of the interview, but I decided to listen in the off chance I'd learn I was erroneous in my convictions. During the interview, the man spoke of how he was previously a drug-addict and became a hustler *(male prostitute)* to pay for his addiction. He said that after he had cleaned up his act, he prayed and became straight. What upset me about this interview is that, millions of people listened to his story, sold on his convictions that *gayness* can be cured, but few realized that this man was not even a homosexual. He was a drug addict, and, like all acute addicts in the height of their need, they'll do just about anything to get their *fix*, including prostituting themselves to whoever will arrange that fix. This man's sexual actions were not a result of a sexual orientation, but rather, clearly the result of his acute drug-addiction.

Comparing homosexuality with prostitution is simply beyond absurd. They're not even related. Prostitution is a *profession;* not an *orientation,* and it's as much a *straight* profession as it is a *gay* or *bi* profession *(it's also a "tri" profession, but I think the whipped cream costs extra, and you have to provide your own jumper-cables).*

Linking *homosexuality* with *promiscuity* is also completely inaccurate. Sexual promiscuity is a mindset regardless of orientation or gender. It's in our nature to want sex, and to want it regularly, and just because we choose to remain faithful and monogamous doesn't mean promiscuity is not on our minds. It has also been suggested many times over that homosexuality is a sexual addiction, however, inasmuch as homosexuals are just as predisposed to sex-addiction as are heterosexuals, scientific research shows that homosexuality is merely a natural expression of human sexuality; it is not an addiction. If it were an addiction, gays would not be able to function without sex, nor have successful lives or normal family lives. Addiction, whether to sex, drugs, gambling, spending or any other vice that takes over our lives, is the result of obsessive behavior, weakness and lack of discipline, and it all yields the exact same results regardless of gender or orientation: *It destroys lives.*

Just because a person is of a different orientation does not imply they are *consumed* by their orientation. Yes, there are sex-addicts among the ranks, but just because some are addicts doesn't mean they're all addicts. I would even venture to guess that the numbers of addicts among homosexuals per capita would not be any higher than that of heterosexuals, if for no other reason than for the in-nate surplus of creative energy most homosexuals seem to exhibit and which serves as a natural outlet for excess sexual energy.

One of the main reasons homosexuality stands out so much in society, and why gays are so segregated from the "straight" world, is because of all the attention society lavishes on homosexuals. Religion plays a huge role in the attention given to homosexuals; there is probably way more attention given to homosexuals due to religion than from gay activism. In fact, the first time I ever heard the word *homosexual,* I was a young child in church, and the preacher *(or fraud or closet-case or whatever...)* was telling the congregation about what gays do and how evil they are.

Incidentally, on a brief note away from homosexuality, when I was fourteen years old, I had no idea who the artist Prince *(known as formerly or currently)* was, but thanks to a church preacher, I, along with the entire congregation, was made aware of a rocker named Prince and his song lyrics referring to him encountering a woman who was in the process of gratifying herself with a periodical in the vestibule of an inn. This anecdote might not have as much to do with homosexuality as it has to do with inadvertent religious glorification of sexual deviancy, but it is yet another testament to what happens when religious addicts preach judgment instead of love.

At fourteen, I knew nothing about my raging hormones, and I was a respectable young man who wanted to be a priest, and I was present on that day to worship God and learn the gospel; not to get ideas about what goes on in seedy hotel lobbies *(and made to wonder where those hotels just might be).* Had I been preached to about loving God, I might have remained focused on my goal that day *(and for weeks later).* Instead, I was taught about gays and having sex in public places with hot chicks and dirty publications, and I was introduced to a sexy androgynous idol that sang and danced and drove a purple motorcycle, and I didn't even have to leave the church pew. Unsurprisingly, I learnt to really appreciate church that day for reasons other than God.

In an *affirmatively conscious* society, homosexuality would not be an issue. In fact, it would not stand out at all. It's unfortunate for the gay community that in the current society, usually the many homosexuals that do get the attention are obnoxious, arrogant, and usually quite tactless and overtly sexually promiscuous. Contrary to what we're led to believe, this obnoxious, arrogant, sex-crazed attitude is not shared by all gays, just as it is not shared by all straights. Many straight men are arrogant, obnoxious and tactless about sex, and this has nothing to do with their orientation; it has to do with their upbringing, with their maturity level, and especially with their level of integrity. Gay or straight, a gentleman will be a gentleman, a lady will be a lady, a pig will be a pig. If you're lucky enough, you'll get a guy or gal who knows where and when to be both!

In many cases of bisexuals, people feel shame for their feelings and will suppress their same-sex attraction, and, because they're able to perform with the opposing gender, they *choose* to consider themselves straight. Choosing one's partner, however, is not like choosing one's orientation. Again, this comes down to denying the *self;* denying one's true essence and true nature.

Even with everything we know about the learning process, humanity is still adamant to believe only what it sees, even when *proof* exists otherwise. The concept of homosexuality and bisexuality wouldn't even be questioned if evidence of it being *naturally occurring* was *visually* apparent, but for some reason, we just won't take the word of the person who is actually a homosexual. If heart surgeons applied this same thought process to their work, we'd all be in trouble. Fortunately, unlike most of us, a heart surgeon knows to look deeper within. A little known fact about the heart is that, beyond the arteries and valves, and beyond the tiny *visible* vessels which indwell the heart, lies an entirely different, incredibly minute system of additional blood vessels that are not at all visible to the human eye. Most of us wouldn't even know how to draw a diagram of our own heart; much less know about these micro-vessels. We just accept our heart as we know it and go on with our lives. Where homosexuality in relation to humanity's progress comes into play, much like the heart, there are vital factors of its function that we cannot *see*, but truthfully, those factors are as important to humanity as the oxygen we breathe is important to our hearts.

For a moment, let's look at sexuality in an uncommon manner, for example, using an example of a hermaphrodite *(a being which possesses both sexes)*. Regardless of the hermaphrodite's sexual orientation, there is no denying that there is a penis *and* a vagina, and in many cases, breasts as well. There is also no denying that, assuming all organs are functioning, the hermaphrodite can conceive life by having their egg fertilized by another, and/or they can conceive life by fertilizing the egg of another. There is no question that this person was born this way, and there is no question that this person did not *choose* to be this way. Usually, in the midst of this phenomenon, it is suggested that a person born into such a body should be surgically altered, but where is the indisputable evidence which proves that this *phenomenon* is a defect? Even with the *visual* evidence, we still remain uncertain of what

God's purpose for such a creation could be, but even in our uncertainty, denying what we just can't seem to wrap our little insignificant minds around, whether or not the evidence is staring us in the face, is costing us more than we'll ever know. The evidence of this fact lies not only in our history, but in the results of our history which have made our current reality what it is today.

We absolutely need to wake up and stop making the concept of sex scary, evil and guilt-ridden, especially when it comes to teaching our children. The guilt factor alone plays a huge role in what we are attracting to ourselves as a result of feeling guilty about sex. Take for example gonorrhea, syphilis, HPV and HIV/AIDS. When it comes to teaching children, if we'd stick to the facts, we'd realize that sexuality is not at all a *sexy* topic, but rather, a topic of human mechanics, emotion, spirituality, nature and science. Teaching children that our most basic need and function is a shameful thing is teaching lies about human nature, and it throws off our natural feelings that come with our natural functions. Furthermore, if it's not bad enough to go through life dwelling in the fear that this beautiful process that gives life can also take it away, could there be anything more detrimental to the mind than to associate an ailment such as HIV with the word *positive?*

Regardless of orientation, sexuality is a natural, wonderful, powerful thing. Inasmuch as responsibility, respect and discipline are important factors to consider when approaching our sexuality, sexuality remains nonetheless one of the greatest aspects about being physical beings. It bonds relationships, it gives life, it heals, and it feels sooo good. So, forget about everything you've ever been told out of guilt and fear and shame when it comes to sex. Sex is a gift, so get it on!

CHAPTER XIX

=WhatDefinesHumans=

**There's more to being human than just walking upright...
Just ask any duck!**

When scientists publish their work, they are ideally supposed to share what they think separates humans from other species. As a scientist, I figure I should *walk the scientific walk*, so, without further ado, here's my theory:

**What separates humans from all other species is
their creativity and their *ability* and *desire* to
consciously alter their basic nature.**

What's powerful about this statement is that the ideal behind it suggests that we truly are different from all other species. The very fact that we'd *want* to change our nature implies many possibilities surrounding our divine purpose. Animals have no reason or desire to consciously change any aspect of their nature, but humans do. Sure, it could be argued that our desire to change our nature has more to do with our ego than anything; things like desiring to become monogamous in order to *get the girl*, and that this same ego-trip is what keeps us separated from each other and ultimately from God, but I have every reason to believe otherwise, if for no other reason than for the evidence of what happens when we do change our nature out of love.

According to this theory, only love has the power to change our basic nature. Yes, we can brainwash ourselves to *believe* something, but brainwashing isn't about changing ideals as much as it is about overriding other ideals. Without love, we are no different than any other species. Sure, unlike dogs and cats, we humans can peel a banana with our hands, but so can chimps, and I won't even get into the eerie things raccoons can do. When it comes down to human nature, humans try, with immense failure, to deny their basic nature, but unless love is involved, we can't succeed at changing our nature, and until we grasp this concept, we're doomed to frustrate ourselves to no end. When trying to change our nature without love, we only make things worse. A cheater will cheat again, an addict will need his fix, and it's only a matter of time before the man inside the transsexual diva gets fed up with his automobile mechanic and fixes his car himself. Until we tune into our true *self* – with love – we simply cannot evolve. We are what we are, and it cannot happen otherwise.

Before I continue with the human thing, let's look at the animals. Yes, a dog or a cat may be of a loving nature, but they won't stop "dogging" or "catting" just because they love you or because you love them. Animals, especially dogs, do things for attention and approval and, of course, for food. Yes, dogs and cats love us, and we've heard the countless stories of how they rescue people every day, but that has more to do with their nature. When it comes to *changing* their basic nature, they are not going to change. A dog will sniff another dog's butt even if the Queen of England is at your house for afternoon tea. Sure you can train them to do, and not do, many things, and if you succeed at training them, they'll comply. However, the change in nature is not of *their* doing, it's of *your* doing. This compliance is purely out of emotional conditioning and denial of expressing their basic nature. It is then an *oppressed* nature; it' is not a *changed* or *evolved* nature.

As humans, we marvel at our advanced abilities in comparison to those of animals, and of course, we should. We can speak, drive cars, use a can opener, understand that the mailman is not the dog-catcher, and even manipulate jumper-cables in ways both automotive *and* intimate. That said, animals are far more advanced than we give them credit for, and we could definitely learn much from their examples.

Animals communicate with each other through instinct and intuition. Ever wonder why your dog likes some dogs and wants to attack others? We don't know what they're saying to each other, but it's clear they're saying something, and it isn't with words. Humans possess the same instinctual and intuitive communication skills possessed by animals, but most of us have all but completely lost touch with these skills. We may think we're so advanced compared to animals, but if that were the case, how come animals know everything from the character of the people who enter our home, to knowing there's going to be an earthquake an hour from now? Animals are connected to everything. If we'd detach ourselves from the false ideals and alleged realities that are like a spell we're under – and our telephones, too – we might rediscover that connection to our own intuition.

If there is anything we can learn from animals, it's their acceptance of their own nature, and their acceptance of the nature of others. A dog doesn't question other animals; it just accepts the facts. It is in a dog's nature to mark their territory, and in its nature to bark. For dogs, there is no judgment. A fat dog is just a dog, a skinny dog is just a dog, and the neighbor's cat is irresistibly chaseable no matter what color or size it is. Those are just facts!

I'm not implying that we must accept our current or ego-based nature and remain the way we are. I'm implying that it is in accepting our nature that we discover that it is *in* our nature to want to *change* our nature, and that this unique human factor is imperative to our advancement. It's also with our acceptance of what's in our nature that we will discover the difference between what we should be looking to change, and what we need to stop struggling with, fighting against, or vainly attempting to oppress.

When it comes to protecting their young, animals don't insult other animals; they simply protect their young by stating their place and saying *go away!* This is a perfect example of an affirmative use of anger. Other animals aren't insulted by it; they're just responding to their own nature. Humans are often afraid to offend others when it comes to protecting our kids, or even when it comes to mere arguments. With animals, however, it's all growling and teeth, and no one questions what that means, and no one is offended by it, and nobody holds grudges.

In the animal world, there are several animals which are monogamously mated for life, like the beaver and the fox. Then there are those animals which are a little bit slutty *(not to put too fine a point on it)*. There are also those in-between animals which mate for life but also like to play the field, like the wolf, for example. In all cases, these animals' mating rituals are not by choice but rather by nature. They do not struggle with their nature, and they make no effort to change their nature or the nature of their mate(s). It is all perfectly natural for them, and it doesn't occur to them to think otherwise, nor to play games. Mr. Beaver doesn't struggle to be faithful to Mrs. Beaver, and Mrs. Wolf does not care that Mr. Wolf is a *player*. For those in the animal world, there is no struggle to be something they're not. At this point, I'll refer again to the term, *"Occam's Razor"*, which implies, *all things being equal, the simplest explanation tends to be the right one.* The reason I mention this is because I want everyone who reads this to understand the simplicity of where I'm coming from, so here goes...

Humans are not inherently a monogamous species *(in other words, we're all slutty by nature)*. This ideal is supported by the very fact that we have so much trouble keeping it in our pants – and I'm not just talking about the dudes! If it were in our nature to be monogamous, it would not occur to us to be otherwise, and it certainly would not be difficult to be monogamous. Unlike animals who just accept their nature, we struggle with monogamy because we've not recognized and accepted that we're *not* inherently monogamous by nature, and therefore, we're fighting a losing battle.

Notice that I use the word *monogamous* and not the word *faithful*. By *monogamy*, I'm referring to basic *human* nature, but when I mention faithfulness or fidelity, this is where our *spiritual* nature comes into play, and, in spite of anybody's belief of the contrary, there is a difference between monogamy and fidelity. The idea that our basic human nature to *run around* is a sin is as insulting to God as it is to humans. It's one thing for someone to question your mate-choice, but it's another thing to question the way

God made you. Like it or not, your nature is a large part of who you are, and there is no escaping it.

So, humans are not inherently monogamous. By this, I mean to say that, being with one partner is not purely in our nature. This is not a limitation of the human being, but rather, it's just another component of our limitless, unconditional capacities. Perhaps this will change as our consciousness evolves, but at present, once again, we are what we are. What does have the ability to adjust our current nature, in current times, is love. Whereas sex with his wife can make a man a father, it is love that makes him a dad. When a man who's known as a *player* finds the right woman, it's typically love that makes him stop *playing*. Fidelity is also encouraged when a man has something to protect, like a good partner and a family. Yes, there are other things which can confuse us into thinking we are in love. Sometimes we're partnered with someone because she cooks like Mom or he's wise like Dad, or maybe she's psychotic like Mom or he's violent like Dad, and those things make us feel *at home*. The key to recognizing the difference between love and dependency is in acknowledging how successful the relationship is, and gauging the relationship's intimacy level. It's also helpful to spend time in silence and come to know one's true *self*. At any rate, assuming it's really love, that's what keeps a person faithfully monogamous. It's amazing what we'll do for love. Love wakes us up.

Of course there are many factors which separate humans from animals, and no other factor separates us more, or rather, defines us better, than human creativity. Unlike animals, humans are inherently creative, and nowhere in our lives is our creativity better expressed than through our sexuality. Yes, I realize that animals have their creative side, but their creativity has nothing on humans. To humans, birds seem to sing, but in reality, what sounds like music to our creative minds is just a bunch of bird-talk; *Yo, dude, that's my nest!* If they were anywhere nearly as creative as humans, their nests would have evolved from the dead twigs and cow-dung construction designs from thousands of years ago. Or, at the very least, they would have invented the roof by now!

Animals are about necessity. Their creativity will excel out of need, like when a fox absolutely needs to feed its young, or when a dolphin needs to save a life. Humans, however, are inherently creative, and our motive to be creative is purely out of an inherent need to evolve. It's the reason we paint pictures, knit doilies, sculpt figures, and do all the other things we do, including sports, acting, dancing, mechanics, science, and all other forms of thought and movement in existence, if for no other reason than to create better versions of ourselves. Even with our sexuality, we're creative. Humans play and try different things, like taking on roles, playing emotional games, and even using toys. Yes, some animals have sex face to face, but again, it's very mechanical and out of necessity, and those animals who do it face to face generally won't do it otherwise; humans will. That's creative!

We are born to create, and those of us who don't create *things* will create *experiences*, even if it's just the drama in our lives which ultimately defines us. As for our most creative form of expression – our sexuality – those who deny themselves their right to their sexual expression and creativity are denying themselves every feeling, sensation, sentiment, emotion, and all the passion with which it all flows, and which moves forth to feed our creative desire and purpose.

So, desiring to change our nature in the name of love, and our inherent creativity, are what separate us from the animals. Acknowledging these factors is what will evolve us from the ancient populace we are today into the deeply advanced civilization we will be tomorrow: The advanced civilization we were, and are, meant to be.

CHAPTER XX

=WorldPeace=

If you want peace, you drop walls, not bombs...

There's no denying that the inhabitants of our planet are at war, and I'm not referring merely to the wars involving jets, guns and grenades, but as well to the wars within our communities, within our homes, and within our *selves*.

There is a constant rumbling upheaval throughout the entire sphere of this planet, and it goes on not in spite of each of us, but rather, *because* of each of us. It's not only because of what we think, say, and do to encourage and reinforce this upheaval, but it's also because of what we don't think, don't say, and don't do to make a difference.

For some people, world peace means having everybody believing in their religion. For others, world peace means having no religion. For almost all of us, it means being able to place our heads on our pillows at night without worrying about our safety and the safety of our loved ones. Often times, whether taking a stand for peace of a nation, or taking a stand for proper coaching in a little league game, the motives behind our silence and complacency have to do with not wanting to make things worse, where-as other times, the motives are in not wanting to be the subject of disapproval. Both of these excuses are fear and ego-based, and they are not good enough reasons to not challenge unjust issues. Sometimes the motive behind our silence is that we're afraid to create war, but make no mistake, the absence of war does not imply the presence of peace, and sometimes, a little *affirmative* upheaval is just what the doctor ordered. I'm not saying there is such a thing as a good war, but a good healthy dose of logic goes a very long way, even if for a while you come off as un-popular.

Whether we're dealing with war, abortion, government, economics, neighbors, family, or ourselves, so much of what we base our decisions of what we should and should not do is based once again on inaccurate ideals about God, religion, ethics, manners and morals. Whether it's in the grand scheme of all things, or in the seemingly insignifi-cant moment-to-moment things, when it comes to God, we've got to use our heads and our hearts, and stop being cowards about speaking up when the need for a voice arises. Regardless of what we think, we do no favors to ourselves, or to humanity, or to God when we live in or act out of fear. We also do no favors by limiting ourselves or limiting others from reaching beyond current states of knowledge or consciousness. When we limit ourselves and our lives, and when we limit others, we limit our ex-perience, and in effect, we are limiting God and God's divine purpose.

Religiously speaking, we personally and socially limit new *ideals* because we fear the possibility of overstepping boundaries set forth by God, but in actuality, God never set boundaries before us. The boundaries were set before us by those who lived before us, and who lived in fear before us. We're afraid to live our lives and break through the barriers which keep us from discovery and from divine consciousness, and even from *basic* consciousness, not only for fear of how others will judge us, but also for fear of how God will judge us when it is time to pass through this life.

The concept of judgment is a human ailment, and it is to the process of life what sour milk is to a nursing child. God doesn't judge. In whatever capacity God acknowledges us, God *observes* and does so with love. God is pure and whole. Judgment is a trait born out of fear, not out of pureness and wholeness. Any parent, clergy or other misinformed individual who uses the idea of God's judgment to *fear* and *guilt* people into subscribing to their limiting beliefs of what life should or shouldn't be, are only breeding more fear and guilt and evil. Whether we subscribe to the ideal of God's judgment out of fear or out of ignorance, or both, spreading the word of God's judgment is truly a thing of evil which goes against all that is good in life, including world peace. I would imagine that if God would say anything, he'd probably tell people, *"Leave me out of this!"* I know I personally don't appreciate it when somebody speaks on my behalf and delivers a message that isn't mine. If anything will ever be judged, it will be the lies and the misgivings that have been spread, and continue to be spread, as the *Word of God*.

When I look at war; take for instance the ongoing unrest in the Middle East, my heart aches for all the blood which is shed allegedly in the name of God. The holy land that is being fought over is connected to the entire planet, and thus, it is *all* connected, and all this land is holy. Whatever energies which may have been beautiful, peaceful and holy in that portion of our world, probably moved somewhere else from the moment the first gun was brought therein. Much of the ideals behind the unrest in the Middle East has largely to do with money, but mostly to do with religion, and not just any religion, but religion and religious ideals which date as far back as anything ever recorded. On one hand, there's a lot to be said for the wisdom and teachings of such ancient knowledge, whereas, on the other hand, just because a religion is the oldest *recorded* religion doesn't make it the oldest *existing* religion. It is merely the oldest religion of which we may be aware.

There is currently no easy answer as to how to eliminate war and civil unrest once and for all, at least not with how we currently see our world. War more often has to do with religion because it is so much like religion. Everybody thinks their purpose is the right purpose and that everybody else is wrong, and all who don't agree are hellbound infidels. As a result, winning is more important than being at peace, and this applies as much to civilians as it does to the military.

I recall some years ago while working at a design trade showroom, a woman who regularly frequented our establishment came in one day slinging verbal arrows about how Palestinians aren't even a real people, and she went on to defend Israel and her *fellow* Jews, and their right to their land and how these *strangers* had no right to invade them. Keep in mind, this divorced Jewish American living in Canada, blasted these ideals to me; a Canadian who voted in the kind of government which currently extends this woman's rights and freedoms to be the person she has *chosen* to be; a bitter judgmental divorcee who barely honors her religion for the benefits of it's convenient holidays. Of course I didn't argue with her, after all, I knew very little about Palestinians, but it did concern me that this woman felt it appropriate to deny others the right to choose to be a *people,* when she herself is a *person* resulting from her right to choose. Palestinians, whether by choice, by circumstance, or by birth, are a *people.* If they are a people by choice, they have every right to be, just as a woman who is in Canada or in America has the right to be a Hasidic Jew to please her G-d, or just *say* she's a Jew in order to reap the benefits of the high-holidays. This is called freedom!

What frustrates me about these *know-it-all* ignorami is, if they truly care about what's going on in their alleged *mother-land*, then why aren't they hopping on a plane and going to their land and fixing the problem? I'm not Jewish. I don't support the many limiting ideals implied by Judaism, but I do know that Jews have the right to their religion, and in light of their obvious current imminent demise, they need all the support they can get, and I for one support them. It would be nice to see more Jews doing the same.

Contrary to popular belief, Jews make up a very small portion of the world's population. At a shockingly small and rapidly declining population of only 14.2 million Jews worldwide, and with a growth rate of less than 0.3%, it's amazing that there is a Jewish community at all. Compare that to the 9.6 million and growing Palestinian population, most of which live in the Middle East as opposed to the Jewish community which are spread all over the globe; a mere 3.5 million in Tel-Aviv, it really seems that it's only a matter of time before the Palestinians all come together and take what they want; if in fact all Palestinians are at all as radical as it has been suggested.

Now, to really place things into perspective; combine the population statistics of both the 14.2 million Jews and 9.6 million Palestinians, and compare that to the staggering 1.6 *billion* (and growing) population of the Muslim community. In this thinker's mind, it really places the Palestinian/Jewish unrest issues into perspective. Muslims – like them or not, agree with them or not, pray with them or not – understand the power of incorporating discipline into their lives. Muslims walk the walk; they do whole-heartedly as the religion advises, like marrying and getting down to the business of having many children, and especially supporting their own. That is why they're growing.

If every person who calls themselves Jewish were truly dedicated to their religion and their people, they'd pay attention to the fact that there is immense strength in numbers. They'd walk the walk, get married, respect their spouse, have many children, and they'd teach the importance of *living* their religion in its entirety. As usual, the problem with the spiraling decline of any religious community is the complacency of those within their community. If I could go back to that fateful day at the showroom and respond to that woman who criticized the Palestinians, I would tell her that *she* is what's wrong with her people and her religion; not the Palestinians. *She* and her lack of integrity, her lack of courage, and her lack of honesty. She with her big mouth spewing words of hatred in a land of peace, instead of delivering words of peace to a land of unrest. Even as a non-Jew, I know the importance of preserving, protecting, and supporting Jews and their heritage. If you are religious, by all means, support your religion. Support it affirmatively and lovingly with all your heart, mind and soul. Otherwise, if you're not going to do something about the problem, please keep silent about it, and let the rest of us work and live and support each other in peace, because your hatred is only breeding more hatred.

When it comes to religion, as with anything else, when we don't have the brains or the courage to make a change, we say *"it's all good"*, but, it's *NOT all good!* It's not all good when, as you are reading this, a child is being raped and tortured in some war-torn location across the globe, and at the same time, it's also happening in your community. It's not *all good* when an ailing retired couple is scammed out of their life-savings. It's not all good when a misdirected twelve year old boy in one state is tried as an adult for his crime because of his large stature, while in another state, a teacher who has molested another twelve your old boy is only tried for having an inappropriate relationship with a minor when she should be tried as the predator she is. When it comes to making things good, it can only be *all good*, and will only be *all good*, when we all take a stand and put our logic and courage to work for the betterment of all humanity. It will be *all good* when we set laws that are strict, and we strictly adhere to them. It will be *all good* when we give as much energy and attention to our children in the same manner of which we give our addictions, vices, habits and hobbies.

I mention in the previous chapter just some differences between humans and animals, but in actuality, there are countless things which separate us from the animals, for better and for worse. We're different than animals in so many ways, and yet, the basic tools we've been given – our talented hands, our creative minds, our speech, and our very nature, are all being abused, misused, overlooked and wasted. This way of living has cost us so much for so many generations, and it will continue to cost us as long as we continue this damaging, destructive cycle of *doing nothing*. I believe this *doing nothing* includes refusing to dialogue with extreme radicals. I agree that we shouldn't negotiate with terrorists, but there is a difference between negotiating with terrorists and extending to them the opportunity to hear and learn logic and see the light of day. I know that many don't agree with this theory, but consider this: We've already been talking to our friends; now it's time to talk to our enemies. If we don't sit down peacefully and endure difficult dialogue, then we will continue to endure worldwide bullying, terrorism and incessant war.

The manner in which distressed relationships, troubled finances, compromised health, and most accidents and other unfortunate events are merely the residual outcome of our actions, and is an outer projection of what's going on inside of us, is the same manner in which the planet's lack of peace is just a projection of our collective way of thinking, and a result of our actions. Those of us in the West who are not experiencing bombs and machinegun fire are every bit as much at war as those in the Middle East. Our fear, hatred and heartache is very much the same because we're all connected in mind and spirit. In order for the guns and tanks to stop firing in the Middle East, and for all sides involved to come to an affirmative agreement, we here in the West must bring peace to our homes, our lives, our relationships and our *selves*. This is because there are more of *us* than there are of *them*, and as such, our love, compassion, forgiveness and concept of peace would spread throughout the planet. Until a greater mass brings peace to themselves, peace cannot be spread across the entire planet, and the entire planet will just continue to suffer.

So many individuals feel powerless to do anything in a world so full of hatred, anger, blame, oppression and war, however, they do have the power to change it. We change it by attending to our own lives. We do this by loving and forgiving all, extending and dwelling in compassion, and not subscribing or succumbing to approval, shame, guilt, lies or fear. We need not worry about what's out of our control or about who's not doing their part. We just need to be our authentic *self* and do what is in our control, and encourage all others – through action and example – to do the same.

Although individual minds react differently, and react according to social environment, the minds of all Earth's inhabitants are nonetheless all collectively reacting to the same issues – hate, anger, fear, blame, oppression, war – because we're collectively infected by one shared virus: *Ill Perspective*. It just takes a few individual minds to help alleviate the *virus* and change the *programming* of our collective thought process. I for one refuse to participate in thoughts of hate, anger, fear, blame, oppression and war, as much as on the other side of the planet as in my own community, my own home, and in my own *self*. I hold tight to love, compassion, forgiveness and to the faith that peace is *possible*, is *probable*, and is *present* now. I refuse to participate in any other form of expression, because love is what I was placed on the planet to *be, do,* and *spread*. This is my job. This is the job of all of us. We can all do this.

When we all do our part, just as much with the small things as with the big things, then we will begin to build that path towards world peace. When we stop acting as if world peace is someone else's responsibility, and when we affirmatively involve ourselves in our own world on every level, and put to good use our talents and abilities, our love and compassion, and our forgiveness and faith, only then will all things be *"all good"*.

CHAPTER XXI

=Politics=

Truth is not something you vote on; it is or it isn't...

One of my favorite things to do is have discussions with people who complain about the government and its doings and how bad and corrupt the system is. It's one of my favorite discussions because it's one of the few times I can actually have direct dialogue with the actual source of the problem – the person complaining about it – the citizen.

Whenever I discuss politics with a complainer, especially one who seems to have all the answers, I can bring the entire conversation to a grinding halt by asking one simple question: *What have you personally done about it?* As you can imagine, this question brings about a moment of silence, and the top two replies are: *What am I supposed to do about it?* (and/or) *I voted!* –End of conversation!

This next tid-bit of information may come as a surprise to many people, but I think it's worth mentioning: *The government works for you!* It's one of the most important things people need to understand, along with: *Voting isn't enough!* It's amazing that in a society as free and open as ours, how little our citizens actually involve themselves in their government. Perhaps we feel if we don't get involved, we won't be held accountable when it all falls apart, but, no matter how we handle it, we are all accountable, because every decision, or lack of deciding, affects us all.

Shortly after Senator Barack Obama became president of the United States, I found myself driving on an Arizona highway, from Phoenix to Flagstaff, following a tanker truck filled with either milk or gas (or both, who knows?). The truck was dusty, and written in the dust on the back of the truck were the words, *He's not my president.* Upon reading that statement, I thought of what I'd like to say to the person who wrote that statement, and to every single person who thinks in the same manner as that trucker.

First off, if they voted, then it meant that at the time of voting, they were in support of the manner of which a president is selected, including acceptance of the majority vote. Second, if they did *not* vote, then they really have no say in the matter because it meant they've left the decision to the people who *did* vote. Finally, if they simply don't like the way things are done, then they should do something to change it rather than expressing disapproval for the results of a process which they either supported or did nothing to change. Otherwise, writing *He's not my president* on the back of your truck after all is said and done only makes you look like a moron, if for no other reason than *he IS your president.* If we accept the process of democracy (the process of voting) then we must accept the results including who gets voted in. If we are continually dissatisfied with the results, then we must change the process, because like it or not, we're all part of the game, we're all part of the process, and we're all part of the problem(s).

Most all current governing processes worldwide are terribly archaic and long overdue to be put out to pasture, The only way this will happen is if every one of us steps up to our responsibility as citizens of our countries and bring enlightenment to people and to government. Many forms of governing in all countries which have been executed a certain way for centuries, are ideals which were set in place by forefathers in relation to their ideals of what was right and/or necessary for their time, not to mention their own body of inaccurate knowledge, their ignorance and their fears, and then of course their dishonest, illegal and immoral motives behind their ideals, and lastly, the ideals imposed upon them by their forefathers which have equally trickled down into our current governments.

In our current time, much of how we govern is largely based on what was written by our forefathers, however, in order to make any change, we must ask ourselves a few questions: Who decided that what was good for *them* is good for *us?* Who decided that we, in the here and now, and in the grand scheme of all things, *must* subscribe to the limitations set in place by others who lived decades and centuries before us? In actuality, our forefathers and ancestors had no more right to limit our life experience, including how we choose to govern ourselves, than we in current times have the right to limit future generations based on what we think is right or wrong and the decisions we make as a result of our own fear and ignorance, and as a result of the limitations imposed upon us by *our* forefathers and ancestors.

The manner in which past generations wanted to govern *themselves* and *their* children was *their* right and *their* business. The manner in which *we* wish to govern *ourselves* and *our* children is *our* right and *our* business. It's time we all make it our business to exercise our rights, here, today, now! If, however, we willingly choose to continue to govern in the manner of which we currently do, we've got to get a mitt and get in the game, and we've got to play the game like we want to win. With every election we're reminded of how important it is to vote, if for no other reason than for the fact that we have the *right* to vote, unlike those in so many other countries. The problem, however, doesn't lie in the fact that not everyone is voting; it lies in whom we're obligated to vote for.

Society has become more accustomed to voting *against* parties than voting *for* them. That's the norm, and in the midst of trying to decide who shouldn't run the country, we've overlooked the very important fact that the answer is, *neither* party should! So we vote against the worst of two evils, and, the lesser of two evils stands tall on his platform raving about how everyone clearly wants him in office. One of the problems with voting against some-body is that, in the process, we don't vote in a party who should be doing the job; we vote in a party who we hope will be less damaging to the country. It has become a game of mere damage control more than anything else. Damage control shouldn't be our main concern when voting in a party because, let's face it; a party who will only *slowly* destroy us, will still ultimately destroy us.

The first step towards social upheaval can always be traced back to the antiquated, backwards thinking behind mismanaged economics. Yes, some things are not always so clear, but other things are as clear as day, and they need to be recognized and implemented. As mentioned in the chapter on religion; everybody should be taxed at the same rate, no exceptions. The limited thinking behind the ideal that the wealthy have more and thus should carry everybody else is unfair, and it's illogical. A man who makes one million dollars per year generally has the education, know-how and experience which brought him to where he is, and he generally works harder, smarter and more efficiently than the guy who makes ten thousand dollars per year. He's also generally more disciplined and focused and has made huge concessions and sacrifices to get to where he is; something most everyday dudes simply don't want to do. If people do not want to work, that's fine, but they shouldn't expect to reap the benefits of the hard work done by others. At any rate, those who make less give less, those who make more give more. This is fact, if for no other reason than you cannot possibly give of what you simply do not have.

For the sake of example, imagine for a moment that everybody's income is taxed at 10%. If one man makes ten thousand dollars per year, he contributes *one thousand* dollars to the economy. If another man makes one million dollars, then his financial contribution is *one hundred thousand* dollars. The man who made one million dollars has contributed what it takes one hundred other men earning a ten thousand dollar annual salary to contribute. Add to this the fact that he probably owns or at least runs a company employing many employees, thereby contributing to people's jobs, livelihoods and constant economic influx. His higher echelon of purchases of products and services also creates more jobs than do the inferior purchases of is lower earning counterparts.

Penalizing people who make more money only removes the incentives for wanting to work harder and better and more efficiently, or wanting to make a company bigger to employ more people, and it makes them think twice about getting a higher education. The ideal that the rich must carry the rest of society also gives little, if any, incentive to those who do little, to do anything at all.

I wonder how quick we'd be to stop being lazy and get to work if we were taxed *more* for making less. Here's the deal: *work more – keep more, work less – keep less!* Of course this tax idea is ridiculous, because it implies we should be getting taxed for doing *nothing*, but how ludicrous is it to be taxed for doing *something*, especially when that *something* is doing more than what others are doing and contributing to our economy? I realize that there are dishonest millionaires holding positions they don't deserve to hold, but contrary to popular belief, they do not make up the general populace of millionaires. Compared to all groups on the planet, millionaires make up a very small portion of the world, and if it wasn't for their work, study, education, visions, knowhow, risk-taking, sacrifices, concessions and so forth, we'd all be in trouble, because their contributions go well beyond income-tax contributions.

As for taxes, I'll say it again: *You don't work for the government; the government works for you!* I understand that if we *want* something from the government, we have to *nourish* the government, but the constant year-after-year tax-hikes in areas of income and property is bleeding us all dry, and the end is nowhere in sight. Where taxes are concerned, if we continue in this manner, it will never be enough; there will always be hikes and this trend will persist until we're all broke! Ultimately, rectifying this issue is about everybody getting involved; something most people simply can't, or won't, be bothered to do.

So what are we to do? The first thing to do is ask yourself some questions like: Who is your mayor? Where's the mayor's office? Have you ever been there? Have you ever written him/her a letter either encouraging or reprimanding him/her? What good have they done? What bad have they done? Have they made good on their promises? If not, why didn't they? If so, what can you do to ensure they win again in the upcoming election? The next step is to follow the same steps with your governor or counselor or president, prime minister or whomever is in charge. Hold them accountable for the promises they make, and if they need support, find a way to give it to them.

If, on the other hand you don't want to do anything to improve the government, at least stop complaining about how things are done and move on to affirmatively changing things you are interested in changing. Any affirmative change in any area of life is a change for the better, and it affirmatively affects everything because everything is connected to something else, including politics.

Several years ago I asked myself – if people are such lemmings who do whatever the government tells them to do – why is it that the great spiritual *leaders* of the past like Jesus, Buddha, Krishna and so forth, simply didn't hold office and merely enforce people to love and respect each other, and turn all governments into one single love-ruling dictatorship. My answer from *within* was: *Love cannot be imposed or enforced*. As such, the great leaders would never have held office in order to enforce, impose or even define Love. To do so, they would have had to *label* Love and God, thereby limiting and conditioning Love and God to mere bureaucratic notions and preventing Love's very evolutionary process.

This is not at all to say that there is not Love or God in government. Government is not inherently a bad thing. Government is just one more living, breathing entity of energy which mirrors its society's level of maturity and consciousness. For all nations, and for the entire planet, government will evolve when its citizens evolve.

CHAPTER XXII

=AmericaTheGreat=

Dear America: Please be great again...

Undeniably, one of the most influential events to rock the world in recent times happened on September 11, 2001, when terrorists *(or somebody)* brought America to its knees by crashing airplanes into significant buildings across the nation. I say *in recent years* because it's very likely that it's only a matter of time before an event of such magnitude – give or take a few thousand innocent lives – takes place in America yet again. Very likely, in fact, considering the way things were and are being handled since the 9/11 crises. I say *very likely* because, when it's so blatantly obvious how easy it is to get away with carrying out such a debilitating task as were said events, it not only makes it clear to those who do this kind of thing that they can get away with it, but it fundamentally suggests an open invitation.

Along with the tragic, heartbreaking catastrophe that was and is 9/11, America was blessed with the ultimate test and definitive opportunity to set the example for the rest of the world, and to the God for which it claims it stands, and of how love conquers all. This was a most splendidly obvious opportunity that the nation's leaders sadly overlooked, and a truly divine test of compassion at which it failed miserably.

There was only one way to successfully handle what happened on that fateful September day, to justify all the life-loss and heartache, and to heal us all. If the situation would have been handled in such a manner, it would have been the first step towards world peace, and to bringing all of humanity to a new level of consciousness, because it would have been the ultimate example of courage, grace, strength and dignity. It would have been the ultimate example of answering the classic question; *What would Jesus do?* It would have been the ultimate example of Love.

When news spread that airplanes had been hijacked and flown into buildings, America's chief shouldn't have gone into hiding while its citizens felt vulnerable and terrified and were desperate for guidance and reassurance from their leader. He should have stood tall and proud from the office in which he was blessed with the honor of occupying and expressed to his citizens that, not only was the country safe to go to sleep that night, but that as a people who put their trust in God, not only would they not be brought down to the level of the terrorists by retaliating in kind, but that all of America should pray for the offending country and wish them peace, for within their peace lies America's. The president should have reminded his citizens to love the unlovable because the unlovable are the ones who need it. Instead of *God bless America*, it should have been *God bless the offender,* because only under God's blessing can the offender understand what they've done. America's leader; this same man who claimed to have placed God at the forefront of his leadership, should have reminded people of the scripture; "*Love your enemies, bless them that curse you, do good to them that hate you, and pray for them that despitefully use you and persecute you.*" (Matthew 5:44). Or, at the very least, he should have placed the Commandment *Thou shalt not kill* at the forefront of his agenda.

Yes, some would argue that the president should not have been at the White House because it could have been terrorized as well, however, if a nation which boasts the kind of power the United States boasts, should it not have been able to protect one building in an effort to prove to it's own citizens, not to mention to the offenders, that America has what it takes to protect the entire country? If the United States government, with all of it's technologically advanced security protocol, couldn't demonstrate its confidence in its own capability to protect the 55,000 square feet of building that is the White House, in order to protect the nation's leader, how could its citizens feel confident that their government could protect them within the confines of over 3.8 million square miles of land?

It's no secret that most countries follow America's lead. America is to all nations what Oprah Winfrey is to television; like her or not, we all wish we had her influence, her success, and especially her power. The world was looking upon America during that tumultuous period, and if America would have forgiven its offender, as preached throughout the Holy Bible of which America allegedly holds in such high regard, the entire world would have witnessed the beginning of a new era, and they would have followed the example.

Instead, the United States stooped to the lowest level of that which the offending nation slithered. In the process,

America taught the planet nothing about faith in God or about integrity. As a result, America failed to meet the challenge of its blessed opportunity to set the stage for an effective new way of handling things, and a brand new beginning for humankind; a new beginning of epic proportions. This beginning would have put America on the map as not only the land of the free, but the land of peace as well. It would have given an entirely new meaning to the phrase, *Home of the Brave.*

At this point you might be asking what my motive is in bringing up the United States in a book such as this, and my answer is very simple: *Wake up, America...the world is watching!*

Even as a Canadian, I grew up understanding that America meant *freedom.* I understood this to the point that I actually thought *America* was the literal translation for the word *freedom.* Today, however, when I think of America, what comes to mind is illiteracy, gluttony, ignorance, greed, and of course fast food, obesity, prescription medication and lawsuits. That said, keep in mind, I actually love America and its people, but imagine what comes to mind for someone who hates America.

In 2007, I was mortified to learn that it was estimated that about eighteen million children worldwide would die from lack of basic necessities like food, water and medication. The cost of eradicating these staggering statistics was estimated to be approximately 2.5 billion dollars. Conversely, in preparation for July Fourth Independence Day celebrations in 2007, Americans spent more than 2.8 billion dollars on fireworks, which amounts to three hundred million dollars more than was required to eradicate the aforementioned senseless, unnecessary deaths which would take place throughhout the world, including within the United States in 2007. I shudder to think what was spent on gas, burgers, beer and bullets during that same weekend. I'm not implying that July Fourth shouldn't be celebrated. On the contrary, in fact. I think it's not taken seriously enough, much like Christmas, where we're ready to party but we forget what we're celebrating.

It makes me wonder how many people spent the same amount of money in one year on charitable donations and tithing as what they spent on fireworks for one night. I also wonder if they knew they could participate in saving eighteen million children this year by foregoing fireworks, video games, MP3 players, or something – *anything* – would they do it?

The United States of America has been, since long, very powerful and influential. If they won't set the examples and the standards and do their part to make the *world* a better place, they have little hope ever making better their own nation. Ultimately, I certainly don't think that it's just America's responsibility to save the world, but as the most powerful nation on the planet, it's at the very least America's responsibility to *set the example*, if for no other reason than to save itself.

CHAPTER XXIII

=TheGrandFinale=

A new beginning...

On September 9, 1999, I was staying at my sister's house in Montreal, and I woke up for no apparent reason in the middle of the night, and I got out of bed only to discover my entire family; my sister, her husband and their two small children, all awake as well, sitting quietly and looking outside at an incredible electrical storm. It was unlike anything any of us had ever seen before. There was no thunder, but the lightning was spectacular. On one level, it was eerie and made us wonder what, if anything, it meant. On another level, it was fascinating and we were not scared. As a matter of fact, I think the energy from all that electricity was stimulating us more than we thought, because, I can remember the next day, even though I barely slept the previous night, having so much energy and feeling so good.

The very next morning, and throughout the entire day, I received all kinds of *prophecy* emails regarding the previous nights date, 9/9/99, and its connection to the end of the world. What's interesting about these ancient prophecies is how they always seem to surface with dates and *conveniently* deciphered descriptions of events only after the events happen. Even more interesting are the people who happen along these prophecies; people completely sold on the alleged prophetic information that some anonymous person sent them, but who still won't listen when you tell them that they're killing themselves with drugs, alcohol, cigarettes and artificial sweeteners.

Since I can remember, there has always been talk of the end of the world, and the fact is, there always has been. My parents told me stories of when they were children and were told of the end of the world, and my grandparents have also told me those same stories of their childhood. I am most certain that one day, I will tell my own children and maybe even my grandchildren, of the time when my generation prepared for "the end".

Admittedly, a large portion of the *end of the world* talk has always come from religious ideals, and these ideals have always been a great guilt-builder and an effective way to ensure people run back to church, and to keep people from moving forward in life. Interestingly enough, most of what the churches are spewing about what we do know about the coming end of a cycle as stated by sources the likes of the Mayan calendar is knowledge that has been discovered *scientifically*. What's bothersome about this is that the religious have since long done their uttermost to prevent and ridicule the findings and advancements of science, yet today as always, they accept those findings and conveniently utilize them in just the right amount as to reinforce fear into their followers, and to claim yet again that the end of the world is at hand. The Religious do this not surprisingly as they continue to prevent and ridicule the many advancements of scientific discovery; the same advancements from which they conveniently borrow their new "apocalyptic" data.

As we approach the year 2012, there is growing concern over the possibility of the end of the world; most of this hype having to do, again, with misconceptions relating to the Mayan calendar, among other sources, and much also stemming from recent movies about catastrophic events to come. Couple this hype with war, economic crises, airplanes falling from the sky and where the world *seems* to be headed, and it's all pretty convincing. In actuality, all of these things have been going on for decades, and many of them for centuries, especially war. Our existence is about experiencing every aspect of life, good and bad, and this includes the misery of war, the joy of war ending, and the lessons which come of it all, should we choose to learn from them; which doesn't seem to be our strong suit.

As for airplanes crashing; since their development, airplanes have always fallen from the sky. It doesn't suggest the end of the world, it merely suggests that either someone didn't do their job, or they misjudged the weather or flight path, and this is simply the price we pay for taking the daily risk of propelling thousands of 80-ton metal machines containing hundreds of humans, 35,000 feet into the air. We haven't perfected flying because, not only are we not designed to fly, but because nothing is ever perfect. One of the greatest assets of being God-Energy is possessing the gift of creation, and the ability to change things. We've learned to lift off, and now we're learning to stay up there. Hopefully great customer service will come into play at some point, but an airplane falling from the sky is not indicative of the end of the world; it's indicative of humans at work creating and improving upon their creations, and it's an indication of humans evolving.

As for where the world is headed, contrary to popular belief, we're in a really good space. Yes there is change on the horizon, but like the seasons, it is not the new season that kills the previous season, but rather, the previous season that relinquishes itself in order to give birth to the new. Sure, our music is getting ruder, advertisements are more risqué, and the family unit has changed, but didn't our grandparents say that same thing during their time, and their parents in times previous to that? When you consider situations of the past like slavery or the holocaust, or the way the women in our world have been treated *(yes, I acknowledge there is still work to do in that arena)* including in western society, there is so much more good today than ever before, and I believe that communication has played a huge role in these advancements.

News-media sells us on all the bad that goes on in the world, but if there was truly so much bad, why would they have to repeat the same story over and again, often within the very same broadcast? So a few frightening top stories make headlines around the world; does it really mean that the end is near? The fact is, although there are thousands of bad things that happen all over the world each day, there are countless billions of good things which happen each day. How unfortunate that very few, or none, will ever make it to the news. Obviously most news programs are negative because the news itself is sensational, yet we all hate the negativity, it scares us and we all talk about it, but, we go back for more. We do this because we either want to be informed or entertained, or both. Actually, most news is more entertaining than it is informative, so if you don't watch the news, and if it's such an important piece of information, someone will tell you about it.

At the time of writing this, I had not had cable television in my home for about four years, yet I've always known the big stories: Bird flu, Swine flu, Tsunamis, Earthquakes, Michael Jackson's death, Oprah ending her show, Ellen coming out, Jet Travolta's passing, to name only a few things I had heard about only minutes after they aired. The interesting thing about all of these news stories is that I could have continued with my life not knowing any of it, and none of it signified the end of the world. I was certainly saddened about the deaths, concerned about the flu, and thrilled for Ellen, but again, I didn't know these people and they didn't know me, so it's not like I would have missed a funeral or a coming-out party. And, since I travel so much, I already wash my hands a lot and I cover my face when someone sneezes on a plane, so I was already prepared to deal with the public flu pandemic. In short, I really needed none of that news, and even without cable television, I was nonetheless inundated with it.

Our constant need to be entertained is largely due to our creativity; we're as intrigued and interested in what others create as we are with what we create. Boredom, however, plays a huge role in our constant search for entertainment as well. Boredom, like idle hands, is not a good thing, but it can be dealt with by keeping busy with affirmative activity. I'm not suggesting that every moment needs to be filled, for *silent stillness* is one of the single most powerful creative processes, and a process which is beyond merely entertaining. However, if you're bored and need to fill a moment, watching the news for entertainment isn't *doing* something; it's turning your brain into mush and filling that mush with more reasons to be scared or lonely or sad or lower than you already feel, or just more bored than you already are.

On a spiritual level, I've discussed the *going within* process with many religious people who insist that God is on the outside, or *"up there"*, but I am not denying God is *up there* and/or around us, I'm implying that God is within us *as well;* this supported by the scripture; *The Kingdom of God is within you* (Luke 17:21). Perhaps the simplest way I can describe how infinitely present God is within us is to once again use computers as an example. During the time of the moon landing, computers were hundreds of times larger than what they are today, yet, their capabilities were thousands of times less efficient than the handheld tele-phone/media devices we use today. What technology developers accomplished since that time is, they discover-ed ways to *compress* memory and data to the point that programs, and thus computers, could be made physically smaller. For most of us it's difficult to imagine how much farther computer technology can go, but these same lim-ited ideals we have about current technology are the same limited ideals we had back during that moon landing peri-od. In this same manner, if we can imagine information being compressed to fit into anything, we can conceive of how God is compressed, or *concentrated,* within each and all of us.

We're an impatient species, and that's okay, because, believe it or not, that's what helps us advance. If we'd be happy with things forever, we'd never advance; just one more thing which separates us from the animals. What appears to be an impatient species that gets bored with things is actually a species that is ready for the next level. Keep a child in kindergarten for ten years and see how long he'll be entertained with the ABC song. For the record, I'm not glorifying impatience; I'm acknowledging that impatience is part of our basic nature. Understanding that we are naturally impatient helps us better understand why we're this way and what good can come of it, and understand the importance of filling valuable time with constructively creative and affirmative activity when we're waiting for things to happen.

In the early 1980's, a computer called the Commodore Vic-20 was introduced to our school, and for many who could afford it, the high-tech gadget of the 20th century was all the rage and proved to be a magnificent tool on so many levels. To give some of you an idea of how obsolete this computer is today, your electronic wristwatch with chronometer probably has more memory and capability than did the Vic-20. To emphasize the computer's current obsolescence, the system's software was on a typical four-track audio cassette which was processed through a separate component called a *datasette*, and you didn't download anything. Come to think of it, aside from a few games and math lessons, I don't recall what the point of the computer was, but for us humans, it was as welcome to our technologically hungry minds as a hunk of chocolate cake is to a famished child.

A short time later, after people got used to – or bored with – the Vic-20, that same company introduced the absolute *must-have* computer called the Commodore 64. The 64 had more memory, and obviously you could do more with it, but it still ran with a cassette-based program, unless you splurged for the floppy disc, which many people did. Back then the Internet wasn't even a thought (at least not for civilians), and even if the Internet had existed, the 64 was not Internet compatible. Nonetheless, we welcomed it into our lives.

Today's computer technology in contrast to that of my youth is not even comparable, yet every day there is new technology, and we're always as hungry for it as those who produce it are hungry to develop it. Like so many misunderstood characteristics of the nature of our species, our hunger for something more is part of who we are and is necessary for the advancement of all of humanity. This discovery is important when it comes to understanding our basic nature because, in a world where we constantly put ourselves down for not being content with life, it completely underscores that our need for change is not an anomaly, but rather, it plays a crucial role in our advancement and survival. This change and advancement is not in vain, because we are headed somewhere, and despite what anybody says, whatever comes our way; we will survive!

As for 2012, here's my prediction: The sun will rise, we will carry on, and we will continue to grow. Yes, things will be different, but not in any way we can't adjust to or ever be happy again. I believe that challenging times are on the horizon for humans, but not any more challenging than the times we've ever experienced and survived in the past, and it's not because we're being punished. It has been suggested by many scientists that this is the most exciting time to be alive in all of history, but in actuality, any time is an exciting time to be alive. Yes, this is a very exciting time, because change truly is on the horizon. The world is changing, shifting, adjusting and growing. There is no shortage of speculation about the world coming to an end, but in actuality, the planet is merely changing, and we are every bit as capable – and likely – of surviving the planet's changes as we are capable of surviving our individual changes. The planet is a living organism, constantly recycling and renewing, constantly healing and repairing, constantly ageing, moving and transforming. Change is part of life, and the planet is not in any way impervious to change. In fact, the planet, as with every existing thing in all of creation, relies and thrives upon change.

There is constant debate over the global-warming issue and if it even exists. Of course it exists; the proof is evident and undeniable, but global-warming is not entirely responsible for all the changes Earth is undergoing. The fact is, Earth consistently changes, and it has been this way since its conception. Sometimes the changes are caused by planetary alignments, other times they're caused by colossal asteroids slamming into Earth, and sometimes they're caused by Earth's inhabitants. Sometimes, like presently, it's a mix of all these factors. Yes, I believe we've caused trouble for Earth's natural healing process. After all, we've depleted much of Earth's natural resources – water, oil, minerals, forests, wildlife – and we've replaced it with garbage landfills. Not to mention, every single car serves as a space-heater which moves about adding more heat to the already sun-heated countless thousands of miles of asphalt roadways encompassing the globe. Admittedly, we are not the cause of change; we're merely dictating whether or not our way of life will be harmonious to those changes.

Everyone is waiting for *the change* humanity is expected to experience in the coming years, but in actuality, we've already been changing. It doesn't happen overnight; at least not according to humanity's *linear* perspective of time, but mark my words; we are already changing.

I believe the future belongs to the strong, the healthy, the educated, and to the kind and compassionate. They will be the survivors. Strong means possessing the emotional, spiritual and physical strength to see ourselves through to the next level. Healthy means feeding the mind and the body with only the very best nourishment available. Educated means continuous learning and deep thinking for the betterment of humanity. Kind and compassionate means allowing all to live, and encouraging nourishing sustenance among our fellow man. Of course these terms mean so much more, but if we can just grasp the basics and put them to use within our current capacity, we're already ahead of the game.

In the midst of this change, I believe there are far more wonderful times in store for us than bad, but we rarely hear about these wonderful things thanks to negative movies, misinterpreted prophesies and the hearsay spewed by the media and by church leaders. Either way, it is our mindset that will dictate what we'll experience in coming times, and dictate what we'll get out of that experience. The biggest problems we face as we approach 2012 are not politics, religion or war, but our thinking, intentions and actions. The thoughts we each carry on this planet are all part of the *Great Collective Consciousness* and what this *Consciousness* thinks and feels. If we all *see* and *fear* the *end of the world*, it will happen.

A few years back, I had an acquaintance who increaseingly spoke of the end of the world, or the "rapture", as she put it. As a spiritual man with great interest in the wellbeing of my fellow human, I listened and honestly tried to digest her words, but the more I digested what she said, and I observed her lifestyle, and the more I considered from where she was getting her information, I realized it was time to spend less time with her and get my spiritual nourishment elsewhere.

It wasn't because I didn't believe or didn't want to believe her – I was really unbiased either way – it was because everything she said was so negative that it constantly brought me down. In my mind, even if she was right and the world would end in 2012, it was then 2008, and I was a good and honest man. I prayed, meditated, recycled, was good to my neighbors, so what exactly was I supposed to do about it if it was true?

For the record, I didn't believe or agree with her findings, not only because the bulk of her information was found on the Internet, usually from *rapture-minded* groups, but also because of her fear-based attachment to her religion. I rarely take issue with people who are religious, but I do take issue with addicts who impose their beliefs on others and don't follow their own rules. For example, if you're Catholic, you are not supposed to get divorced, plain and simple. If you divorce and get remarried, your union is not recognized by the church. This particular woman was divorced and remarried, thus breaking a most crucial rule according to her faith, and then she claims to prophetically receive extraordinary *holy knowledge* about the end of the world.

This woman was also convinced about what was to come because of her nightmares, yet, when I suggested that her dreams might be caused by the hormone medication she was taking for her menopause, she insisted that it wasn't the meds. I know I'm not a physician, but even being a male in my thirties at the time, I was aware of the negative effects menopause medications can yield, yet she was so adamant to be right about the end of the world that she was willing to forego asking the doctor about the medication, and she allowed for all the horrifying nightmares to continue.

Perhaps the greatest loss to this woman's life was her *life* itself. Her friends couldn't handle her negativity, people thought she was losing it, and in one year she had aged to what seemed like twenty years. This wouldn't have mattered if she was at least enjoying her life, but she was clearly lonely and unhappy. She was a religious lady who forgot to live for God and love her fellow man, instead, wishing and praying for the end, and dwelling in fear, and instilling fear in others while pulling away from everyone and making no contribution to her community, to her church, and thus to her world or to the universe or to God.

For those who don't know, the term "rapture" literally means – among other things – *to be transported from one place to another*. This transportation, should it ever come to be, could very well signify a *conscious transformation* as much as it could signify a physical or spiritual change. Dwelling on the idea that it has to be a painful punishment of epic proportions is as unrealistic as it is illogical, and, such idealism is only conducive to a miserable existence until it actually happens, if it ever does happen.

In actuality, our world ends every day, but we don't acknowledge it because we still live in the residual of what was yesterday. We do this by holding on to yesterday's arguments and circumstances. Once we truly grasp the concept that our circumstances don't have to be our experiences, we can allow ourselves to move forth into each new day and each new world. Just as there has always been, there is currently so much fear regarding the end of world, but just as we've almost always failed to learn from history, we've again failed to realize that the only thing we're really afraid of, is change, even if change is one of the blessed concepts which clearly propels our nature.

Every time the world changes and something new happens, something else comes to an end, but there is no evidence of the actual *world* coming to an end. The Mayan calendar is a mathematical calculation of cycles, and although we have every reason in the world to believe that it implies the end of a planetary cycle, there is nothing to indicate the end of the world.

Upon that up and coming fateful December day of 2012, we will go about our business. Anything negative we may experience as a result of the cycle change, or cycle renewal, will be largely brought on by one or both of two factors; one being our failure to prepare for this change which includes all the damage we've done to the planet which may very well compromise a harmonic shift when the cycle renewal takes place, and two, the very fact that most of us, as the days draw closer, are thinking catastrophically rather than affirmatively in terms of those coming days.

For those wondering how we'll deal with the change, the answer is; we're already dealing with it. This change we're all expecting is already in effect. It began long ago, and everything from being closer to God, to the changes, or mutations, in our DNA, to the way our children are being born, to the shift in our personal, global and thus universal collective consciousness, has already begun. Other than this, contrary to what *doomsday* thinkers have in mind about that fateful day in 2012, I'll say it again: *The sun will rise.* The pain and anguish we are allegedly due to experience at the end of times is happening already, and it has been going on for centuries. This pain is not punishment for being bad, but rather, are growing pains which come from reaching new heights and crossing uncharted boundaries, and they should be looked at as trophies which mark our advancements in our mission to survive against all odds.

In our constant search, nature, science and change have honestly revealed that tomorrow is not doomsday, but rather, merely natural change just unnaturally disturbed by a residual of past and current actions carried out by the planet's inhabitants. The only way we can ever change the negative residual of today is to affirmatively change things here in the now. This is an investment in tomorrow. This is an investment in humanity. This is an investment in ourselves and in God.

CHAPTER XXIV

=SomeFinalThoughts=

From one human to another...

Some writers think that readers should feel honored to read their works. I, however, am immensely honored that anybody would take their time to give these ideals a chance to be absorbed into their consciousness. For your consideration and for your time, from the very core essence of my being, I thank you; the reader, for taking your precious time to have opened your mind to these ideals. Whether or not you agree with these principles is unimportant *(all doubts can be addressed by reviewing chapter 11)*. What's important is that perhaps somewhere within these pages, something made you think beyond where you usually stop thinking, and perhaps you're better for it. If this is the case, then the world is a better place, and I've succeeded with my intention.

I've mentioned it a few times throughout this book, and it bears repeating: *I'm just a regular guy*. I'm not any different than anyone else. I'm not above or better than anyone else. I'm just a guy who wanted to write an open letter to my planetary brothers and sisters to make a difference in the world, and I kept writing until the letter became too big to fit into an envelope. Yes, I want to make the world a better place, as much for myself as for my family, my friends, my country and my planet, but I know I can't do it alone. I can encourage people to be kinder, think deeper and work smarter, harder and better. I can promote *Conscious Affirmative Living* until it's bleeding out my pores, and I can do my best to set an example for anyone who cares to observe. Beyond this, however, the real changes will come to be when the role of raising the bar and adhering to higher standards of consciousness becomes the responsibility of more than just one man.

Admittedly, it took me a long time to discover that when you want something, all you have to do is ask. Furthermore, when you're clear about what you want, and clear about where to get it, you don't waste time; you go directly to the source. Therefore, I am humbly appealing to you; the reader, to bring the best of yourself to our planet, through whatever your capacity, whatever your talent, whatever your passion, whatever your dream, whatever your inspiration. I'm asking this, from one human to another – from one precious child of God to another – in the name of all that is honest and pure and good and True, to take simple steps towards the betterment of *you* for the sake of the betterment of all of humanity.

Whether this means being a more attentive parent, a kinder boss, a superior employee, a straightforward politician, an honest lawyer, a responsive physician, a devoted teacher, a thoughtful neighbor, a courageous teen, an involved senior, a millionaire with a generous streak, a little person with a big idea, a daring underdog, a secret hero, or anything else that will make you into the ideal *you*. One small step each day; this is all I ask.

There's so much we can do in our day to day lives to make changes that count; things which really take no more energy to do than what we're currently doing anyway. Obvious simple things like, yielding right of way to another motorist, obeying the speed limit, filing an accurate tax declaration, sincerely wishing a beautiful day to a discourteous individual, holding a door for a few people, holding an elevator for someone who's clearly trying to get to it before it closes, picking up litter off the street, tending a neighbor's garden or shoveling the walk while they're away. These little things may seem insignificant or miniscule to some of us, but those little things add up over the span of a year and go an incalculably long way, especially when carried out by millions of people each day.

Even if most of the people you do this for are oblivious to your kindness, somewhere along the line, somebody's life will be changed. Someone you held the elevator for might have landed the job that afforded them to send their child to university; the same child who becomes the researcher who finds the cure for cancer. The person you gave right of way to in traffic might have just made it to the hospital in time to say goodbye to a dying relative, or might be the doctor who makes it just in time to save a life; and he could be both. It's also possible that the miserable person who served you your morning coffee thinks that nobody in the world cares, and it might just be your smile that gave her the courage to smile at the man of her dreams; the same man who will stand by her throughout her cancer treatments. All you do and all the good that comes of it is *energetic*, and it all comes back.

For those up to the challenge, the next time you hear somebody say, *"Why doesn't somebody do something about...?"* Ask them, *"Why don't 'you' do something?"* This is a great way to get people to do something or be silent about it. It's also a great way to lose *friends*, but you need to do away with the whiners and complainers anyway, and on an affirmative note, there are millions of people out there who would love to be your friend – literally millions!

Throughout this book, spirituality has been at the forefront of almost every chapter. This is not because it's a spiritual book, but rather, because most of the planet's inhabitants are religious or spiritual, and it is the general populace to which this book is directed. If you're not religious or spiritual, it's as much your duty to respect the rights of others to believe what they believe as it's their duty to respect your right to not believe what you don't believe. Respect, peace and harmony are everyone's duty. I've heard just as many nonbelievers suggest how stupid the religious are for dwelling in their convictions as I've heard the same said by the religious about nonbelievers. These statements from both sides are as unfair as they are unintelligent and immature. The fact is, there are intelligent believers and nonbelievers. If you want to know which of the believers and nonbelievers are intelligent and mature, here's a hint: *They're the ones not casting judgment.*

Tolerance, compassion, forgiveness, patience; these are what we must extend to each other, for they are the removers of walls, of conditions, of limitations, and they are the healers and nourishment which help us grow and move forth. As much as we must extend these gifts to each other, we must also receive them, because we're all imperfect; we all need tolerance, compassion, forgiveness and patience. Simply put: We all need love.

This – in the midst of everything that humanity has ever been through, and will ever go through – is what will save us. This, in the midst of our imperfection, is what should define us.

This Is Love. This is God's Language.

Claude La Vertu writes and speaks on personal and global
development concepts surrounding
"Conscious Affirmative Living".

For more information, log onto:

www.claudelavertu.com

The Companion Series

The Companion Series is a collection of follow-up workbooks intended to accompany GiraffeNeckSoup. Each title contains overviews of from this book and includes additional insights, concepts and tips. Each companion book also includes therapeutic exercises, questionnaires and journaling geared towards each topic.

The Success Companion
How to succeed at anything with one key in one year (or less)
Outlines how, with one key, in just one year (or less), you can succeed at achieving your dream or goal.

The Affirmative Companion
A Meditative Introspective Workbook & Journal
A compilation of effective teachings, affirmations, meditations, prayers and exercises for all people of all faiths.

The Relationship Companion
A Relationship Introspective Workbook & Journal
An introspective guide and workbook for achieving, healing and repairing relationships.

Also by Claude La Vertu:

-Clairvoyant Being
-LoveDare (Novel)
-A BETTER MAN - A LoveDare Story (Novel)
&
Claiming & Maintaining Peace Of Mind
A Guide To Attaining A Perpetual Sense Of Wellness
Offers guidance on how to heal emotional wounds and maintain a personal sense of wellbeing which promotes, invites and attracts a true *peace of mind* state of being. An essential read for victims of violence and sexual abuse who seek to make peace with the past once and for all. Includes exercises and journaling for personal growth.